THE HUDSON-MENG SITE: AN ALBERTA

BISON KILL IN THE NEBRASKA HIGH PLAINS

by

LARRY D. AGENBROAD
Chadron State College

APPENDIX I   Hudson-Meng Chipped Stone
Bruce Huckell, University of Arizona

APPENDIX II   Molluscs from the Hudson-Meng Site
S.-K. Wu, University of Colorado
Charles Jones, Bendix Field Engr. Corp.

APPENDIX III   Use of Opal Phytoliths on Paleo-Environmental
Reconstruction at the Hudson-Meng Site
Rhoda O. Lewis, University of Wyoming

APPENDIX IV   Vegetation and Flora of the Hudson-Meng
Bison Kill
Lawernce W. Young, II, University of Wyoming
Ronald R. Weedon, Chadron State College

Copyright © 1978 by

University Press of America™

division of
R.F. Publishing, Inc.
4710 Auth Place, S.E., Washington, D.C. 20023

ISBN: 0-8191-0530-9

Library of Congress Catalog Card Number: 78-57606

To

Albert and Bill

CONTENTS

LIST OF FIGURES

LIST OF PLATES

Available as a separate order from:

University Press of America
4710 Auth Place, S. E.
Washington, DC 20023

LIST OF TABLES

ACKNOWLEDGEMENTS

An excavation which involves six field seasons, plus three years of initial testing with support from volunteers, field school participants, paid crews and participants from Educational Expeditions International, with support from multiple funding agencies can only partially acknowledge everyone who helped to make the project a success. Foremost in such an endeavor is the expression of my thanks to Albert Meng and the late Bill Hudson, for whom the site is named. The development of the site is a tribute to the professional desire and interest of these two men, who repeatedly tried to promote professional interest in this bone deposit over a considerable period of years.

From the beginning, outstanding cooperation and interest in the project has been demonstrated by the U. S. D. A.-Forest Service: Pine Ridge District, especially in the persons of C. Van Doren, W. Chesboro, and B. Tice.

Colleagues from other institutuions gave immeasurable assistance in shared information, publications, pre-publication manuscripts and discussions of similar and dissimilar aspects of other sites. The members of the Department of Anthropology, of the University of Wyoming were outstanding in their cooperation. In particular, George Frison, John Albanese, Mike Wilson, George and Sandy Zeimens, Charles Reher and Jean Bedord, gave quantities of information with regard to procedure and comparative studies. Joe Ben Wheat, with his study of the Olsen-Chubbuck site, plus the accumulated experience from a number of other Paleo-Indian sites, was an invaluable resource person. Marie Wormington gave freely of her knowledge, experience, expertise and encouragement, as did Dennis Stanford, Dick Shutler, Vance Haynes, Don Crabtree, Paul Martin, Dick Forbis and countless others. They made rap sessions on-site, and at numerous Plains Conferences and Society for American Archaeology meetings, profitable experiences which are reflected in the total outcome of this investigation.

Support of the project varied from non-existent to generous. Initial and continuing support came from the Chadron State College Research Institute. The National Science Foundation became a major source of funding for a three-year period (GS-38000). Educational Expeditions International participated with funds and personnel for two seasons. The Nebraska Legislature provided funding during the last two seasons, under a bill sponsored by Senator Richard Lewis.

A very important aspect of support was that of the participants in the field crews. From volunteer efforts to financial support in the form of course fees during the seasons we operated as a field school, to ideas, questions which led to ideas, suggestions and efforts beyond which they were compensated for, the success of this investigation is due in large part to the individuals who participated as part of the entire "crew." Thanks troops!

1971

Without the voluntary efforts of more than fifty persons, the 1971 excavations could not have been accomplished at the Hudson-Meng Paleo-Indian site. Acknowledgement of those persons, who worked around classroom and job loads and work schedules is minimal compensation for their efforts. Volunteer crew: Dale Anderson, Larry Berlin, Pam Bowen, Mr. & Mrs. Dave Carlson, Peggy Corman, Teresa Chase, Mr. & Mrs. Gary Enlow, Wayne Farrens, Pam French, Jane Habur, Dave Hansen, Mr. & Mrs. Bill Hudson, Chuck Holmgren, Willy Levine, Mr. & Mrs. Everett Larson, Gary Luoma, Mr. & Mrs. James McCafferty, Skip McCafferty, Duff McCafferty, Darrel McDonald, Mr. & Mrs. Mike McVay, Mr. & Mrs. Albert Meng, Tom Moss, James Musso, Mr. & Mrs. Jim Nelms, Gregg Ostrander, Mary Paulson, Sigrid Paulson, Alan Rainbolt, Carl Rath, Mr. & Mrs. Richard Scott, David Scott, John Sims, John Slader, Nancy Spahn, Arthur Struempler, Larry Wickersham, Lynn Watt, Larry Watt, Mr. & Mrs. Jake Yost.

1972

Field crew: Dale and Pam Anderson, Peggy Corman, Maybelle Cox, John Ducca, Pam French, Terry Frye, John Hartley, Joan Kennedy, Gary Luoma, Ralph Miller, Enrico Miozzi, Glen Mitchell, Dale Mundorf, Dan Meyers, Chris Nelson, Helen Spencer, Bill Stolldorf, Frank Witzel.

Field volunteers: Cynde Adcock, Mrs. Dan Fisher, Amy Fisher, Mike and Zula Lewis, Albert Meng, Wess Pettipiece, Kathleen Russell, Lanna Scott, Dale Tracy and family, Darwin Troyer, Rosemary Wagner, Sandra Uridil, Marty McCafferty.

1973

Dig Foreman: Frank Witzel; Assistant Forepersons: Enrico Miozzi, Peggy Corman.

Crew: Karen Alderman, Dennis Aldinger, Madelyn Anderson, Dallas Balhorn, Rhoda Cogswell, Peggy Corman, Neil Ellington, John Fox, Linda Gaipl, Clyde Gibb, Betty Gibson, Chris Grosh, Cheryl Johnson, Robert Johnson, Cheri Landrey, Gayle Leonbardt, Mike Lewis, Dave Moody, Richard Saunders, Robert Willis, Zdenka Uridil.

1974

Assistant Director: Charles A. Jones; Dig Forepersons: James Mead, Peggy

Corman.

N. S. F. Crew: Mike Lewis, Rhoda Lewis, Cheri Landrey, Mary Ann Jones, Reginald Cedarface, Rodney Cape, Gary Mason, Bill Sydow, Jeanne Bork, Paula Downen, Phyllis Kraus, Brett Agenbroad, Wanda Agenbroad.

E. E. I. Crew: John Atkins, B. Eddie Cain, Jerald Gooden, Greta Lichtenheld, Georgia Powell, Cindy Ruskin, Joanne Thede, William Warm, Sally Becker, Steven Bell, Patricia Carson, Douglas Gelb, Nancy Goglia, Margaret King, Leslie McCament, Anne McConnell, Leo Trusclair, Steven Wadley.

1975

Assistant Director: Raymond C. Leicht; Dig Foreman: James Mead; Cartographer: Barb Dutrow.

N. S. F. Crew: Rick Koza, Rhoda Lewis, Lanna Timperley, Margie Hatton, Jay Jones, Betsy Marquart, Robert Ely, Don O'Malley, Brett Agenbroad, Wanda Agenbroad.

E. E. I. Crew: Georgia Powell, Roslyn Parker, Arianne Dworsky, Hallie Finucane, Greg Duerksen, Eugenia Ellison, Caroline Kenner, Debra Landry, Michael Melius, Diana Girsdansky, Barry Hoff, Stephen Brennan, Katrina Roch, Teresa Young, Susan Rodgers, Richard Panning, Sally Williams, Wendy Gillman, Alan Campbell, Kirk Wallis, Charlotte Haldenby, Don Hassel, Carolyn Chace.

1977

Dig Foreman: James Mead; Dig Foreman and Cartographer: Barb Dutrow.

Crew: James Fitzgibbon, Marianne Fitzbiggon, Matt Rohde, Arkie Snocker, James Landon.

Photographic credit is due Allison Habel, Con Marshall, Jim Mead and Monte Weymouth. The ink drawings of the artifacts were done by E. Steve Cassells. Field crew were kept in good food and high morale by four field cooks: Pam Anderson, Jeanne Bork, Wanda Agenbroad, and Barb Dutrow.

Backhoe work was provided by Blair Ditching of Hot Springs, South Dakota, for the four initial seasons. Radiocarbon dating was provided by Southern Methodist University, supported by National Science Foundation Grant DES 72-01582 A01, to C. V. Haynes.

A great deal of credit is due the students who worked in the laboratory, on the analysis of the faunal remains, and lithic studies. Several undergraduate and graduate research papers were generated and presented at the Nebraska

Academy of Sciences and the Plains Conference meetings. The results of several of these papers are presented in this volume.

Last, but certainly not least, gratitude and acknowledgement is given to the efforts of those persons who helped produce the preliminary and final reports, by typing and mapping. Field maps of the initial season were drawn by Nancy Spahn. Peggy Corman was cartographer for three field seasons, followed by Barb Dutrow for the final two seasons. I was assisted in final map compilation by Susan Sauser and Barb Dutrow. Typists for the various version of the preliminary papers and final draft of the manuscript include: Wanda Agenbroad, Susan Sauser, Leanna Scott Timperley, Jeanne Bork, Cheri Landrey, Rhonda Grantham, Barb Dutrow, and Robin Wasserburger. Dorset Graves proof read the final draft to help insure continuity and the ommission of major grammatical errors.

CHAPTER 1

LOCATION AND SITE HISTORY

LOCATION

The Hudson-Meng site (25-SX-115) is located in Northwestern Nebraska (Figure 1). It is located approximately 23 miles (37 km.) northwest of Crawford, Nebraska, near a topographic high, a landmark, known locally as Round Top (Lookout Butte on the U.S.G.S. map). On U.S.D.A.-Forest Service land, the site occupies portion of Sections 17 and 18, Township 33 North, Range 53 West, Sioux County, Nebraska. The geographic coordinates are 42° $44'$ $22''$ north latitude and 103° $36'$ $10''$ west longitude. The elevation of the site is approximately 4200 feet (1280 m.) above sea level.

PHYSIOGRAPHY

Sioux County is divided into several topographic and geomorphic areas, primarily by stream systems. To the south, the major influence is controlled by the Niobrara River and the White River, both of which drain in an easterly direction. North of U.S. Highway 20, there is a major topographic feature known as the Pine Ridge Escarpment; an erosional feature caused by stream action (the Hat Creek and White River drainage systems) on the Tertiary beds tilted by final phases of the Black Hills uplift. Drainage is northward to the Cheyenne River by way of Hat Creek and its tributaries, or east to the Missouri River by way of the White River and its tributaries.

Topographically and physiographically, the site occurs at the boundary of the High Plains and the Missouri River Short Grass Prairie (Figure 2). The High Plains were described by Webb (1931) and Johnson (1901) as the "undisturbed fragment, or fragments, of the original debris apron." The debris apron, to which they refer, is the alluvial and fluvial material deposited on older marine sediments, which are inclined toward the east. The formation of this debris apron was due to precipitation in, and erosion of, the mountains; the sediments were carried to the base of the uplands and deposited eastward due to the change in gradient and the high evaporation rate of this sub-arid region. Rivers either dwindled and died to the east of the mountain front, or they had sufficient discharge to flow through the Plains to the Missouri River. The Platte River, to the south of the

1

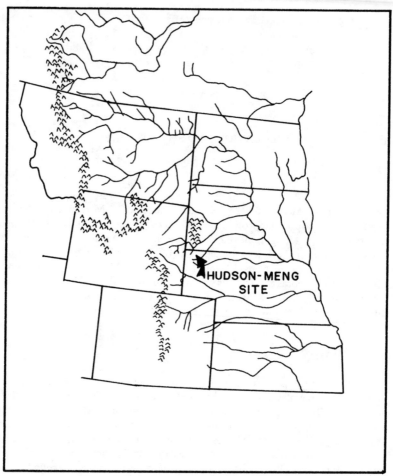

Figure 1. Location map of the Hudson-Meng
Paleo-Indian Bison Kill.

Pine Ridge, is an example of the latter type. As the water of the streams dissipated, due to aridity or infiltration, the sediments were deposited, choking the stream bed and causing lateral migration of the channels. In this manner, an alluvial deposit of up to 500 feet in thickness accumulated east of the mountains, yet west of the Missouri River. Later erosion on the arid, western edge of this region was accompanied by humid environment erosion on the eastern margin. The result was a remnant, dissected surface known as the High Plains.

Locally, the site occurs on the northern slope of the Pine Ridge, on the headwater reach of a branch of Whitehead Creek, a tributary of Hat Creek. The controlling feature for the drainage system and for the site location is the presence of a large perennial spring. Located some 100 yards up gradient from the site, this spring was undoubtedly the attraction for the coincidence of bison, man, and a natural feature which served as the jump.

CLIMATE

Thornthwaite (1941) describes the Great Plains as "the largest uninterrupted area with semiarid climate in North America." The region outlined in that statement includes the High Plains, just described, and the Hudson-Meng site. A region of high variability in temperature and precipitation, it is probably not too different presently, from what it was 9800 years ago.

Records for Chadron, Nebraska, (1931-1960) give an average annual precipitation of 15.32 inches (38.91 cm.), with a maximum of 21.6 inches (54.86 cm.) and a minimum of 10.64 inches (27.02 cm.). Fort Robinson is closer to the Hudson-Meng site, and is probably more representative of the local conditions. Records for the same period, at that location, indicate an average annual precipitation of 17.81 inches (45.24 cm.), with extremes of 29.42 inches (74.73 cm.) and 10.78 inches (27.38 cm.). At the Fort, the mean annual temperature is 47.8° F. (8.8° C.) with extremes of -35° to 105° F. Winds of up to 80 miles an hour are recorded at the Scottsbluff, Nebraska weather station. In winter months, the wind-chill factor carries the effective temperature to much lower extremes than the air temperature indicates.

SITE HISTORY

The spring and the area surrounding the site was homesteaded by F. E. Nance. After several years of work and two grass fires which destroyed his buildings, he sold the land. It eventually became Forest Service property in 1954 and remains so to the present time, though grazing rights are leased.

Spring effluent had cut a relatively deep arroyo to the north. The west bank of this drainage and a small headcut extending west of the main drainage had revealed an exposure of bone, under several feet of overburden. This bone bed had attracted and interested Albert Meng since he first noted it. Keeping watch on the deposit for several years, he began to attract professional attention, to see if it warranted excavation. Over a period of years he tried to interest several institutions, witnessed a portion of the bone bed destroyed by construction and with the help of Bill Hudson, brought it to my attention in the spring of 1967.

A U.S.D.A.-Soil Conservation Service dam was constructed on the spring drainage in 1954. At the time of construction, the bulldozer operators concentrated on the west side of the drainage "where the fill was softer." In doing so,

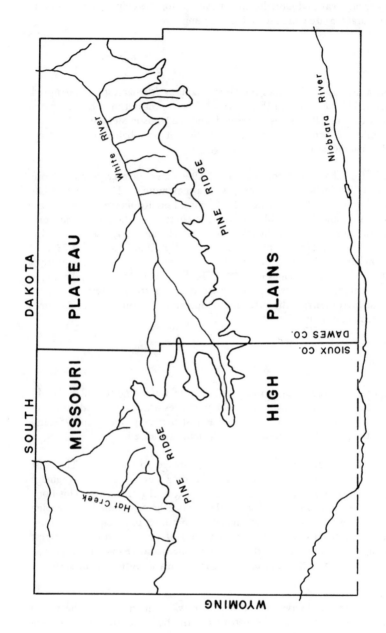

Figure 2. Physiographic Map of Northern Sioux and Dawes Counties, Nebraska (after Witzel, 1974).

4

they cut through the bone bed. Work was shut down while they contacted local authorities as to how to proceed. Ultimately it was decided the bones were of sheep and dam construction continued. An estimated 20 to 25% of the original (pre-construction) bone bed appears to have been included in the dam fill.

Having been shown the deposit in 1967 by Albert and Bill, it was decided that Chadron State College would at least conduct test excavations to determine the extent of the bone bed, whether or not it had cultural materials within it and its relative antiquity. Securing a federal permit, in the falls of 1968, 1969, and 1970, we excavated hand dug test pits to bone bed. The bone was examined, undisturbed, to determine the faunal elements present, their abundance and distribution.

The model we had in mind at the time was that of an Olsen-Chubbuck arroyo, paralleling the modern one, having served as the receptacle for waste bone from a butchering operation. Accordingly, test pits were dug along a rough north-south alignment paralleling the modern drainage.

Results of the test pit excavation were puzzling and inconclusive. Numerous individual bison remains had been observed over a relatively large area (pits were dug within the area disturbed by the dam constuction). It was estimated we had proven the remains of at least twenty to thirty animals in the test program. No cultural materials were discovered and it was noted that we had not found any skulls or hoof elements, notably low meat yield portions of the bison carcass. This data led to discussions with George Frison and Joe Ben Wheat, who had noted similar absences in archaeological sites. With this information and experience, it was decided to open one portion of the bone bed in an intensive, controlled excavation in an attempt to prove whether the deposit was purely paleontological, such as a blizzard-kill of a number of animals, or whether it had cultural materials, indicating an archaeological site.

In the fall of 1971, after the academic year had begun, a crew of 12 volunteers headed for the site area for a weekend of intensive excavations. The weather being uncooperative, we stopped at Crow Butte to decide whether to continue the operation or not. A flip of a coin sent us to the field and excavation began, as the weather improved. Twelve students were aligned in a north-south orientation, given a meter wide area to excavate, and work commenced.

By 11:30 a.m., in response to a request for bone identification, I went to the central portion of the excavated area. In the meter square adjacent to the one from which the request originated, one of the students, Garry Luoma, had just uncovered the base of a Knife River Flint projectile point that had Paleo-Indian characteristics, proving archaeological affinity and creating the Hudson-Meng Bison Kill site.

CHAPTER 2

LAYOUT AND METHODOLOGY

Results of test pits from 1968 and 1969 indicated a north-south concentration of bison bone beneath an area of overburden which had been, at least partially, disturbed by bulldozer operations during the construction of the Soil Conservation Service dam. In addition to the test pits, weathered, fragmented bone could be observed protruding from the grass roots above the dam spillway to the north of the dam. The topographic configuration, on the west bank of the spring effluent, suggested the bone bed would be a narrow, linear accumulation such as the Olsen-Chubbuck site in southeastern Colorado.

SITE LAYOUT

With this model in mind, a steel reference point was driven into the spillway floor, north of the known exposure of bone. This point was given a 00 + 00 designation, allowing a grid (Figure 3) to be set up with reference points measured in meters to the north, south, east and west of this position. Stations were then referred to by their north or south and east or west direction and distance from the 00 point. This allowed the grid to be extended in any direction the bone bed was revealed to go. The one meter grids were identified by their northeast corner coordinates and all artifacts, bones, etc., were referenced to that corner stake.

Early in the excavation, each metric square was assigned a number as well as being referenced by its northeast coordinates, as explained above. After two seasons of field work, the numbering of each square was abandoned for the northeast coordinates, as the bone bed was widening in all directions and the original system of square numbering was becoming confusing.

METHOD OF EXCAVATION

The first field season caused us to abandon the Olsen-Chubbuck model for the configuration of the bone bed. Areal and test excavations revealed an extensive bone bed, one unit thick, widening in all directions.

Excavation procedure developed the first season, and was carried out

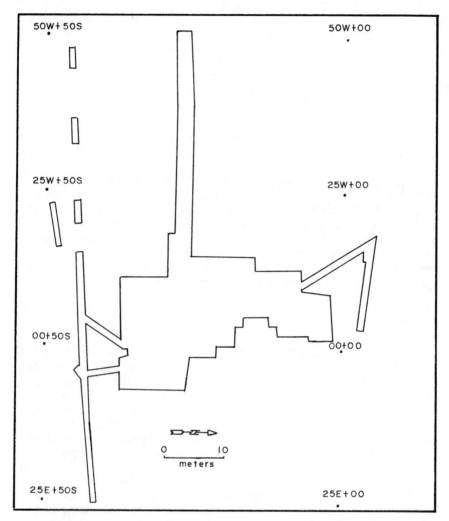

Figure 3. Planimetric Map of the Areas of Excavation.

through the entire investigation. The method was to lay out a portion of surface area which could conceivably be excavated with the funding, crew size, experience and time allotted to that field season. Test excavations had proven the overburden to be sterile with regard to human artifacts. This allowed us to remove the overburden by backhoe, to within approximately one foot of the bone bed, which was known from test pits.

Once the majority of overburden was removed by the backhoe, a metric grid referenced to the 00 + 00 stake was laid out, and each of the crew members were assigned an east-west meter strip. Each excavator began at the western limit of his or her assigned area and, using hand tools, began to expose the bone bed. Bone which was exposed was pedestalled, left in place and left as undisturbed as possible. By initiating excavation of the west edge of the seasons area of excavation the bone was left undisturbed, as it was exposed, with the excavator moving eastward, on unexcavated ground so as not to disburb the bone once it was exposed.

All overburden was screened through one-fourth inch mesh screens until lithic waste flakes were encountered. Then use of a one-eighth inch mesh screen was employed to recover the smallest flakes. In several areas of unusual concentration of lithics, window screen was also employed to recover the very small waste flakes. Screening was done dry, although some wet screening was done in two seasons, primarily for the recovery of gastropods from the bone bed. No notable occurrences of other relevant materials were recovered from the wet screen process.

A program of test pits and trenches was initiated prior to the first field season and was continued as a part of each successive season's work. At first, due to lack of funding, these exploratory excavations were hand dug through up to nine feet of overburden. With increased financial support, backhoe pits and trenches were sunk in areas of exploration.

It is with some degree of frustration I must admit that, after six field seasons, we do not yet know the north, south or west limits of the bone bed. In spite of more than 600 square meters of total excavation, plus more than 100 meters of test trenches and pits, these limits to the bone bed are still unknown. The only limits clearly defined are to the east, where the bone bed was destroyed by construction activity when the dam was built. An apparent northwesterly limit to the bone bed was noted with the second field season and is apparent on the bone bed maps (Plates 1, 2, & 3). Testing beyond this apparent limit did reveal scattered bone at bone bed level, however.

Test trenches and pits were usually oriented so as to give us the most data with regard to stratigraphy and areal extent of the bone deposit. It should be noted here that, at no location where we were able to dig to bone level, did we fail to encounter bone.

MAPPING

Having tested the bone bed, to find it a single unit over an extensive area, we decided to map each bone in place, to scale, so that eventually a map of the bone bed as it was originally deposited would be produced. A wooden frame was constructed with one-meter inside dimensions. A string grid on 10 centimeter

9

spacing was constructed within the frame.

The grid allowed the mapper to draw the bones, to scale, in the same relationship (Figure 4) as they were deposited, on metric graph paper. In addition,
each square meter was photographed, usually with the grid in place, to provide a
photographic record, as well as a graphic record of the unidsturbed bone bed. The
photographs also proved to be a valuable aid in compilation of the final maps and
in cross checking problem areas on the graphic maps.

Funding did not allow a sophisticated photographic procedure. Photographs were usually taken from a six foot step ladder, with a Polaroid land
camera, to provide instant prints, of acceptable exposure, prior to disturbing or
removing the bone. There was no attempt to take each photograph at the same
elevation above bone or to correct for parallax, distortion, etc. The photographs
were considered a supplement to and a cross check of the graphic map, not a sub-
stitute or replacement for it. A controlled photographic map such as the one generated by Dennis Stanford at the Jones-Miller site near Wray, Colorado, is the ultimate in reconstructing the spatial distribution of faunal materials in a kill site or
butchering and processing area. The graphic mapping, however, is more easily produced within the range of most project budgets and equipment potentials. In my
personal opinion, for most research purposes, models and model testing, etc., the
graphic production of a map (with an inexpensive, uncontrolled photographic
cross check) is completely satisfactory.

With multi-seasonal generation of maps, plus changes in mapping personnel,
it is important to train the mappers in the same type of techniques, as well as to
be able to join units or segments of the bone bed, as they are sequentially produced. Excavation and mapping with strict coordinated control allowed a smooth
compilation of map segments produced over a period of years, by different carto-
graphers.

In an attempt to produce continuity, the same field cartographer was main-
tained for as many seasons as possible. Replacement with an equally competent
individual who was already thoroughly familiar with the style of the previous person, from extensive laboratory and field experience, allowed a smooth transition
which is undetectable in the final map.

From the first field season, it became clear that there was spatial variation
in the distribution and concentration of the elements comprising the bone bed.
It also became apparent that there was both random and non-random distribution
of certain faunal elements. From these observations, two sets of models and
methods for testing them were derived.

Bone density maps, defined as the number of bones per square meter, were
constructed as a prospecting tool, to guide both exploratory trenches and test
pits, as well as future excavation. The construction of these maps was simply to
count the bones in each metric square, either from the map or photographic data,

Figure 4. A Portion of the Bone Bed Showing Mapping Frame in Place.

plot the numerical value on a satisfactory grid and contour the values, as one might contour a topographic plot. The resulting contour configuration indicated a definite trend to the area of highest bone concentration. Conversely, it delineated trends of low bone-yield, whether as isolated areas, or linear, or spatial regions.

From the initial bone-density map, a strong northeast-southwest trend of maximum number of bones per meter was noted. This trend, tied to the contours indicating sparse bone occurrence to the northwest and southeast, guided the excavation efforts of the following year. The second year's excavations served as a test of this newly developed model of the site. It proved, in each successive year, that the maximum density trend was valid and is a cultural feature of the site, one which calls for an explanation and one which was still unmistakeably evident at the end of the current field season (Figure 5).

In addition to spatial distribution and density maps, a map of the paleo-topographic surface, the surface on which the bone was deposited, was produced (Figure 6) as a guide to understanding the configuration of the bone bed and as a prospecting tool. The paleotopographic surface was identifiable due to the pedestalling of the bone, leaving the bone at rest on the surface on which it was

11

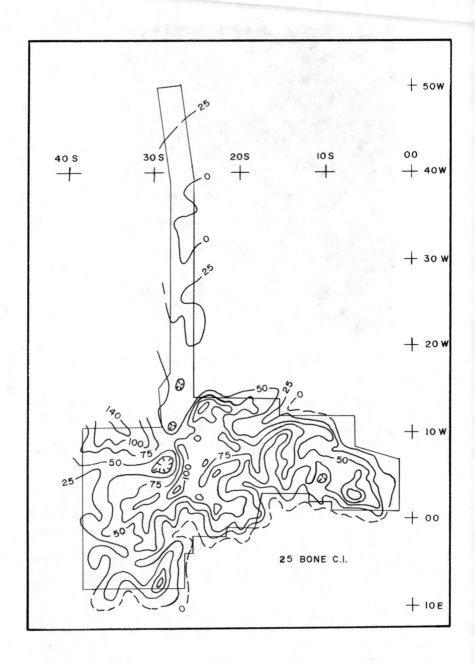

Figure 5. Bone-Density Map.

deposited. Once an area was excavated, an elevation survey by transit and metric rod produced the numerical data for a contour map of this paleotopographic surface.

From the initial paleotopographic map, it was evident that the bone bed had both a westward and northern tilt, or inclination. The northern tilt was readily explained due to the gradient, past and present, of the spring effluent. The westward tilt was less easily explainable and could only be interpreted as a remnant, planar surface dipping toward a deeply buried drainage system to the west of current excavations. Again, this information was verified and sequentially expanded with each seasons increment of new information. The model generated was one which called for a terrace surface on the east bank of a drainage channel which was as yet unknown in location, or size.

Our initial model was an Olsen-Chubbuck type of bone bed. With this model in mind, early excavations and test pits and trenches were aligned in parallel to the modern drainage. Testing to the west of the suspected alignment produced more bone, and at a slightly lower elevation than original areas of testing and excavation. It was at this point in time that the Olsen-Chubbuck model was abandoned in favor of a "terrace-east-of-the-arroyo" model. This model proposed a bone deposit representing a butchering-processing area to the east and above the actual kill site, on a terrace sloping westward toward the arroyo drop. This model held out until the 1975 field season and was modified by further evidence at that date.

The combined information and models generated by the bone-density maps determined the prospect-trenching efforts for the remainder of the investigation of the site. Both sources of data, especially the paleotopographic information, prompted the excavation of a trench into the ridge to the west of the known areas of the bone bed.

Trenching was begun in a more or less central position on the maximum bone trend, and at an angle to it. The trench was oriented east-west for both topographic and mapping purposes. Each year, the trench verified and added to the information gained from the mapping. As more westward extensions were created, excavated and mapped, the density trends and topographic configurations were strengthened.

An increasingly serious problem with westward expansion was the depth of overburden. To augment excavation data, a portable auger drill was acquired and a drilling program initiated to test the depth of Quarternary fill and the configuration of the valley bedrock. An east-west line coincident with the trenching and grid network was established from the top of the ridge west of the site, through the site and across the drainage, the eastern ridge, the east arroyo and onto a bedrock exposure several hundred meters east of the bone bed.

The drill string had a maximum penetration of thirty feet. To augment this depth, we set up the drill in the trench, giving it a vertical advantage of up to

13

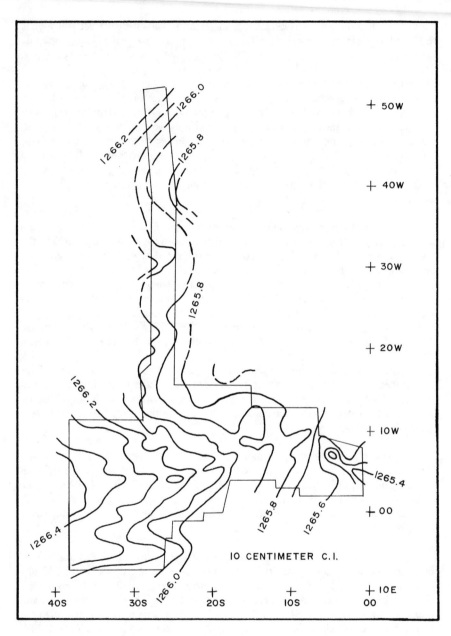

Figure 6. Paleotopographic Contour Map.

twenty feet below modern surface. Drilling was begun on the crest of the ridge west of the excavations. Bedrock (Oligocene Brule formation) was encountered at less than one meter, easily recognized by difficulty in drilling and in the physical characteristics of the drill cuttings. At 10-20 meters west of the trench limit of the 1974 season, bedrock could not be found with maximum penetration of the drill string. Placement of the drill in the trench, then drilling through the bone bed to maximum penetration, still failed to yield bedrock. It was not until the drill was placed east of the dam (and modern drainage) that bedrock was again encountered, at very shallow depth.

The results of the drilling information (Figure 7) indicated a very deep Quaternary alluvial fill extending to approximately fifty meters west of the original bone exposure. Not only was the fill more extensive laterally than expected, it had proven to be deeper than anticipated. This information gave the physical evidence of the possibility of a paleo-drainage, deeply buried, to the west, as indicated by the paleotopographic maps. The testing of this model became the primary exploration project of the 1975 field season.

Beginning with zero depth near the 00 north-south line, more than 25 feet of overburden was encountered at the western limit of the trench, at 53 meters west, in the 1975 season. Simple backhoe excavations and trenching, coupled with hand excavation, were inadequate. In the 1975 season, we rented a P & H power shovel with a 19-foot boom capacity. Even this was insufficient to reach bone bed level until we excavated in steps, with the machine.

The evidence gained was worth the effort and expenditure. The bone bed was encountered at 25 feet below modern surface, where the static water table was encountered and vertical excavations ceased.

These data, plus the expanded information of the bone density and paleo-topographic mapping, modified the model of the kill site. It became apparent that the original model of an arroyo drop with steep walls to the west and east at a meander bend must be modified slightly. With the new information, it appears that the model is a meander bend, with a steep west bank which was used as the fall, and a point bar-terrace gradation on the east bank, which served as the butcher floor surface.

In addition to an accurate, small-scale representation of the site, the bone map allowed testing of several hypotheses which were generated in the several seasons of field work. The initial season presented information which indicated a random scatter of certain faunal elements, such as mandibles. At the same time, other faunal elements appeared to be non-random in their dispersal. Portions of the site seemed to be areas which had abnormal amounts of articulated skeletons or skeletal portions. Still other areas of the bone bed appeared to be low in bone density, but correspondingly high in lithic debris and artifacts, or evidence of hearth areas.

15

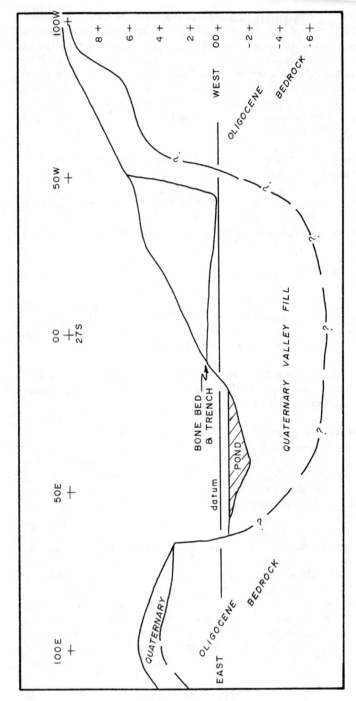

Figure 7. East-West Geologic Profile.

THE HAT CREEK DRAINAGE ARCHAEOLOGICAL SURVEY

Realizing the potential of other Paleo-Indian sites within the Hat Creek drainage, a surface survey was initiated in 1973 and carried out through 1974. The purpose of the survey was to locate new sites, recover a representative surface collection of archaeological material from the area adjacent to the kill site, and to provide some notion of a paleo-environmental control for the location of sites of all ages in this drainage system.

The Hudson-Meng site is located in the southeastern extremities of the north-flowing Hat Creek drainage, a tributary to the Cheyenne River. The area affected is all of Sioux County, north of the Pine Ridge escarpment, and a portion of Dawes County, in Nebraska. Funding nor manpower allowed a 100 per cent survey of the area, but the areas which were surveyed were totally covered.

No large scale topographic maps of the area are available, so mapping and site location were done on acetate overlays of 9" x 9" U. S. G. S. air photos, at a scale of 1:17,000. All sites, fossils or artifacts collected were plotted by resection, using a Brunton compass and prominent topographic features. Artifacts collected were given field numbers and later given permanent numbers reflecting the air photo sheet which covered the location at which they occurrred, plus a sequential site number for that sheet, allowing absolute provenience to be recorded and easily cross referenced.

A total of 148 projectile points were collected, 118 of which were classifiable. Of these points, 35.6% were Paleo-Indian types, 45.8% were corner notched varieties and 18.6% were side notched varieties. One hundred thirty-three scrapers, two hundred eight knives and utilized flakes, twenty-one drills and gravers, eighteen chopper tools, twenty-three ground stone tools and nine ceramic sites were located in the two year survey. One hundred eight, *in situ* hearths were located, most in stratified context.

The above results indicate that approximately one-third of the surficial artifactual material is classifiable as Paleo-Indian. There is an apparent lack of artifactual material dating the interval between the Cody Complex (*ca.* 7000 B. P.) and McKean (*ca.* 3800-4500 B. P.) suggesting abandonment, or marginal habitation of the area during the proposed Altithermal (Antevs, 1955).

Seven major drainages are tributary to Hat Creek. Of these, all but one have their sources in the escarpment, at perennial springs such as the one at Hudson-Meng. Most of the archaeological sites, of all ages, cluster along these drainages, as one would suspect. Most of the Paleo-Indian sites located in the survey appear to be covered by one to seven feet of reworked Oligocene materials and eolian deposits (Hartley and Luoma, 1974; Luoma, 1975).

17

CHAPTER 3

THE BONE BED

From the initial exposure of the bone bed, in the walls of a segment of a tributary drainage and from the area disturbed by construction, plus the rather narrow configurations of the modern topography, it appeared that the bone bed would most likely be a rather sinuous, linear feature not unlike the Olsen-Chubbuck site (Wheat, 1972). Excavation and testing in the initial field season proved that model to be wrong. Rather than a narrow, linear feature, all evidence led to a broad, widespread accumulation.

Test pits dug to as much as four feet below the bone bed level revealed no further occurrence of bone. All excavations through overburden failed to reveal any stratification of the bone deposit or any younger cultural material. The bone bed was one unit, usually no more than one or two bones in thickness, spread over an extensive area. This information argued for a single event, or for several smaller events, which with later data as to the time of year, occurred in a short time-period.

As previously indicated, a portion of the eastern margin of the deposit was destroyed by construction work. In addition, a strong northeast-southwest trend of the area of highest density of bone had been delineated. There was an apparent limit to the bone bed along a northwesterly line, although scattered bone and lithic materials were encountered in test excavations in areas northwest of this limit. Also, areas of cultural activity other than butchering or processing were delineated, such as hearths and lithic workshops.

CONDITION OF THE BONE

When first exposed, the bone was not overly dissimilar from the carbonate-rich earth in which it was entombed. In fact, inexperienced excavators often went through a "sculpt-your-own-bone" routine when the area of excavation was still damp. As the earth and bone dried upon exposure to air, the bone became increasingly harder and whiter allowing it to be cleaned up and any excavating errors, such as imaginary bones, to be identified.

Calcium carbonate impregnated the overburden and filled the root-casts

19

of former plants. These carbonate root-casts were conspicuous markers on the osteological or lithic material from the bone bed.

Once the bone air-dried, it became hard enough to handle and could be removed to the laboratory and studied, without the use of artificial preservatives. Only in the case where broken bones were reunited in the laboratory was glue or impregnating agents used. There is scant evidence from the bone bed for long exposure to the elements, after deposition. In fact, what evidence there is convincingly argues for a rather rapid burial of the deposit, most likely by eolian materials.

One bone shows worm burrowing, indicative that at least this bone, or portion of the bone bed, was possibly exposed through fly-season of the year after deposition. A few bones show rodent gnawing; however, this could have been done by burrowing gophers, moles and similar creatures, underground, rather than a phenomenon associated with a duration of surface exposure. No evidence of large carnivores, either domestic or wild, is present in the bone bed.

METHOD OF EXCAVATING THE BONE BED

Once enough testing and excavation had been completed to realize the bone bed was a thin, lateral unit, like a blanket of bone on the ancient land surface, we could plan our excavation of it. Initial work was done in the areas of bulldozer-disturbance for several reasons. It was here that the bone bed was most likely to be disturbed by the activities of cattle, by amateur excavation, or by natural forces such as erosion, freezing and thawing, or deflation.

As information accumulated with each season's excavations, it became clear that the deposit was more continuous and much more extensive than we had expected. It was also tilted toward the west, into what is presently a rather formidable ridge. One geomorphic feature on that ridge, a rather continuous and noticeably abrupt change in slope, suggested a modern form which might reflect a paleo-feature, such as the west bank of the old drainage system.

It was decided to test this possibility by cutting a backhoe trench, east-west, at about 25 meters south. The trench exposed bone, in increasing density as it was extended westward.

At this point, we also experienced excavation difficulty. The bone bed was inclined westward; at the same time, the modern surface rose westward at an even greater angle. The result was that as we progressed westward with the trenching, we exceeded the depth-limit of the backhoe boom.

The next season brought a bigger backhoe, with greater debth capability, and a new plan for testing the western extent of the bone deposit. It was decided to cut a trench approximately three meters wide, narrowing it to the west as the depth limit was encountered.

In this manner, we exposed sixty-six square meters of the bone bed, in the trench, to the west of the large areas of excavation. We could notice a thinning of bone concentration, yet the bone continued, as did the dark, organic stain associated with it, as far west as we cut the trench. Much of the overburden had to be removed with hand labor and wheelbarrows, making this area expensive in time and effort.

The combined trenching and auger-drilling program suggested the Oligocene bedrock could not be more than ten to twenty meters west of the end of the trench extension in the 1974 season. In the 1975 season, a P & H powershovel with a nineteen foot boom was used to extend the test-trench farther west in an effort to intersect the alluvium-bedrock contact, which would most likely also expose the cross section of the jump area.

Even with the nineteen-foot boom and added power and speed of the large shovel, we had to adopt a "step" method of excavation. We cut as deeply as the unit would dig, then opened an area to a greater depth below surface, approximately six feet, moved the shovel to this lower elevation, and dug the trench floor deeper.

In this manner, we were able to cut the trench floor to approximately 25 feet below the modern surface. The bone-bed was encountered, primarily as the dark, organic stain, but containing bone. Beneath the bone horizon, a stream-sorted sand was exposed. Hand excavation of a pit to twenty-seven feet below the surface exposed a continuum of stream sediments, grading to coarser sizes with depth, ending in cobbles which probably indicated the channel floor, at twenty-seven feet below modern surface. Water table was encountered at this depth, making further vertical testing infeasible.

The information gained from this extension, plus the paleotopographic map compiled over several years, led to a new interpretation of the geomorphic configuration of the jump at the time of the kill. From a steep-walled arroyo model, the new information rather conclusively indicated a wash cutting against the Oligocene bedrock on the west bank, at a meander bend, with a point-bar grading into a terrace on the east.

This interpretation is also substantiated by the density of concentration configuration of the bone bed and by the paleotopographic map. A schematic sketch of the kill site is presented in Figure 8.

Bone was not removed from the site after the middle of the 1973 season. At that point in time, we had more than two hundred animals represented in the laboratory. This population was considered more than adequate for a statistical study of the faunal elements. It had also been proposed that a portion of the site be developed as a permanent exhibit of a Paleo-Indian bison kill.

21

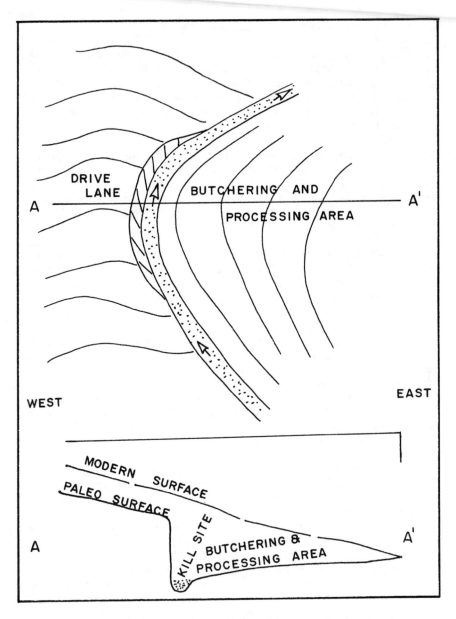

Figure 8. Schematic Sketch of the Kill Site with a Cross-Section showing
the Modern and Paleo surface.

With this prospect in mind, plus a large sample in the laboatory, the bone bed was excavated, mapped and identified, but left in place. The bone which was removed for laboratory study was from that area of the site which had the greatest potential of disturbance or destruction by erosion, pot hunting, etc., due to shallow burial. Most of the area in which bone was removed was the portion of the site from which overburden had been removed for construction of the dam.

The 1977 season was initiated in order that we might excavate and map a portion of the bone bed that would unite the maps of all seasons. The area had been partially excavated in 1975, but was uncompleted due to a week of heavy rain at the close of that field season. A secondary goal of the field season was an exploration program for an associated campsite, satellite to the location of the butchering floor and kill site. This goal was not reached, nor was the exploration program even initiated. We were prohibited from such exploration, and even from opening any new surface area, by the conditions of the new permit.

CHAPTER 4

DISTRIBUTIONAL ANALYSIS OF FAUNAL REMAINS

In an attempt to identify butchering patterns, or other cultural attributes of the bone bed, we carried out a distributional analysis of selected cranial and post-cranial elements.

The methodology applied was a color-coded plot of the elements on the final map of the bone bed. Since each bone was identified and given a number on the field sheets, we had the provenience of each bone within the site. Separate plots were made for scapula, humerus, radius, metacarpal, sacrum, pelvis, femur, tibia, metatarsal and cranial elements. After the individual elements were plotted, front limb and hind limb elements were plotted; each was grouped in a different color code, to further identify processing areas or procedures.

In the field excavation and identification of the faunal elements, it became apparent there were more concentrated areas of certain elements, though no deliberate stacking of units, such as at the Jones-Miller, Olsen-Chubbuck or Casper sites, were observed. As the plots were finished and hung, side by side on the laboratory walls, it became apparent that a pattern did exist. It was not a pattern which correlated with planned, specialized butchering of selected elements in given portions of the butchering floor. Rather, it appeared that all bones, regardless of their anatomical position, were randomly scattered in circular patterns throughout the bone bed, with the presence of a hearth area serving as the center for each of these patterns.

Front limb elements and hind limb elements as well as cranial fragments displayed approximately the same patterning; essentially a random scatter in the circumference of each "butchering circle."

At least six such "hearth-centers" were identified within the excavated portion (Figure 9) of the bone bed. An additional circle is suggested, without a hearth, in the northern portion of the bone bed. This activity area (A) is coincident with the second highest concentration of lithic debris and tools found in the site. The abundance of artifacts (8 projectile points, 2 flake tools, 2 scrapers, 1 abrader) recovered in this area, and the fact that the majority of these tools displayed reuse and reshaping, may signify the last butchering center to be utilized, with discard of expendable tools upon the completion of the work.

25

The fact that each butchering/activity center contains a hearth suggests: 1) roasting of portions of the carcass during the butchering operation, which would be a logical expectation and is evidenced by broken, burned bone in each hearth area; 2) below-normal temperature, indicating fires for heat suggested by the time of year (October-November) derived from the dental erruption patterns; 3) the need for light, carrying the butchering operation, non-stop, to completion once the kill had taken place. The size of several of the hearth areas suggests large fires to allow butchering activities to be carried on after nightfall; 4) a combination of any, or all, of the above.

Speculation as to the number of persons involved in the actual dismembering and fleshing of the carcass is gained by the spatial distribution of the butchering centers and the space limits needed to function in and around these centers. These interpretations are presented in the section on utilization of the products of the Hudson-Meng Bison Kill.

Articulated segments of skeletal units within the bone bed were rather common. A plot of articulated units showed the general butchering center/hearth area distribution described earlier. Articulated limb elements and vertebral sections were the most common units noted. More abundant than articulated units, the isolated bones attested to complete butchering, involving dismembering the skeletal unit in extracting all possible flesh.

In the entire bone bed, only six animals were found that could be considered intact (skeletal); all other animals were nearly completely dismembered. Initially, we suspected a butchering sequence which would fit our initial trap model, i.e., a steep banked arroyo with a butchering-processing area on a terrace surface to the east of the actual kill. This model of the kill site gave rise to a sequential butchering process which would involve: 1) rough butchering at the kill site, including dismemberment of the carcass into handling units (halves or quarters); removal of desired portions of the cranial units and discard of the skull caps; removal of the viscera; 2) transport and distribution of the handling units to specific areas of the terrace surface for finished butchering; 3) finished butchering on the terrace to remove muscle packets from the skeletal elements and process the meat packets from the skeletal elements and process the meat to its final stage.

Both geomorphic evidence and the distributional analysis of the faunal elements indicate the original model of the kill site to be erroneous. The modified model calls for a steep drop on the west bank, with the butchering-processing activities carried out on a point bar-terrace to the east of the actual kill site. The same general process of butchering is thought to have taken place, however. The major discrepency in the original model was the lack of evidence for specialized handling (areas) of selected portions of the carcass, within the butchering floor. On the contrary, it appears that all portions of the carcass derived and transported from the rough butchering area were handled, without discrimination, at the hearth area/butchering centers.

Throughout the six field seasons, the absence of skull caps was an anomaly. Cranial elements were present throughout the bone bed; however, the location of the skull caps with horn cores is still unknown, with the exception of a single skull cap with one horn core (Figure 10). Cranial elements were most commonly represented by mandible fragments, usually paired (both halves) scattered throughout the site. It was assumed that the mandibular presence and distribution represents tongue removal, by removal of the mandible (White, 1953). Maxillary teeth and portions of palates were also rather common, attesting to removal and salvage of the nasals. The remaining cranial elements were petrous portions and basal-occiptal fragments derived from brain extraction.

It has been suggested verbally, and in print (Wormington, 1957: p. 127), that the absence of skull caps in a butchering floor of this type might be explained by their use in ceremony or ritual. That such activity was a part of some kill and butchering stations is highly probable.

It seems more plausible that the removal of nasals, tongue, brains and perhaps eyes, left a large quantity (470-600) of heavy, cumbersome, low value skull caps, which were simply discarded in the rough butchering area.

The 1975 extension of the western trench was undertaking to delineate the paleotopography of the kill site and to explore the possibility of finding the rough butcher area, marked by the presence of some plus 400 discarded skull caps. As described in an earlier section, the vertical exploration in this trench was halted by intersection with static watertable, most probably controlled by the USDA-SCS dam and pond level.

Recovery and analysis of skull caps was a desired product of the excavations in all field seasons. Bison speciation is primarily dependent on skulls and horn cores (Skinner and Kaisen, 1947). In the absence of such data, we resorted to post-cranial metric analysis and the comparison of these data to published reports from other bison populations, modern and extinct (Landrey, 1974: Uridil, 1973).

Major units of the appendicular skeleton are presented in Table 1. The totals for each bone category reflect the excavated portion of the bone bed. It was from these data that the distributional plots were derived. Considering these skeletal elements as paired bones, we derived the maximum and minimum count for the bison population in the excavated portions of the bone bed. Humerus, metacarpal and metatarsal counts all yield more than 370 animals represented, and radii count gives 348. Based on these counts, I feel it is safe to state that approximately 400 animals are represented in the excavations at the Hudson-Meng site. Femur count indicates as many as 474 animals. The excavated portions of the site represent approximately 50 to 60 per cent of the known limits of the bone bed, as based on test pits, backhoe trenches, and excavation units. A conservative estimate for the total population of animals is approximately six hundred. It is noteworthy, that axial elements reflect only approximately one-fourth the total count given by the appendicular elements. This is further support of rough

27

Front Limb Elements	1971	1972	1973	1974	1975	1977	Total	Min. # Animals
Scapula	30	176	141	113	143	19	622	311
Humerus	56	172	206	145	193	20	792	396
Radius	44	145	166	117	202	22	696	348
Ulna	30	184	104	40	104	15	477	239
Metacarpal	35	194	230	97	186	15	757	379
Hind Limb Elements								
Pelvis	10	75	120	114	123	10	452	226
Femur	28	220	261	195	223	21	948	474
Tibia	50	157	188	177	196	24	792	396
Astragalus	40	360		82	72	9	563	282
Calcaneum	32	304		55	70	10	471	236
Metatarsal	43	182	224	107	163	20	739	370
Patella	1	34		8	6		49	25

Minimum number of animals – paired bone count . . . 226
Maximum number of animals – paired bone count . . . 474

Table 1. Major Appendicular Skeletal Bones from the Hudson-Meng Site.

28

	1971	1972	1973	1974	1975	1977	Total	Min. # Animals
Mandible	26	78	82	76	69	13	344	172
Axis	6	20	14	23	21	5	89	89
Atlas	2	15	13	22	17	2	71	71
Cervical	38	66		59	94	12	269	54
Thoracic	45	332		288	280	58	1003	78
Lumbar	27	80		106	103	6	322	54
Sacrum	--	13		27	25	6	71	71
Caudal	--	6		--	--	--	6	1
Unidentified	--	682		34	93	37	846	--
Phalanges								
1st	109	414	503	131	202	21	1380	345
2nd	84	357	394	95	117	17	1064	266
3rd	20	74	65	18	33	6	216	54

Minimum number of animals - axial element count. . . 54
Maximum number of animals - axial element count. . . 172

Table 2. Major Axial Skeletal Elements from the Hudson-Meng Site.

29

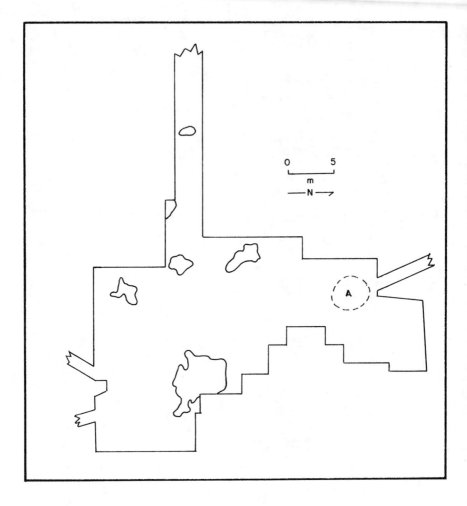

Figure 9. Hearth and Butchering Center Locations.

butchering at the actual kill site with selection and discard of portions of the carcasses.

All evidence from the site (geological, archaeological, paleontological) has convinced me that this is a single component site, used for one brief time, possibly as a result of the coincidence of man, animals and an effective natural trap. Whether the kill site represents one large animal drive, or whether it represents several smaller drives in a short period of time is unknown. Either possibility is acceptable in the light of the evidence produced by the excavation. Analysis of the dentition (Russell, 1973, 1974) has indicated that the kill took place from mid-October to mid-November, based on the tooth erruption pattern of the

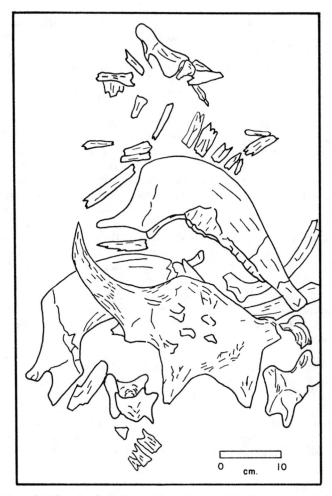

Figure 10. Sketch of the Single Horn Core and Skull cap recovered from the Hudson-Meng Bone Bed (after Pokorski, 1973).

calves. Mass kills, both natural and planned, are recorded in the literature. An animal drive yielding 600 bison is certainly not outside the realm of possibility. Equally acceptable is the alternative theory: several smaller kills over approximately a month's time. My personal feeling is that the evidence indicates a single event.

In an attempt to estimate the physical conditions of an arroyo trap, we calculated the volume of portion of the modern arroyo, just east of the field campsite. This arroyo, (Figure 11) cut since 1935, serves as a reasonable analog of the volumetric requirements of a trap for a herd of bison. Calculations based on the linear measurements provided by Wheat (1972, p. 85) for mature bison cows were used to estimate the volume of an animal. Cows were used, rather than bulls, as the predominant members of the Hudson-Meng herd apparently were cows. Using 1.52 meters as the height to shoulder and 2.13 meters as the length of the average bison cow, excluding the legs and idealizing the shape somewhat; estimating the width as .73 meters, a bison cow has a volume of approximately 1.46 cubic meters. This compares to a volume of .85 cubic meters (30 ft.^{3}) estimated for a 1000 pound steer (Ivan Rush, personal communication) by the Nebraska Cooperative Extension Service. Adding ten per cent for an estimated size difference between modern bison and those from the Hudson-Meng bone bed, a value of 1.61 cubic meters was used in the calculations. The larger values used for bison, as compared to domestic cattle, give an added, conservative, estimate of the space needed.

The arroyo was considered to be V shaped. The width of the arroyo, bank to bank, and the depth measured at mid-width gave the base and height to solve the triangular cross section. The width (base) was 7.98 meters and the height was 4.41 meters. Each ten meter length of the arroyo gave a volume of 176 cubic meters and would accommodate 109 bison cows. A fifty-meter length of the arroyo would accommodate 545 animals. Figuring some calves and immature animals, instead of mature cows, would increase the number of animals that could be packed into such a space.

The foregoing calculations are simply a weighted estimate of the number of bison which could be obtained in a 50-meter length of an arroyo such as is present to the east of the site today. These figures indicate that it would be quite possible to handle the nearly 600 bison represented by the bone bed, in the natural trap which produced the butchering floor. The bone bed is known to be continuous for more than 40 meters in a north-south dimension, which would be parallel to the paleo-drainage and therefore to the bank over which the animals were driven.

In all jump sites in which I have been involved, especially a series of seven jumps in southern Idaho (Agenbroad, 1968, 1976), animals were deflected from drops less than twelve feet (3.2 meters) by stone fences. It would seem safe to assume that the fall used at Hudson-Meng site was at least of this magnitude.

One portion of the bison carcass was apparently ignored at the kill and butchering site. There is no evidence in the bone bed of the utilization of the marrow. Several burned, broken, smashed fragments of long bones do occur in the hearth areas, which indicate at least a casual usage of this resource, but no bone breakage or collection occurs in the majority of the site. The long bones are scattered in the same butcher center patterns as previously described. There is no noted deliberate breakage to gain access to the marrow cavities. What long bone breakage there is apparently came from the fall or by the pressure of overburden and the bone position, as the site was buried. Some bone had certain portions

Figure 11. A Modern Arroyo just East of the Site, Which serves as
An Analog of the Kill Site Arroyo.

removed in butchering, as is discussed under the following section.

Of the plus four hundred animals represented in the excavated portion of the
bone bed, only six remain in articulated position, all in the southwestern portion
of the site. These animals may represent cripples who struggled eastward onto
what became the butcher floor before they were dispatched. They were most
probably left where they lay and butchered at that location, without the dismembering and transport which those in the kill area received. It is highly
unlikely that several hunters would attempt to carry or drag a complete carcass
to those positions. An assessment of their positions suggests that the actual kill,
or drop area, is west, or northwest of the location of the carcasses.

One such animal (Figure 12) was exposed in 32S, 8W. The damaged skull is still in articulation with the vertebral column, extending to mid-thoracic. The right forelimb is still in relative position, as is a portion of the rib cage. The remainder of the skeleton was destroyed by the hearth area of 33S, 8W. Most of the recognizable skeletal units which were in relatively complete articulation were found in that portion of the bone bed bounded by 26 to 33 south and 4 to 6 west.

Figure 12. An Articulated Skeleton in Square 32S, 8W.

CHAPTER 5

BUTCHERING PATTERNS: HUDSON-MENG SITE

As noted earlier, the butchering activity in the Hudson-Meng bone bed apparently took place around "centers" identified as hearths. It has already been suggested that this pattern is probably due to cooking, heat and light. With six hearth-butchering centers identified, we account for the more than 700 excavated and partially excavated squares and can predict the patterns which continue into the unexcavated areas.

We have postulated two major butchering activities, i.e., "rough" butchering at the actual kill site and "finish" butchering around the hearth centers in the bone bed. This model explains the absence of skull caps, lower extremeties, etc., which are low-meat yield portions of the carcass, discarded at the "rough" butchering location.

In assessing the appendicular skeletal elements (Table 1), humeri, radii, and metacarpals are the most abundant representatives of the front limb. Femora, tibiae and metatarsals are the most abundant in the hind limb. This is logical in that the hind quarters (ham) and the shoulder contain the largest muscle packets on the carcass. The hind quarter also contains the choicer cuts, with exception of the loins, hump and ribs. These limb units are the ones I would have predicted to be most common, even prior to excavation.

Articulated segments of the axial skeleton (vertebral column) were also noted (Table 2), many sections still having rib heads and 4-6 inches of the rib still attached. Sacral units were rarely encountered (61 in the entire bone bed) indicating that they, like the skulls, were discarded elsewhere, during the dismembering process.

Pelvis count is low and probably due to destruction of the flat, thin blades of the ischium and illium, plus the rather narrow, delicate arches. It is also probable that the hind legs were cut free of the pelvis in the rough butchering stage. Several pelvi with the femur heads still attached were in the bone bed, indicating the breakage of neck of the femur in the separation of the hind limb from the pelvis.

Approximately half as many ulnae as radii appear in the bone bed. The

35

absence of this bone may be due to its destruction in the butchering practice, in the separation of the upper and lower front limb. The fact that many of these bones are not fused to the radii is further indication of a large portion of the herd being adolescent, or young (less than three and one-half years).

The usage of bison bone as butchering tools is not apparent at this site, only one possible humerus tool (Figure 13) was noted. Although evidence for tibia choppers, humeri tools, etc., were searched for, none were noted. The abundance of bone butchering tools at the Casper site, (Frison, 1974) and the Jones-Miller site (Stanford, personal communication), as well as younger sites such as the Boarding School site (Kehoe, 1967), caused us to look for evidence of such tools. A mule deer humerus was the only bone butchering tool recovered (Figure 21) from the site. With the exception of one antelope scapula, slightly above bone bed, this tool is the only non-bison large mammal bone from the site.

Any analysis of butchering procedure is dependent on a number of variables: preservation of the bone, type of tools used, time available to butcher and process meat, number of animals to be processed, working force, formalized or random butchering patterns and many others. With greater antiquity, the chances of recovery of such data are smaller, as there is less chance for evidence to be preserved. Excellent analyses (Frison, 1974, 1976; Wheat, 1972) have recently been published, giving us a much greater insight into this cultural aspect of mass kills.

From the initial test excavations at the Hudson-Meng site, it became apparent that there was some selectivity on the part of the butchers, as to the portions of the carcass that would be encountered on the butchering floor, as represented by the bone bed. An early observation was the absence of skulls and infrequency of lower limb elements (phalanges in particular). With later analysis, it became apparent that skulls were present, though represented primarily by basal-occipital portions and petrous portions. One skull cap with one damaged horn core (Figure 10) was recovered from the more than four hundred bison represented in the excavated portions of the bone bed. A total of only 65 sacral units were recovered from the entire bone bed. Caudal vertebrae were represented by only six specimens, the rest apparently having been taken with the hides during skinning. The initial observation of few hoof units was particularily true for the third phalanx (enough for only 53 animals). Second and first phalanges were more common, in that order.

Major post-cranial bone were examined for breakage, occurrence, evidence of tool manufacture, or butchering marks. With the carbonate encrustation present on the Hudson-Meng bone, no butchering marks such as cut marks were observable, to allow detailed butchering analysis. Patterned breakage was noticeable on some elements. The absence, or relative absence, of other elements argues for differential handling of portions of the carcass.

HUMERI: Ninety-six per cent of the humeri were partially destroyed in the

36

butchering. The proximal end showed the major damage. In particular, the head, neck and lateral tuberosity were partially to totally destroyed.

All specimens were examined for the possibility of blow marks from stone or bone tools; with the exception of the damage already described, no such breakage was observed. Modification of humeri to make bone tools, such as those described at the Casper site (Frison, 1974), was not noted in the field work. Of the 317 specimens examined in the laboratory, only one humerus (Figure 13) resembles the bison bone tools described by Frison (1974, 1976).

FEMORA: Eighty-six per cent of the femora removed from the bone bed, and analyzed in the laboratory, display breakage. Of this number, sixty-three per cent show both ends damaged; nineteen per cent show proximal damage only; and eighteen per cent show distal damage only. A high frequency of detached femur heads within the bone bed argues for either a large number of young animals, or detachment of the femur by breakage of the neck of the femur, leaving the ball attached to the pelvis. Distal breakage suggests separation at the femur-tibia joint.

TIBIAE: All the tibiae collected were given close examination in the laboratory for blow marks or secondary usage as butchering tools. No pattern was noted except the near total destruction of the tibial crest on the proximal end (Figure 14). Of 213 proximal specimens collected from the bone bed and inspected in the laboratory, all but eight (3.8%) had this prominence partially or completely destroyed. The inference is that the lower limb was separated from the upper portion at the femur-tibia juncture. The destruction of the tibial crest was the result of the destruction of the patella and the anterior portion of the tibia in joint separation. No break marks, such as hammerstone blows or the manufacture of tibia choppers were noted.

PATELLAE: Only 49 patellae representing 25 animals, were recovered from the site. The abundance of femora and tibiae indicate patellar destruction, or discard, in the butchering pattern.

METAPODIALS: Metapodials display a very similar damage pattern. Metacarpals show 22 per cent proximal damage only; 39 per cent distal damage only; and 39 per cent with damage to both ends. Metatarsals show 19 per cent proximal, 42 per cent distal, and 39 per cent with both ends damaged.

SCAPULAE: Scapulae were relatively undamaged. It appears that the damage done to bone in separation of the scapula-humerus joint was primarily carried by the humeri.

VERTEBRAE and RIBS: Few vertebral dorsal spines were deliberately broken. Most thoracic vertebrae were intact, as were the lower cervicals. Lumbar vertebrae often displayed damage to the transverse processes, but not commonly enough to be interpreted as a butchering pattern. The most common vertebral

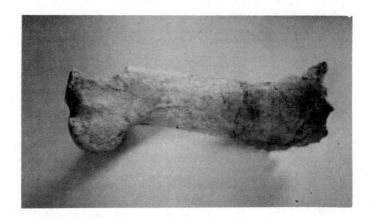

Figure 13. Possible Bison Humerus Butchering Tool.

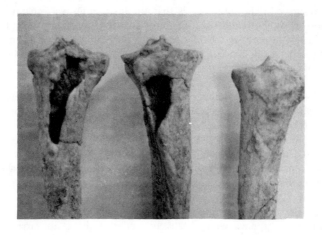

Figure 14. Tibiae, Displaying Characteristic Damage of the Tibial Crest.

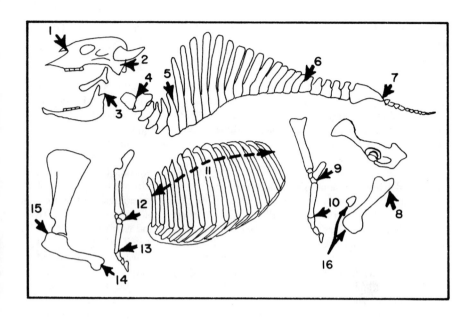

Figure 15. Patterned disarticulation points (modified from Frison, 1976) of the Hudson-Meng bison. (The number sequence is for explanation only, it is not meant to imply a sequence of butchering activity.) (1) separation of the nasals at the nasal/frontal suture; (2) separation of the skull cap from the basal-occipital and temporal bones along suture lines; (3) separation of the mandible by detaching the ascending ramus, or the mandibular condyle; (4) severing the skull from the vertebral column at the atlanto-axis juncture; (5) separation of the thoracic and cervical vertebrae; (6) separation of the thoracic and lumbar vertebrae; (7) separation of the caudal vertebrae (probably with the hide); (8) separation of the femur from the pelvis, often by breaking the neck of the femur, leaving femur heads in articulation with the pelvis; (9) separation at the astraglus-calcaneum / metatarsal; (10) separation at the metatarsal/1st phalanx; (11) breakage of the ribs at 5-8 inches from the vertebrae (dashed line indicates the practice was common, but not universal; (12) separation at the radius/metacarpal joint; (13) separation at the metacarpal/phalanx; (14) separation at the distal end of the humerus; (15) separation with considerable damage to the proximal end of the humerus at the scapula/humerus junction. (16) separation of the femur/tibia with removal of the patella.

pattern was to find segments of the vertebral column, still in articulation. Often rib segments up to six or seven inches long (Figure 16) would remain attached. Most ribs were whole, however.

From the analysis of bone damage considered to be due to butchering practices, a group of major steps in butchering pattern used at Hudson-Meng appears. Using a diagram published by Frison (1976), arrows indicate the major points of disarticulation of the Hudson-Meng skeletons (Figure 15). It should be kept in mind that not all animals were dissected in the same manner.

The absence of complete skulls, after two field seasons of excavation, prompted laboratory analysis of skull fragments recovered from the bone bed. In particular, petrous portions had been noted from the earliest analysis of the bone bed. It was decided to plot the distribution of these elements and any identifiable skull fragments, as well as the occurrence of atlas and axis vertebrae. The results of the initial analysis were reported by Hartley and Pokorski (1973), and Moody (1974). One conclusion, made during their studies, was skull removal at the atlanto-axis juncture, a procedure also noted by Wheat (1971, p. 99) and Frison (1970, p. 22). At the Hudson-Meng site, the axis and atlas vertebrae showed nearly 100 per cent breakage (Table 3). In the bone bed, atlas vertebrae were often associated with skull fragments, whereas the axis was more commonly associated with the cervical vertebrae.

Brain removal customarily takes one of two patterns in prehistoric sites: through the forehead, or through the basal-occipital portion of the skull. The former method is described most commonly in prehistoric and historic accounts (Wheat, 1972; Kehoe, 1967; Frison, 1970).

At the Hudson-Meng site, the evidence supports the latter method of brain extraction. The majority of skull fragments are from the basal-occipital and temporal regions of the skull. The most common clue of skull butchering encountered in the excavation was the presence of a single or paired petrous portions. In analysis of the skull fragments recovered from the bone bed, Hartley and Pokorsky (1973) postulated that the method of opening the skull was to remove the triangular unit of the basilar portion of the occipital. This unit, outlined by suture patterns (Figure 17), was most represented by fragments of skull from the site (other than petrous portions). Fragments of the Bulla Tympannicus were also relatively abundant.

In an attempt to reconstruct the method of butchering the skull, using a prehistoric tool kit, Hartley and Pokorski obtained several cattle skulls from a local slaughter house and used a hammerstone and quartzite chopper as tools. The result of their experimentation leads to the conclusion that the basal-occipital portion was removed, selectively, along suture lines. The laboratory experimentation produced a very clean, easily extracted brain, with minimal work. The process used by Hartley and Pokorski (*ibid.*) is described:

AXIS		ATLAS	
Spinous process broken	33%	Only anterior articulatory surface present	35%
Right posterior portion missing	8%	Dorsal arch broken or missing	45%
Only anterior articulatory surface remaining	42%	Right or left half of vertebra missing	20%
Only ventral surface remaining unbroken	9%		
	100%		100%

Table 3. Atlas-Axis Vertebral Damage
(After Hartley & Pokorski, 1973)

Figure 16. Thoracic Vertebrae with Dorsal Spines Broken and 5-7 Inches of Rib Head Attached.

First, we broke the zygomatic arch, if it was not already broken by removal of the jaw. Next, we perforated along the suture between the parietal and the squamous temporal regions, and the supra-occipital bone laterally above the median occipital crest. After chopping through the nares posterior to the palatine process, slight raps ventrally to the occipital condyles will separate the basal portion. After cutting minor attachments of the meningeal membrane to the cranial cavity the brain will remain with the basal portion. This method leaves the brain free of bone chippings and fragments. Our first attempt at this method took approximately 15 minutes. We reduced our time by half in our second attempt. Subsequent attempts have not been made, but we are confident of reducing our time of butchering further. This method leaves skull parts in articulation exactly as basal

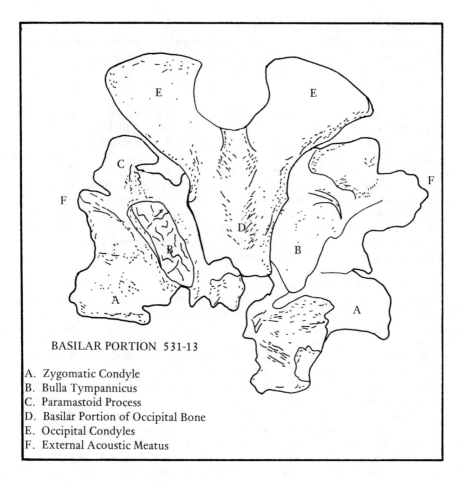

BASILAR PORTION 531-13

A. Zygomatic Condyle
B. Bulla Tympannicus
C. Paramastoid Process
D. Basilar Portion of Occipital Bone
E. Occipital Condyles
F. External Acoustic Meatus

Figure 17. Basal Skull Fragment - "Typical" Skull Butchering Unit.
(Hartley and Pokorski, 1973).

portion (531-13). The basal portion would seem to indicate that this method was employed at least once. The highly fractured nature of the majority of the skull elements and their distribution, would seem to indicate that the basal portion was deliberately removed by smashing blows to the temporal and basal region. It might be important to note here that we observed a number of femur heads in close association with various skull elements. It might be theorized that fresh femurs were used to disarticulate the basal section of the skull.

Mandible scatter throughout the site, often in pairs, indicates the removal of the entire mandible in extraction of the tongue. Approximately 70 per cent of the mandibles have the ascending ramus broken. White (1953) states this to be the earliest method of extraction of the tongue, removing the mandible and tongue as one unit.

The third portion of the skull that was butchered, with evidence left in the bone bed, is the nasal cartilage. It was not uncommon to find maxillary teeth associated with and, in some cases, in proper position with mandibles and, occasionally, palate. From the evidence, it appears that the entire nasal region was removed from the skull by chopping along the suture between the maxillary and malar bones on both sides of the skull, then chopping upward to the dorsal juncture of the maxillary-nasal sutures. The nasal-frontal suture is then chopped and the nares severed posterior to the palatine process. The nasals could have been removed by random blows, but maxilla with teeth from the fourth pre-molar to the third molar, still in place, are scattered through the bone bed. Random smashing or chopping of the nasal would produce few complete units.

An attempt was made to identify the broken burned scrap bone from a large hearth area centered at 00 + 25S. In thirteen square meters, 971 bone fragments were collected, and positive identification of only 86 of these fragments (8.9%) was possible. Though most portions of the skeleton were represented by at least one specimen, the majority of identifiable scrap was: phalanges (30%); petrous portions (14%); metapodials (9%); ribs (8%). An additional 14% can be accounted for by combining "joint elements" such as carpals, calcaneum, astragalus, and ulnar fragments. Of the identified fragments, 75% are of low-meat yield portions of the carcass, indicating an on-site use of such portions for consumption during the butchering process. The extreme fragmentation of all the bone scrap in the hearth areas suggests marrow extraction from these bones, whereas the majority of the bone bed gives no evidence for marrow extraction. An alternate explanation would be that those portions of the carcass were thrown in the fire as discard. Such an explanation fails to account satisfactorily for the intense fragmentation and high incidence of spiral breakage displayed by the bone fragments.

CHAPTER 6

MEAT PRODUCTION AND UTILIZATION

Any attempt to reconstruct the time spent in butchering and processing the kill represented by the bone bed will be speculative. Two major considerations are: 1) was it a single kill involving some six hundred animals? or 2) was it a series of smaller kills spread over a month period? All evidence supports the idea that whichever option is correct, it could be considered a single event. The absence of stratified bone layers, the continuous homogeneity of the bone bed and the distribution of faunal elements within it, plus the artifacts and butchering patterns, all argue for a single event by the same group of people. Whether the butchering was done in a few days, processing a large kill, or in three or four weeks processing several smaller kills seems to be less important than the fact that a group of hunters processed some six hundred bison at this location, at a point in time (October-November) some 9,820 years ago.

Although speculation and assumptions have to be made, it is worth the effort to get at least a weighted concept of the amount of meat processed, the number of people involved, the time to conduct such an operation, and the handling of the final products. Wheat (1972) has done an outstanding job of researching published data with regard to butchering time, methods, yield, and disposition of final product. He has more control of the data from the bone bed, in that skulls allowed aging and sexing of most of the animals. From comparison of modern bison, he adjusts the figure to account for larger, extinct forms.

The bone bed at Hudson-Meng has been analyzed in a similar manner, with some modifications. The butchering time figures, butcher ratio, and conversion factor of fresh to dried meat have been adopted from Wheat's values. The yield per animal has been adjusted, so as to be intermediate between modern bison and *Bison occidentalis*.

Estimates of the amount of meat butchered and processed at the Hudson-Meng site are based on the work done by Wheat (*ibid.* p. 114) at the Olsen-Chubbuck site in southeastern Colorado. The figures used for *Bison bison* calculations in Table 4 are the result of averaging the values he gives for cows and bulls. The table presented is a modified form of the one given for the Olsen-Chubbuck site. We lacked the sex differentiation, due to lack of skulls. Estimates made from the graphic plots for metapodials and phalanges were not consistent enough to

45

infer validity. The data presented are an approximation, a conservative one in my opinion, of the amount of meat produced and processed at the site. The actual amount of meat handled is unknown; these estimates allow comparison with other sites and estimates of the number of persons involved in the total operation. Since the metric analysis of the post-cranial elements suggests a form of bison intermediate with modern bison and *Bison occidentalis*, as used in the Olsen-Chubbuck calculation, I have been chosen a twelve per cent increase over *Bison bison* as representative of the increase in size. Wheat (*ibid.* p. 114) used a twenty-five per cent increase for his calculations.

Destruction of a portion of the bone bed by U. S. D. A. - S. C. S. dam construction prevents any analysis of the number of animals represented by the total bone deposits. Based on the density maps and bone bed configuration derived in six field seasons, it is estimated that 10-25 per cent of the original extent of bone was destroyed in the construction efforts. This estimate would alter any of the analyses and calculations made on the yield of meat products and processing time. The portion of the site which was destroyed lies in a low bone density area as seen on the bone density map (Figure 5). The disturbed portion is in the east-northeast portion of the site. Using the estimated percentages given above, an additional sixty to one hundred-fifty animals could be added to the total faunal population represented by the bone bed.

Such an addition was not considered in the calculations. The estimates and resulting calculations are considered conservative and have been deliberately kept on the conservative side, to produce minimum figures in an attempt to get a more realistic model of the total operation, rather than create an impression of great magnitude and volume. Any figures used or derived could easily, validly, be adjusted upward. The conservative estimates give us additional "safety" factors in the consideration of meat yield and persons involved.

The calculations as to time requirements for butchering the animals are considered to be the same as used by Wheat (*ibid.* p. 116), one and a half man hours per bison, even though the Hudson-Meng bison are probably somewhat smaller than the ones he reports. Of the 400 animals represented in the bone bed, only 1.5 per cent were still in articulated position indicating less butchering of these animals. Projecting this percentage to the estimated 600 animals in the bone bed, we can assume eight were partially butchered and 592 (98%) were totally butchered. These figures multiplied by one and one-half hours for total butchering and one hour for partial butchering (per animal) yields figures of 898 hours (total) and 8 hours (partial) for a total of 906 hours spent in butchering.

These figures call for a butchering work force of at least 25 men over a continuous period of 36 hours, or from one and one-half to three and one-half days. Considering the time of year suggested by the tooth erruption, it is conceivable that such a time estimate is within reason.

Based on the foregoing estimates and calculations using those figures, I

Computed # Bison	(+4 yrs.) Adult (17%)	(1-4 yrs.) Immature (68%)	(-1 yr.) Juvenile (15%)		
	68 (17%)	272 (68%)	60 (15%)		
wt. of usable meat per (50% butcher ratio)	(lb.) 475	188	50		
	(kg.) 220	85.2	22.7		
total wt. of usable meat in kill	(lb.) 32,300	51,136	3,000	(43.22) 86,436	tn. lb.
	(kg.) 14,960	23,283	1,362	39,605	kg.
total estimated wt. of meat butchered with 12% increase for 400 H-M Bison	(lb.) 36,176	57,272	3,360	(48.40) 96,808	tn. lb.
	(kg.) 16,755	26,076	1,525	44,357	kg.
total estimated wt. of meat for H-M bison with an estimated 600 animals	(lb.) 54,264	85,908	5,040	(72.61) 145,212	tn. lb.
	(kg.) 25,133	39,114	2,288	66,535	kg.

Table 4. Age Distribution of the Hudson-Meng Kill with Analysis of Yield of Usable Meat. (Age groups from Table 7)

47

conclude that a group of sixty to eighty persons (men, women, and children), having at least 25 men and adolescent boys, could have handled the entire herd represented by the bone bed, in less than four days. This statement represents the time and labor needed to butcher and jerk (woman's task) the meat from approximately 600 bison. This is substantiated in part by Wheat (*ibid.*, p. 110), quoting Denig (1930, p. 533) with regard to a small camp of Assiniboin being able to skin and butcher from three hundred to six hundred bison in two to three days.

One can speculate on the number of persons in a "small camp," on the completeness of butchering, on sex ratios and adult-child ratios, etc. The fact of a pedestrian hunting group at the onset of a High Plains winter must also be taken into account. It is hard for me to accept an estimate of 200-300 persons involved in a kill operation such as the Hudson-Meng site. I will concede the possibility of a prearranged communal hunt between several bands. To make this coincident with game animals and a temporary, fortuitous natural trap at a given locality is improbable.

One other factor, the possibility of two to four smaller drives in a month's time, would even more easily be handled by a small group of people. The immediate disposal of the meat and meat products is not as great a concern as it would have been for the people at Olsen-Chubbuck. The season of the year differed; early summer (Wheat, *ibid.*, p. 1) for Olsen-Chubbuck and late fall-early winter for Hudson-Meng. With the temperature lows associated with western Nebraska nights in late October to early November, meat spoilage would be greatly reduced. The season is reminiscent of the home butchering of beef in my own boyhood. We slaughtered, skinned and dressed the carcass, then suspended it from the boom on a hay derrick (used for high stacking of long hay) for several days, to age. The usual time for such an operation was October, after the flies had been eliminated and the night cold chilled the meat through the day, while it was suspended thirty to forty feet above the ground.

With the climatic conditions of the bison kill, meat spoilage would be slowed, allowing an extra time for butchering, if needed. The two to four days suggested earlier are well within reason, both as to time requirements for handling the meat, as well as to time requirements due to spoilage.

The desired end product of a communal hunt of this nature is a storable surplus of meat and meat products such as jerky or pemmican. The number of animals and tonnage of raw meat preclude any notion of fresh meat consumption as the total desired result.

Fall hunts take the animals in their prime condition. They allow the accumulation of a supply of meat products to take the group through the disagreeable conditions for hunting and procurement that High Plains winters produce.

With the calculated estimates as to the total yield of meat and jerky produced at this kill, one is then faced with consumption and transport analysis. A population approaching ridiculous size would have to be postulated for a pedestrian group, carrying their possessions, to transport the yield from such a kill. Alternate interpretations allow efficient use and transport of the same total, by a reasonable population, such as the sixty to eighty persons derived in earlier estimates.

Perhaps the most awe-inspiring figure from the calculations is that of the total yield of meat and even the total of jerky processed (Table 5), from that meat. The immediate transportation of such a supply by so few individuals is an impossibility. The removal of a minor amount, such as could be carried in addition to all the other belongings, requires some method of storage, a cache, for the remainder. Several methods could have been employed. Hanging jerked meat, suspended in fresh skin pouches, from tree limbs is one feasible method. A hide-lined cache pit, dug in the wash bank and covered with two to three feet of dirt, would provide a concealed storage which could be re-entered at will, even in frozen ground conditions, by building a fire over it to thaw the enclosing top layer of earth. It could be resealed after the removal part of the contents, for re-entry at a later date.

The physical setting of the Hudson-Meng Kill site does not have much appeal for a winter camp. The winter storm track would cause the most severe wind and snow conditions on the north slope of this projection of the Pine Ridge escarpment. Much more desirable campsites occur along the White River, some twenty miles southeast. High bluffs offer shelter from the wind; timber, grass, water and game are concentrated along the meandering stream. As the need for jerky arose, a party could be sent to the kill site to open the cache and retrieve a new supply. Even the Sand Creek drainage, a mile south of the kill, would provide better shelter, fuel, and comfort than the north slope of the ridge.

No evidence of either cache or camp areas has been discovered. The cache model is called for due to the improbability of the population needed to carry several tons of dried meat, even with the help of dog packs or travois.

If calculations are made as to the total amount of meat eaten by dogs and the postulated human population, the total yield of meat for processing into jerky is reduced. Using the figures used by Wheat (*ibid.*, p. 122) of ten pounds per day per person and eight pounds per day per dog; using the maximum estimate of persons at Hudson-Meng as eighty and estimating one hundred sixty dogs, we can make some hypothetical calculations. Eighty humans consuming ten pounds of fresh meat a day would dispose of 3200 pounds in the four days postulated for butchering. One hundred sixty dogs would consume an additional 5120 pounds in the same time period. This gives a total consumption of 8320 pounds of fresh meat consumed in a four-day period by such a postulated human and dog population.

Some factors which should also be kept in mind are that the figures given

49

Total Meat Yield		Process 75% of meat	Process 50% of meat	Process 33% of meat	Process 25% of meat
600 animals (total bone bed)	(1b.)	21,781	14,521	9,584	7,260
400 animals (excavated bone bed)	(1b.)	14,521	9,681	6,389	4,840
400 *Bison bison*	(1b.)	12,965	8,644	5,705	4,322

Table 5. Dried Meat (Jerky) (1/5 ratio) Production from Fresh Meat Yield. (Based on the figures of Table 4).

consider only the yield of fresh meat. They do not consider the tongue, brains, heart, liver, lungs, nasals and other "soft" portions of the carcass. Any, or all, of these portions used would alter the total meat consumption. In the same manner, scraps and discard to humans are readily acceptable to dogs. As a final qualifying statement, there is no evidence of dogs being with the hunting party. The inclusion of dogs in the calculations is an assumption based on the need of a pedestrian group for a pack animal.

Table 5 is an attempt to quantify the amount of processed meat at the site assuming that 75%, 50%, 33% and 25% of the meat was ultimately processed into jerky. Even at the 25% figure, the six hundred Hudson-Meng bison would have produced over three and one half tons of dried meat; at the 75% figure, the total would have been nearly eleven tons of dried meat.

Using Wheat's (*ibid.*) figures for transportation by humans (100 pounds) and dogs (50 pounds) and considering a hypothetical twenty-five men and adolescent boy population as used earlier, an equal number of women and adolescent girls and approximately thirty children, all loaded (men and women equal 100 pounds, children equal 20 pounds), one gets a figure of 6400 pounds for transport by eighty humans and one hundred sixty dogs, carrying only dried meat.

Again, such calculations call for storage of meat in some type of cache. Even at the 25 per cent production figure, there was a need for storage of that which couldn't be carried under the extreme conditions mentioned above.

As stated earlier, such calculations are hypothetical and based on assumptions. They serve, however, to give a close approximation of the yield from such a kill, the total hours of butchering time, and the possible yield of jerked, storable meat products. They also serve as a means to quantify the total human population involved. Such calculations indicate that a kill of this magnitude could be handled by considerably fewer than 100 individuals; that efficient processing of the carcasses could be done in a short time period, and the end product of such an enterprise was a large quantity of storable food surplus; part of which had to be stored at, or near, the kill in some manner.

The bone bed itself, by the evidence of complete butchering for 99 per cent of the animals, substantiates an efficient, high-yield operation. The only resource which apparently was not fully utilized was that of bone marrow; Wheat (*ibid.*, p. 121) derives a figure of 7.5 pounds (3.3 kg.) of marrow per animal. With a population of six hundred animals, we can consider the waste of 4500 pounds (1980 kg.) of bone marrow. That some marrow was used probably during the butchering is evidenced by burned, split and broken marrow bone fragments in the hearth areas. Most of the marrow bones were not used for marrow resources, however. No estimate has been made as to the tallow and fat resources, though data for such calculations are available in Wheat's excellent monograph.

51

Pemmican production is another possibility that could be pursued. It is dependent on the production of jerked meat, therefore, the previous calculations are considered relevant to the bison kill and its food production. Further processes and processing are of secondary importance to the consideration of the kill site and butchering/processing activities.

CHAPTER 7

THE HUDSON-MENG BISON

POST-CRANIAL COMPARISONS

Post-cranial analysis of the bison bones was undertaken in 1971 and continued through 1973, which was the last year that bone was removed from the field. The initial procedure was that used by Lorrain (1968) at the Bonfire Shelter in Texas. Preliminary comparisons (Farrens, *et al.*, 1972; Uridil, 1972) were made with the Bonfire bison (Table 6), as this site contained separate bone beds of extinct and modern bison. From the initial analysis, the trend was set: the Hudson-Meng bison were intermediate, in post-cranial attributes, to extinct and modern forms of bison.

Bone Bed 2, at Bonfire (extinct bison), lacked the skull caps and tail bones, as did the Hudson-Meng deposit. The absence of caudal vertebrae is considered to be a consequence of skinning (Wormington, 1957, p. 26, 146) and was the case at both Bonfire and Hudson-Meng. The Olsen-Chubbuck and Casper sites report a relative abundance of caudal vertebrae. The missing skull caps and horn cores are added similarities between Bonfire and Hudson-Meng and are, again, in contrast to the deposits at Olsen-Chubbuck and Casper. Another similarity of the Bonfire bone deposit is that Bone Bed 3 (modern bison) "is concluded to represent the remains of a single herd of some 800 animals," comparing with the estimated 600 plus animals at Hudson-Meng, in what is considered a single event.

Initial comparisons were made with the astragalus, naviculocuboid and calcaneum. The analyses were later expanded to include all of the major long bones (Urdil, 1973; Landrey, 1974). As analyses were expanded, so were comparative collections, allowing greater geographic and temporal range. In part, this was also prompted by the small sample size (as few as four bones) for some of the Bonfire material.

Initial attempts at sexing the population were made using scatter diagrams with plots of transverse width at shaft center as opposed to overall length of the metapodials. Duffield (1973) states: "No reason could be found why this paricular index should indicate sexual dimorphism." He refers to the index developed by Lorrain: $I = \frac{L}{TWCS} \times 100$. Referring to Empel and Roskoz's data (1963) on European bison of known sex, he notes overlap between the indices. Since some

	(Extinct) Bed 2 Bonfire	Hudson–Meng	(Modern) Bed 3 Bonfire
ASTRAGALUS			
LLS	83.1	77.4	73.5
LMS	77.3	72.5	69.0
TWPE	49.2	48.7	44.1
TWDE	54.5	49.6	47.3
APWC	46.1	41.4	44.9
V (cm.^{3})	114.0	88.4	77.0
NAVICULO–CUBOID			
L	50.1	45.2	45.7
TW	66.3	57.3	59.5
APW	64.2	55.2	56.7
CALCANEUM			
L	166.2	151.6	146.0
TW	49.1	47.5	42.6
APW	65.9	59.7	57.8
TWPE	41.2	35.5	35.2
APWPE	42.2	38.2	38.4
RADIUS			
L	383.0	323.1	303.2
TWPE	103.3	87.3	82.4
APWPE	52.4	46.2	44.9
TWDE	96.0	79.2	76.0
TIBIA			
L		388.6	366.0
TWPE	117.0	108.5	100.8
TWDE	74.9	69.7	65.5
FEMUR			
TWPE	151.7	125.0	120.5
TWDE	98.7	101.2	89.8
APWDE	137.6	132.6	107.5
Diam. (Head)	57.3	53.8	51.6
HUMERUS			
L		304.7	289.0
TWDE	96.4	86.9	81.7

Table 6. Metric Attributes of Selected Hudson-Meng Post-Cranial Skeletal Elements Compared to the Bonfire Shelter (Dibble and Lorrain, 1968), (After Uridil, 1972, 1973; Landry, 1974).

	(Extinct) Bed 2 Bonfire	Hudson—Meng	(Modern) Bed 3 Bonfire
FIRST PHALANX			
L	75.1	68.4	66.2
TWPE	37.6	32.8	32.2
APWPE	40.4	36.1	34.1
TWDE	36.8	31.7	30.8
SECOND PHALANX			
L	49.5		43.8
TWPE	39.3		31.5
APWPE	40.3		32.7
TWDE	32.8		26.8
THIRD PHALANX			
L	75.2	65.0	68.3
TWAS	28.2	24.3	23.9
APW	53.8	46.3	45.6

Table 6 (continued).

Explanation: L = length; LLS = length, lateral surface; LMS = length, medial surface; TW = transverse width; TWPE = transverse width, proximal end; TWDE = transverse width, distal end; TWAS = transverse width, articular surface; APWPE = anterior-posterior width, proximal end; APWC = anterior-posterior width, center.

of the individual indices fall within the range of the opposite sex, they could be considered to be either male or female, depending on where the division was made. Duffield suggests use of the index developed by Lorrain, plotted against the greatest width of the distal end of the metapodial. This plot will produce two clusters: those with higher values will represent males; those with lower values will represent females. Such plots (Figure 18) were made for the analysis by Landrey (1973). The result of these plots on metacarpals (fused, partially fused, and unfused) for the 1973 season suggests 7-9% males, 11-18% male or female, 73-82% female. It is also noted that, even with Duffield's method, some adolescent males could be represented in the female population.

DENTAL ANALYSIS AND COMPARISONS

Russell (1973, 1974), Russell-Painter (1975, personal communication) analyzed the bison population on the basis of dentition. Population size was based on the count of mandibular first molars, divided by two. The count was then cross-checked by a count of all mandibular first molars, by side. The latter count was taken as the population, when it gave larger results than the count halved. This analysis gave a total population of 222 animals removed from the bone bed and analyzed in the laboratory. Beginning with the latter part of the 1973 season, bone was left, *in situ*, in the field.

Ages were assigned to the mandibles using the procedures explained by Frison and Reher(1970) and Reher (1973, 1974), Frison, *et al.* (1976). This analysis of age groups is presented in Table 7. It totals 34.2% less than two year old; 49.1% from two to four years old, and 16.6% greater than four years of age. The dentition data provide different statistics, and are more reliable than the information gained from the metapodial fusion.

On the basis of post-cranial metric analysis of more than 200 animals (Uridil, 1972, 1973 and Landrey, 1974), the bison at Hudson-Meng are larger than modern bison, yet smaller than the more common forms of extinct bison. Comparative studies (Table 8) were made with Bonfire Shelter in Texas (Dibble and Lorrain, 1968), the Olsen-Chubbuck Kill, Colorado (Wheat, 1972; Bedord, 1974), the Casper Site (Bedord, 1974), and Hawken Site (Frison, *et al.*, 1974) in Wyoming, the Wasden Site in Idaho (Butler, Gildersleeve and Sommers, 1971), the Duffield Site in Alberta (Hillerud, 1966), and the Birch Creek Bison Cave in Idaho (Butler, *et al.*, 1971). This comparative material includes extinct and modern bison, in dated horizons.

Most of the work was done on metapodials, as was done in the comparative reports. Radii, humeri, femora, astragali and tibiae were also compared, where data exist. From the earliest comparisons, on small samples, to the final data on the bone removed to the laboratory, the Hudson-Meng specimens are intermediate between older forms and more modern forms of bison. It is therefore proposed

56

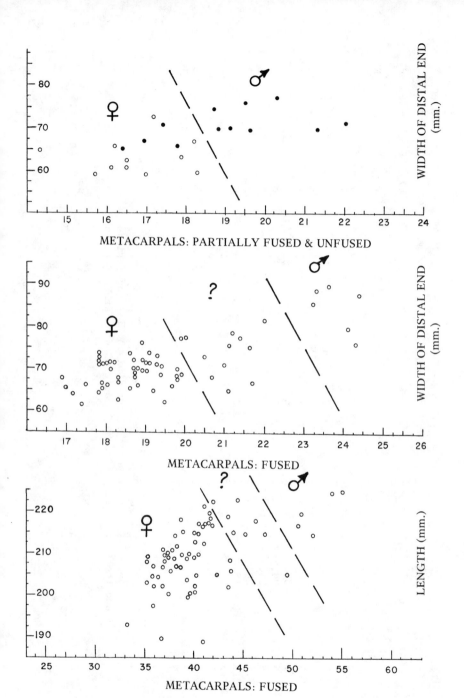

Figure 18. Metacarpal Dimensions Plotted against $I = \dfrac{\text{length}}{\text{TWCS}}$

age group	CASPER Reher, 1974 (9,830–10,060 BP)		HUDSON-MENG Russell-Painter, 1975 (8,990–9,820 BP)		WARDELL Reher, 1973 (990–1,170 BP)		GLENROCK Reher, 1970 (210–280 BP)	
	ht	N	ht	N	ht	N	ht	N
.5		18	51.2	34	48.5	2	54.1	2
1.5		0	48.4	42	44.3	1	46.3	3
2.5		5	42.2	90	41.0	6	38.2	3
3.5		4	38.2	19	36.5	14	34.7	12
4.5		4	35.1	5	33.5	11	28.2	14
5.5	32.2	8	29.4	7	31.0	7	25.4	8
6.5	29.8	7	26.9	5	27.6	9	22.5	7
7.5	26.1	11	23.5	9	25.2	12	20.4	8
8.5	20.5	9	22.0	3	22.3	12	17.0	9
9.5	15.4	3	18.0	3	18.7	8	13.2	17
10.5	11.2	4	15.2	5	14.8	6	9.3	9
11.5	5.0	1			9.9	1	5.6	13
12.5					5.5	2	2.5	5
13.5					4.0	2	0.0	11
14.5					.1	2	0.0	

Table 7. Comparison of Selected Bison Kill Populations And the Average Height of Measurable Mandibular M_1 Metaconids.

Table 8. Comparison of Metapodial Metric Attributes.

METACARPALS	Bonfire Bed 2 (10,230 B.P.)	Olsen-Chubbuck (10,150 B.P.)	Casper (9,830-10,060 B.P.) Mature	Hawken (4,520 B.P.) Mature	Wasden (8,000 B.P.) Mature	Hudson-Meng (9,820 B.P.) Mature	Duffield (8,000 B.P.) Mature	Birch Creek (2,600 B.P.)
L	216.9	215.7	213.4	209.6	214.8	209.9	208.6	205.0
TWPE	74.2	73.3	71.7	71.4	70.8	66.3	71.6	67.9
TWDE	78.4	76.3	75.5	75.4	71.5	71.3	73.1	71.9
TWCS		44.0	43.0	42.5	40.3	40.5		45.4
APWCS		29.9	29.6	28.5	27.6	28.0		30.1
APWPE		44.2	42.8	42.6	41.3	39.7	41.7	40.9
APWDE		40.9	39.7	38.7	39.4	37.1	38.3	37.9
MTWS		43.6	43.0	42.0	40.2	40.0	40.6	44.3
MAPWS		28.1	27.6	26.8	26.5	26.6	29.1	27.0

METATARSALS	Bonfire Bed 2 (10,230 B.P.)	Olsen-Chubbuck (10,150 B.P.)	Casper (9,830-10,060 B.P.) Mature	Hawken (4,520 B.P.) Mature	Wasden (8,000 B.P.) Mature	Hudson-Meng (9,820 B.P.) Mature	Duffield (8,000 B.P.) Mature	Birch Creek (2,600 B.P.)
L	263.5	258.7	261.2	256.7	267.86	257.75	252.43	252.00
TWPE	56.3	58.7	57.2	56.7	55.40	53.20	54.4	52.6
TWDE	70.5	70.8	68.5	65.9	66.3	65.6	63.6	62.9
TWCS		37.0	38.2	34.0	33.4	33.7		35.1
APWCS		37.2	34.3	33.7	33.8	33.6		36.1
APWPE		57.7	55.2	53.4	53.7	52.2	51.0	50.5
APWDE		41.4	40.3	38.2	39.6	37.2	37.4	37.3
MTWS		36.0	33.9	32.9	33.1	32.5	30.0	33.3
MAPWS		32.2	31.0	29.8	29.4	30.4	32.4	30.0

Table 8. (continued).

that the animals whose remains comprise the Hudson-Meng bone bed represent an intermediate or transitional form in what might be considered as the quantum jump from *Bison antiquus,* or *occidentalis* to *Bison bison.* That is, they reflect one point on a transitional curve from the larger, extinct forms, to the smaller, modern forms of bison.

Extinct bison from the 6470 year old Hawken Site (Frison, *et al.,* 1976) are reported as *Bison bison occidentalis,* "intermediate in size between the smaller *Bison bison* that were present by at least 2500 B.C. . . . and the larger *B. bison antiquus* that were present at 8000 B.C." The data from the younger Hawken Site support the evidence from Hudson-Meng, although no diagnostic skulls were present at the Hudson-Meng site. In the absence of cranial material, even with the extensive post-cranial analysis, no definitive assignment can be made for the speciation of the Hudson-Meng bison. At our present state of knowledge with regard to Holocene forms, they could be considered *B. bison occidentalis,* or *B. bison antiquus.*

POPULATION STRUCTURE

Using data from Deevey (1947) and Skinner and Kaisen (1947), Reher (1970. 1973, 1974) has contrasted the death assemblages from the Glenrock, Wardell, and Casper bison kills with models as proposed by Voorhies (1969), for attritional mortality and catastrophic mortality. He states (1974: 117,121) that a herd taken in the fall or early winter should reflect a catastrophic mortality of a "cow-calf" herd. Based on the analysis of several sites, he concludes that such populations do not represent such catastrophic mortality, as the juveniles and "calves are almost universally underrepresented in kill sites."

Using the only measurable specimens of mandibular elements, (Table 7) the Glenrock, Wardell, and Casper sites are compared with the Hudson-Meng population (Figure 19). It is at once apparent that the calves and juveniles are very abundant at Hudson-Meng, as compared to the other populations. Using McHugh's (1958) data for pregnancy and survival, in a manner similar to Reher (1974: 118), an additional 58 calves and 17 juveniles could be added to the total measured population. Such an adjustment (not graphed) would present a population very closely approximating the generalized model for a catastrophic mortality—even without the addition of the bulls.

The absence of calves and juveniles from a number of bison kills, where faunal analysis and age structures have been done, has led to the interpretation of removal and separate processing for juvenile animals. The physical environment of the trap is an added phenomena, to be considered. One alternative explanation for the absence of 1.5 year olds and relative absence of 2-5 year olds, for the Casper site may be the type of trap used. The use of parabolic a sand dune trap would work best on heavier, older animals, and calves, which naturaly tend to stay with the cows. Absence of high numbers of 1.5 to 4.5 year

61

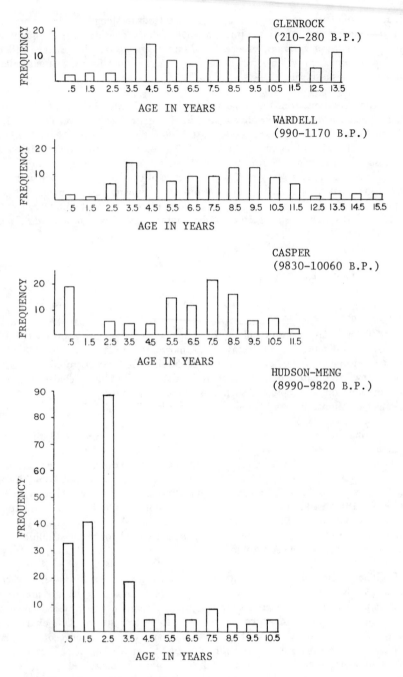

Figure 19. Age-group Structure Comparisons.

62

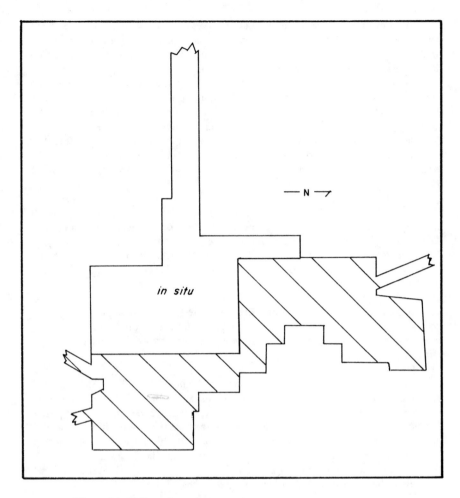

Figure 20. Delineation of Areas of the Excavation From Which
Bone was Removed, or Left *in situ*.

old animals at Casper may be due to the relative agility, strength, and lighter
weight of this group of animals. These factors may have been sufficient to allow
some of them to struggle over the sides of a parabolic dune trap and escape the
hunters. At Glenrock, the jump cliff should have been of sufficient magnitude to
represent all age groups of the herd. It is possible that differential treatment of
animals is the explanation here, and at Wardell, which was a pound, or corral
trap. Hudson-Meng appears to be an arroyo bank jump, or a bedrock cliff
enhanced by an arroyo meander. No differential treatment of age groups or portions of the carcasses is apparent from distributional analysis of the bone bed.

As previously stated, an additional 58 calves and 17 juveniles could be added to "smooth" the age-group structure curves. The remains of these "missing" animals may be around other activity areas in the bone bed, as the laboratory population reflects only those animals removed from the bone bed prior to the mid-1973 field season (Figure 20). It is assumed that the relative abundance of the measured populations reflects the total population, as there was no evidence to the contrary, in later excavations where the bone was left *in situ*. One additional possibility for the absence of calves and juveniles might be the distance and pace that a herd is moved. Even with strong cow-calf ties, it is possible that long distance, fast pace drives might cause calves and juveniles to drop out. In such cases, they would probably be dispatched at a distance from the major bone bed.

Reference to the average height of the mandibular M_1, metaconids (Table 7) indicates greater metaconid height (less tooth wear) on younger site populations. Glenrock, Wardell, and Casper provide average molar wear of 3.2, 3.3, and 4.2 mm. per year, respectively (Reher 1974: 120). The average for the Hudson-Meng population is 3.5 mm. per year, falling between the values for Casper and Wardell, as might be expected.

A survivorship curve was not plotted for the Hudson-Meng population, due to the need for estimation of a "total population" age-group distribution to fit a generalized model. It was decided to compare populations on the basis of field data.

In comparison of the age-group graphs (Figure 19), Hudson-Meng is well represented by the younger age groups, with a sharp decrease in animals 4.5 years of age and older. With the data from Glenrock, Wardell, and Casper, the opposite is true (with the exception of Casper calves). In these three populations, it would appear the herds were made up of older animals. If cultural conditions (such as removal of the young animals) are inferred from these data, just the opposite is true for the Hudson-Meng population, and cultural explanations must be derived to explain the relative absence of animals greater than 3.5 years old.

CHAPTER 8

CULTURAL MATERIALS

Several categories of cultural materials were recovered from the excavation. The bone bed and distribution of faunal elements within it were culturally determined but are discussed elsewhere. In addition to bison bones, a bone tool and four pieces of worked bone were recovered. Several categories of lithic materials constituted the remainder of the cultural items.

BONE ARTIFACTS

No bison bone tools such as those identified at the Casper site (Frison, *et al.*, 1974), or the Jones-Miller site (Stanford, personal communication) were recognized at the Hudson-Meng site during field work periods. Laboratory analysis of more than 200 animals removed from the bone bed did not produce bison bone tools derived from or used in the butchering and processing of the animals.

The only bone butchering tool recovered at the site is also the only large mammal, non-bison bone recovered from the bone bed. This tool, made from the distal end of a rather robust mule deer humerus (Figure 21), exhibits polish on the broken end, away from the joint. It is probable that this tool was used as sort of a gouge to separate packets of muscle from bone during butchering. A suite of stone-tool butchering marks appears on this tool. Cut marks appear where the skin and muscle attachments were apparently cut, as well as where the tendons of the joint were severed.

Butchering marks were not evident on the greater majority of bison bones from the site. In part, this is due to the calcium carbonate encrustation of the bison bone. Removal of this crust would also remove any butchering marks that might be present.

WORKED BONE

Four pieces of worked bone were recovered from the excavations of the bone bed. Two items were fragmentary and may represent broken implements, or haphazard bone carving done during butchering operations.

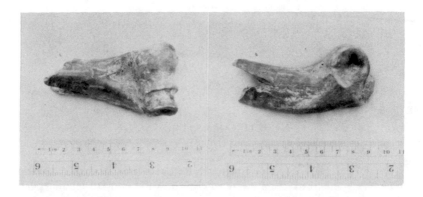

Figure 21. Mule Deer Humerus Butchering Tool.

The largest specimen (Figure 22, top) is a rib fragment which has been split along the rib axis and one end has been cut diagonally (the other end is broken). It has a series of parallel grooves, at opposite diagonals, along the edges of the rib. These grooves were initially considered to be rodent gnawing. After cleaning the bone and examining it through a microscope, the grooves are interpreted as being "rough marks" to create friction for binding, as in a handle for a knife.

A second piece of worked bone is rather non-descriptive (Figure 22, left) in that it appears to be a random piece of bone whittling. No functional use is apparent, although the entire object was shaped and carved.

The third bone artifact (Figure 22, middle) is a fragment of a rounded, smoothed implement. Small, close spaced striations at right angles to the length of the bone and the grain of the bone indicate that it was purposely abraded and shaped, possibly to function as a foreshaft.

A fourth piece of shaped bone (Figure 22, right) has been shaped to a "peg-like" form. A suggested use would be an atlatl spur.

LITHIC ARTIFACTS

The lithic artifacts can be separated into several categories and the chipped stone artifacts are discussed in detail in the appendix on lithic analysis (Huckell, this volume). In general, however, there are the following categories of lithic, cultural materials from the site: 1) projectile points, 2) butchering and processing tools, 3) "production" tools, 4) waste flakes, and 5) anomalous lithics.

66

Figure 22. Worked Bone from Hudson-Meng.

PROJECTILE POINTS

A total of twenty projectile points and fragments (Figures 23-26) have been recovered from the bone bed excavations. Two of these fragments were picked up from the dam and spillway, shortly after construction activities, by Albert and Bill Meng. With the initial discovery (Figure 23:001) we were unsure how to classify the point, typologically. It was definitely within the Lithic stage, as defined by Willey and Phillips (1958), and even more closely resembled the late Lithic of the Plains, identified as the Plano by Jennings (1955). The discovery point displayed the characteristics of Paleo-Indian points, i.e., lanceolate in shape, basal grinding, percussion flaking with pressure retouch, and was of high quality lithic material which characterize most Paleo-Indian technologies. Its descriptive attributes drew attention to similarities with the Scottsbluff point (Barbour and Schultz, 1932; Schultz and Eiseley, 1935) and with the Alberta point (Wormington, 1957). With only one specimen, we referred to it as "Scottsbluff-like" or "Alberta-like" with the emphasis on the "like."

As more projectile points were recovered from the excavations, they began to show a suite, or grouping of characteristics which ultimately, prior to any

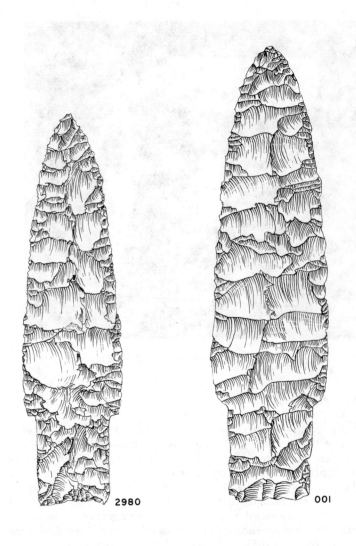

2980

001

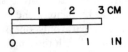

Figure 23. Alberta Projectile Points from the Hudson-Meng Site.

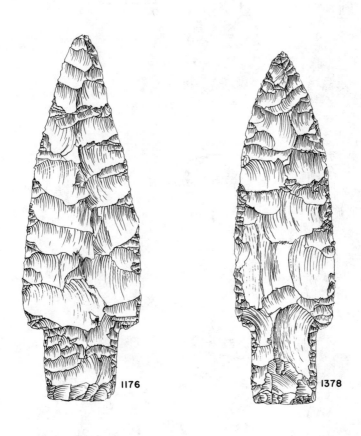

1176

1378

0   1   2   3 CM
0   1   IN

Figure 24. Alberta Projectile Points from the Hudson-Meng Site.

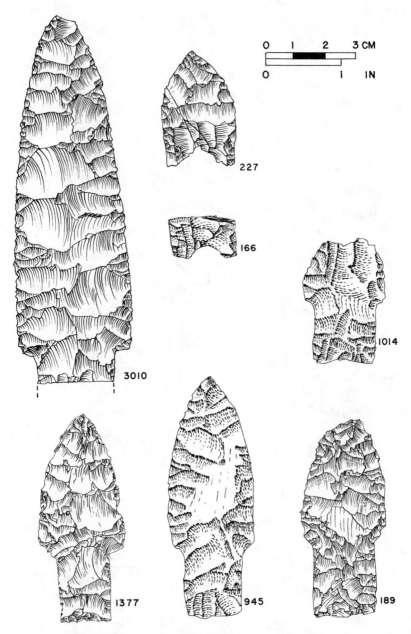

Figure 25. Alberta Projectile Points from the Hudson-Meng Site.

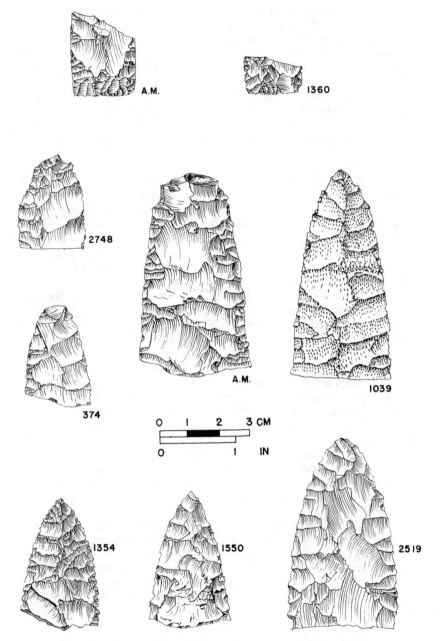

Figure 26. Alberta Projectile Points from the Hudson-Meng Site.

radiocarbon dates, caused us to decide in favor of the Alberta designation. These characteristics included the large flake scars, indicative of soft hammer percussion. Most of the points displayed heavier, larger flake scars than of the "classic" Scottsbluff points. We even considered the artifacts to be transistional between the older Alberta points and the younger Scottsbluff points, as in the stratigraphic sequence shown at Hell Gap, Wyoming (Irwin-Williams, *et al.*, 1973). When several of the points were excavated, due to their similarity (even with different lithic material) in shape, type of manufacture, etc., we classified them as Alberta points. To support the technological basis for the Alberta designation, radiocarbon dates, first on bone and later on charcoal, provided a temporal span older than Scottsbluff and younger than Plainview, in keeping with the stratigraphic positioning at Hell Gap.

Two anomalous, indented base points were recovered from the bone bed excavations (Figure 25:166, 227). A third, somewhat different, indented base point was found earlier on the surface, in the area of disturbance, after construction of the U. S. D. A. - S. C. S. dam at the site. At first, these points caused us to reconsider the interpretation that the kill and butchering/processing area represented a single event. As evidence mounted, the former theory, i.e., that a single component, single (temporal) event kill site was represented by the bone bed, regained favor. The anomalous, indented base points are probably best explained by the reworking of broken tips by indenting, rather than reworking a shouldered stem. Similar basal indention was noted on some of the Hell Gap points recovered from the Jones-Miller site near Wray, Colorado (Stanford, personal communication). Wheat (1977, pp. 134-135) describes and illustrates such practices at the Jurgens site near Kersey, Colorado.

That the Hudson-Meng points were reworked, and reworked extensively, can be demonstrated from an analysis of the collection. Only four of the complete projectile points (001, 945, 1378, 3010) do not give evidence of having been resharpened at least once. In some cases, they were resharpened to serve as projectile points, again. In at least one rather spectacular example (Figure 25: 189) a broken point appears to have been selectively resharpened on one side only and used as a butchering tool. The right edge retains the original shape and flaking of the projectile point, whereas the left edge, showing heavy retouch, is dulled and demonstrates heavy usage as a butchering tool, after the tip was broken.

It is quite probable that the projectile points were hafted to a detachable foreshaft which would permit them to be utilized as butchering tools, after the kill had taken place. The fact that the majority of the points recovered are asymmetrically reworked, and possibly even discarded after the butchering and meat processing had taken place, cannot be ignored. One of the unmodified points was still in place in the vertebra of one animal (Figure 25:945). Its position and angle of emplacement suggests the dispatching of a downed, wounded animal, by severing the spinal cord, near the base of the skull.

The majority of projectile points were manufactured from the brown

72

chalcedony known as Knife River Flint. The quarry sites for this raw material are along the Knife River in west, central North Dakota, approximately 320 miles northeast of the kill site. The abundance of lithic waste flakes of this material in the bone bed attests to tool manufacture as well as sharpening, suggesting that preforms of Knife River Flint were carried in, in addition to the finished artifacts.

Quartzite is the second most abundant material for lithic artifacts in the bone bed. It was considered that the material was probably derived from the extensive quarry sites at Spanish Diggings, near Lusk, Wyoming. Petrographic analysis (Witzel and Hartley, 1973) disclosed a Black Hills source area as more similar in grain size, accessory minerals, and color.

Two projectile points were manufactured from the metamorphosed shale (Figures 25:1377; 26:1550), peculiar to underground coal fires in northeastern Wyoming and in Montana. Nearly identical raw material was collected in the field (Witzel, 1974, personal communication).

A broad category of chalcedonies, jaspers, and cherts comprise the last type of lithic raw material. Source areas for these materials are presently unknown. Many of them could have been derived in the gravels of Miocene river channels now present, due to inverse topography, as ridge crests just two to three miles north and east of the kill site.

An analysis of the quarry areas, at least as to general geographic location, gives some idea as to the range of travel and exploitation that characterizes a group of prehistoric people (Figure 27). As previously stated, the major lithic resources of the hunters at Hudson-Meng were Knife River Flint, quartzite, meta-morphosed shale and "local" cherts, jaspers, and chalcedonies from the area adjacent to the site. The Knife River Flint quarries are well known and described in the literature (Clayton, et al., 1970). The other categories of lithic resources are harder to trace, and prehistoric quarries for the material are less well known.

Perhaps the best known quarry in the local geographic area is Spanish Diggings in east-central Wyoming, near Lusk, approximately fifty air miles west of Hudson-Meng. Early descriptions (Dorsey, 1900; Holmes, 1919; Renaud, 1931) assign such names as "Mexican Mine" and "Spanish Diggings" to the locality, under the mistaken assumption that the activities were due to a search for precious metals. The quartzite occurs in rocks of Lower Cretaceous age, originally assigned to the Lakota Formation in current nomenclature (Witzel and Hartley, 1973). Nodules of jasper are present with the quartzite, and were probably a highly desired product of the quarrying, as well. Anyone who visits these quarries cannot help being impressed with the amount of labor represented by the quarry pits, waste piles, and the extent of the quarry operations.

Flint Hill, in South Dakota, is another quartzite quarry. Located approxi-mately forty air miles north of the Hudson-Meng site, in the southern flanks of the Black Hills, the quarry is also in the Lower Cretaceous Lakota Formation. The

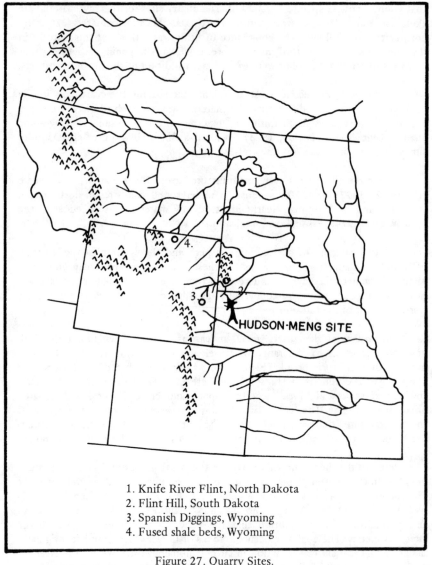

1. Knife River Flint, North Dakota
2. Flint Hill, South Dakota
3. Spanish Diggings, Wyoming
4. Fused shale beds, Wyoming

Figure 27. Quarry Sites.
(O denotes approximate location of known lithic sources).

material occurs in lenses and pods in a silica enriched sandstone, very much like the Spanish Diggings material.

Petrographic studies (Witzel and Hartley, *ibid.*) of quartzites from the two areas, compared to the waste flakes and tools from the Hudson-Meng bone bed suggest Flint Hill as the most probable quarry, of the two areas examined. The possibility of other quartzite quarries in eastern Wyoming and western South Dakota precludes a definitive statement as to the source area.

Red jasper flakes are abundant in Knapping Locus C (Huckell, Appendix I, this volume). The texture and coloration of this material is similar to jaspers derived from the Phosphoria Formation outcrops in north-central Wyoming.

The "fused" or metamorphosed shales are relatively common in North-Central Wyoming and Southern Montana. Extensive outcrops can be seen from the highway in the vicinity of Buffalo, Wyoming. These units are the result of coal bed fires, many of which were subterranean, which fused the overlying and under-lying shale units. To pick one location as the source area would be as difficult as it would be erroneous. The general area does give a relative range, however.

In an attempt to compare the projectile points from Hudson-Meng with known Alberta points, we did a metric analysis of several collections (Table 9). The largest comparative collection from a single site was that from the Fletcher site (Forbis, 1968). Four specimens from Hell Gap, Wyoming, are also included. Several private, surface collections are included to give a greater representation of the range of variation within this point style. Of special importance are those specimens in the private collection of Bill Hudson and those at the Nebraska State Museum. These collections were derived primarily from Sioux County, Nebraska, and are so similar in every aspect, as to indicate a tight grouping of cultural-technological attributes.

From the metric analysis of the specimens, the most consistent attributes, due to resharpening of point tips, etc., should be those of the length and width of the bases, which in turn give us an approach as the diameter of the foreshaft and the depth of hafting. Of twenty-six specimens which retained base lengths, the extremes were 16.0 to 31.4 mm. with an average of 24.09 mm. length. Basal width on twenty-eight specimens varied from 16.6 to 27.0 mm. with an average of 22.50 mm. In general (68%), the basal length was slightly more than basal width, though a few speciemens (22%) had bases whose width exceeded their length.

Plots of projectile point dimensions and indices, for Cody (Scottsbluff and Eden points) and Firstview, San Jon points (Wheat, 1972) compared to Hudson-Meng Alberta points (Figure 28), show several interesting facts. In graphic plots, the Alberta materials cluster outside the compared point types on the basis of width, whereas length varies greatly and is coincident with the compared types: however, two specimens exceed the Eden in length.

The plot data for Alberta points differentiate between points which have been reworked (retipped) and those which have not. In both total length/blade width and blade length/blade width plots, Alberta points cluster in two groups. With two exceptions, all of the lower cluster points have been reworked. Upper cluster points include two reworked points which, even after retipping, are still

I.D.	Length	Max Width	Thickness	Length Base	Width Base	Re-Worked	Mtl.	Base
Hudson-Meng								
001	156.2	38.1	9.7	31.4	26.9	No	KRF	Cc.
166	--	--	--	--	21.9	--	Qtzite.	Cc.
189	--	28.5	7.8	23.9	21.5	Yes	V. Jasp.	St.
227	36.6	24.6	6.9	17.0	23.0	Yes	Chalc.	Cc.
374	--	(21.3)	5.3	--	--	--	Chert	--
945	75.9	28.0	9.4	21.9	19.3	No	Qtzite.	Cv.
1014	--	26.7	6.9	19.7	20.5	Yes	Qtzite.	Cc.
1039	--	(32.8)	8.7	--	--	--	Qtzite.	--
1176	117.0	39.3	9.0	23.2	24.9	Yes	KRF	St.
1354	--	(25.8)	9.2	--	--	--	Chalc.	--
1360	--	--	--	--	18.6	--	KRF	St.
1377	67.0	29.0	8.3	21.3	17.4	Yes	F. Shale	Cc.
1378	112.3	33.5	8.1	23.7	20.8	No	Chalc.	St.
1550	--	(26.9)	8.9	--	--	--	F. Shale	--
2519	--	(36.5)	7.8	--	--	No	Chalc.	--
2748	--	21.7	4.9	--	--	Yes	KRF	--
2980	124.7	32.1	8.6	29.0	23.0	Yes	KRF	Cc.
3010	(117.5)	38.3	9.6	--	26.3	No	KRF	--
	--	36.1	8.4	--	21.4	--	Chalc.	St.
Harvard-Hell Gap	(63.7)	27.5	--	26.6	23.1	Yes	?	St.

Table 9. Metric Attributes of Alberta Points.

I.D.	Length	Max Width	Thickness	Length Base	Width Base	Re-worked	Mtl.	Base
Fig. 43	--	--	--	20.7	21.3	broken	?	St.
	(53.6)	28.7	--	(19.9)	22.2	Yes	?	--
Smithsonian Lindenmeier								
71 i 442320	(64.9)	32.9	9.1	(26.4)	25.9	Yes	KRF	--
71 j 443267	53.5	23.0	4.8	17.9	16.9	No	B. Jasp.	St.
Holyoke, CO SIC-69-1	120.0	40.7	9.5	27.6	26.8	No	R. Jasp.	Cc.
TX Panhandle	(45.4)	21.9	6.2	19.8	16.8	Yes	R. Jasp.	Cv.
Hell Gap, WY.-Surf.	--	27.9	7.1	17.0	24.2	?	P. Chalc.	Cc.
F. Powers Collection Sunrise, WY	44.9	19.8	6.3	16.9	15.5	Yes	KRF	Cv.
	48.9	23.7	7.1	19.0	15.5	Yes	Chert	Cv.
Nebraska 7264	143.0	33.0	7.6	24.0	22.3	No	KRF	Cc.
	--							

Table 9. (continued).

I.D.	Length	Max. Width	Thickness	Length Base	Width Base	Re-worked	Mtl.	Base
SX 7355	--	37.4	7.5	23.3	24.4	?	Grey Chert	St.
7435	--	33.8	9.0	--	25.6	?	Qtzite.	--
DW 7354	--	27.0	9.0	27.3	24.3	No	Chalcedony	St.
GD 7494 (?)	--	32.8	8.2	28.7	23.0	?	Grey Chert	Cv.
Fletcher, Alberta:								
F:6-7	117.0	37.0	11.0	28.0	27.0	No	Weld. Tuff	Cv.
F:2	--	35.0	11.0	--	26.0	Yes	Weld. Tuff	--
F:11	--	--	7.0	--	16.6		Basalt	Cv.
F:8	--	28.0	7.8	22.0	22.0	?	Basalt	Cc.
F:9	42.0	22.8	6.6	16.0	17.0	Yes	Chert	Cv.
F:Dyck (h)	(160.00)	35.0	10.0	--	26.0	No	Basalt	--
AF 13 56-2	--	31.1	10.0	--	21.6	No	Qtzite.	--
Hudson Collection								
Sx-1	(112.5)	36.6	8.4	26.4	24.0	Yes	KRF	--
Sx-2	(60.0)	30.5	8.3	--	22.6	Yes	KRF	--
Sx-3	--	30.9	8.9	26.1	24.1	?	Qtzite.	Cv.

Table 9. (continued).

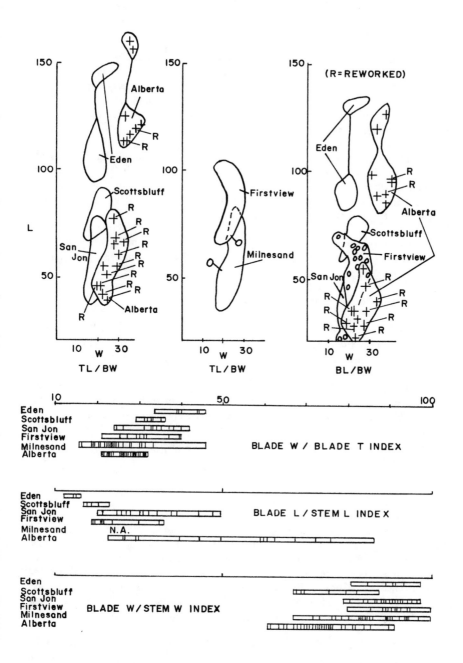

Figure 28. Projectile Points: Dimensions and Indices (after Wheat, 1972).

within the range of length of original points.

Comparison of the blade width/blade thickness index with the material presented by Wheat *(ibid.)* shows the Alberta points to be tightly clustered in the index range of 20-32, with the majority in the 25-32 range, nearly duplicating the "relatively thin" Firstview points. The plot shows near duplication for the lower range of the plot for Firstview materials as well as the Milnesand points which tend to be somewhat thinner.

The blade length/stem length index is less diagnostic, in that the Alberta points in Table 9 show the widest range of the types plotted (22-85) with only minor clustering from 22-30. What is reflected here is the blade length reduction due to reworking, noted earlier in the dimensional plots. The higher index values represent the heavily reworked points.

Of more importance is the blade width/stem width index, which indicates the presence of pronounced shoulders on the Alberta specimens. The range of values from 59-91, with the majority from 65-75, gives the most pronounced shoulders of the groups plotted. The range for Alberta duplicates and overrides the Scottsbluff I material that was plotted by Wheat *(ibid.)*.

On the basis of the dimensional plots and indexes of the Alberta points, compared with the data presented by Wheat, the Alberta points cluster in two groups: those whose length is as great as, or more than Eden points, while also having much more blade width; and those which are near duplicates for San Jon and Milnesand length but are wider. The latter group is represented by reworked specimens. A similar conclusion is gained in the plot of blade width. The blade width/blade thickness index indicates the Alberta specimens to be relatively thin, resembling Firstview and Milnesand and thinner than Scottsbluff I, or Eden. The blade width/stem width index shows pronounced shoulders, also characteristic of Scottsbluff I.

BUTCHERING AND PROCESSING TOOLS

Butchering and processing tools are represented by knives, flake knives, and scrapers (Figures 29-32). The 1974 season provided the unexpected occurrence of a Cody Knife. This distinctive butchering tool is generally associated with Scottsbluff and Eden projectile points. To my knowledge, this is the first occurrence of a Cody Knife with Alberta projectile points. Such an occurrence, with typologically and chronologically older Alberta materials, calls for a reassessment of the Cody Complex in the High Plains (Agenbroad, 1978).

The Cody Knife from the Hudson-Meng bone bed (Figure 29) was discovered in the western trench extension of the 1974 field season. The artifact was one of several tools, in a cluster near the location at which the bone concentration diminishes rapidly. At this position, the bone bed was beneath nearly seventeen feet

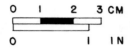

(a)   3016

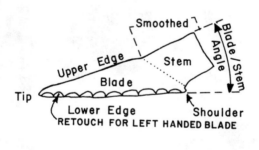

(b)

Figure 29. Cody Knife from the Hudson-Meng Bone Bed (a) and Cody Knife Terminology (b) (after Dick and Mountain, 1960).

81

Figure 30. Gravers and Butchering Tools from the Hudson-Meng Site.

82

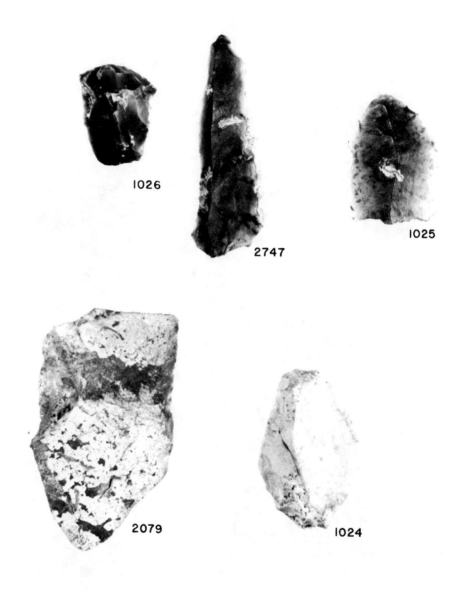

Figure 31. Additional Butchering Tools and Scrapers.

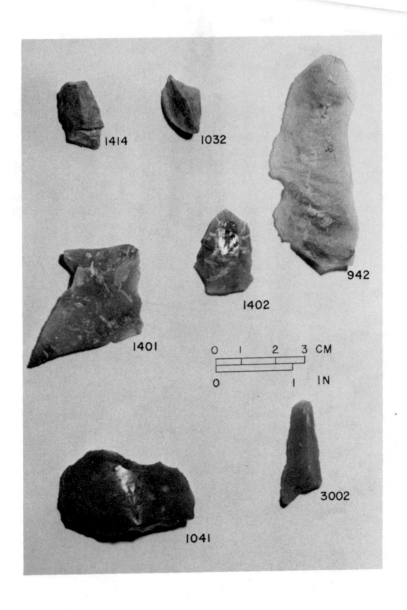

Figure 32. Additional Butchering Tools and Scrapers.

of fill. Metric attributes of this butchering tool and comparative local specimens are given in Table 10. Its discovery in an Alberta culture bone bed gives greater antiquity and new associational data. The Cody Complex must be revised to inlcude Alberta points as well as Scottsbluff and Eden points.

Cody knives from the Claypool site were described by Dick and Mountain (1960). I have followed their descriptive table (*ibid.*, p. 230) and added one category which I shall define as right- or left-handed blades. This distinction is made with the tang of the knife place in an upright position (Figure 29) and the blade, in particular the retouched or cutting edge of the blade, toward the viewer, designating right- or left-handedness as illustrated.

The paucity of published information on Cody Knives, other than the Claypool site, has led to the descriptive analysis and distribution pattern of this "diagnostic artifact" (Agenbroad, 1978). The distribution (Figure 33) is essentially the eastern High Plains from New Mexico to Alberta and Saskatchewan. Most specimens have one shoulder, as illustrated in Wormington's book (1957, p. 267) and in the Claypool specimens (Dick and Mountain, 1960; p. 226). The Cody Knife from the Hudson-Meng site, and the one from Moose Jaw, Saskatchewan, display two well developed shoulders.

At the time of discovery, the Hudson-Meng Cody Knife appeared to have been a heavily used tool. The transverse blade has a slight concavity, which was puzzling until the tool was placed in a haft, during a discussion with Dennis Stanford at the Jones-Miller site. It became apparent that the last row of resharpening flakes driven from the tool intersected the haft elements and the tool was then considered expended.

In addition to the Cody Knife three gravers, fourteen flake knives, one preform and three scrapers, were recovered from the excavations. The metric attributes of these tools are given in Table 11. These tools vary from rough flakes displaying what may be considered "use retouch," to well designed tools. The butchering tools are illustrated in Figures 30-32. Two of the artifacts (Figure 30: 3105; 31:2079) were in close association with the Cody Knife. Of these latter tools, Figure 30:3105 represents a composite tool, executed on a very thin jasper flake, having a heavily worn cutting edge from the bulbar end, along approximately two-thirds of its ventral side. The opposite end of the flake has been flaked to produce a very delicate graver. The dorsal edge of this tool has been dulled by breakage, either intentionally or as a product of striking the flake; intentional breakage to produce this "back" is suggested by the abrupt termination of this edge. Two additional gravers (Figure 30:1038, 764) were found, one exhibits heavy damage.

Also in association with the Cody Knife and composite tool just described is the heaviest butchering tool recovered from the site. Fashioned from a large flake of mottled grey chert, this tool (Figure 31:2079) has the entire ventral edge and one end, to half the dorsal edge, unifacially retouched. Somewhat less

SPECIMEN	MATERIAL	THINNED BASE	STEM LENGTH	STEM WIDTH	BLADE LENGTH	MAXIMUM THICKNESS	STEM/BLADE ANGLE
Hudson-Meng HM-3016	grey chalcedony	yes	14.8	15.0	51.7	5.8	35°
Hat Creek CSC-HC-158	brown jasper	yes	12.7	15.3	--	4.2	15°
CSC-HC-187	jasper	yes	18.2	20.4	--	7.8	27°

BLADE FLAKING	STEM GROUND	BLADE	REMARKS
Transverse	yes	left	Concave (expended) blade; double shoulder; diamond/lenticular cross section
Transverse	yes	right	Double shoulder; lenticular cross section
Transverse	yes	left	Concave blade; single shoulder; lenticular cross section

Table 10. Metric Attributes of Cody Knives-Hat Creek Drainage.

Figure 33. Geographic Distribution of Reported Cody Knives.
Solid circles denote stratified locality.

Specimen	Max. Length	Max. Width	Max. Thickness	Tool Type	Material	Remarks
HM-2079	68.8	41.3	9.9	Unifacial Flake Knife	Chert	Retouch on entire ventral, ½ dorsal edge
-3105	57.0	23.8	4.7	Composite: Flake Knife	Brown Jasper	Unifacial retouch on entire dorsal. One end a denticulate graver tip.
-1025	36.9	27.4	5.5	Utilized Flake	KRF	Use retouch on bulbar end and ventral unifacial retouch
-1042	49.0	24.5	5.5	Utilized Flake	KRF	Unifacial retouch on entire ventral edge
-1614	59.4	36.1	8.4	Semi lunate Knife	KRF	Unifacial retouch, entire concave edge
+1008	26.1	20.1	7.1	Utilized Flake	Chert	Unifacial retouch of entire ventral edge
017	--	35.5	8.2	Preform Knife?	Chalcedony	Bifacial retouch, entire edge-broken with only three fragments recovered
-1024	45.3	30.8	14.3	Keeled side Scraper	Quartzite	Unifacial retouch, 2 sides and possibly on broken end

Table 11. Metric Attributes of Butchering Tools. (measurement in mm.)

Specimen	Max. Length	Max. Width	Max. Thickness	Tool Type	Material	Remarks
-1026	29.0	23.0	10.7	Keeled end and Side scraper	Jasper	End and one side with unifacial retouch slight spur
-1041	43.8	26.4	10.7	Side and end Scraper and Obtuse angle	KRF	Unifacial retouch on end and both edges. Obtuse angle "plane" on keel with heavy use polish.
-2747	62.7	21.9	8.1	Side Scraper	KRF	Unifacial retouch, one edge, one a blade
-3002	(32.2)	(13.8)	9.8	Side Scraper with spur	Chalcedony	Thick blade with spur
+1404	(39.6)	(20.9)	3.0	Utilized Flake	Grey Chert	Thin flake with one utilized edge
+1181	--	(29.0)	5.2	Utilized Flake	KRF	Bulbar flake portion with utilized margins
+1359	46.5	24.0	6.9	Utilized Flake	Grey Chert	Utilized margin
+ 764	--	--	2.3	Graver Tip	Pink Chalcedony	Fragment with graver tip
+1038	27.8	23.5	4.2	Graver	KRF	Shattered graver tip on bulbar portion of flake
- 942	66.7	26.3	5.4	Utilized Flake	Chalcedony	Marginal use retouch

Table 11. (continued).

Specimen	Max. Length	Max. Width	Max. Thickness	Tool Type	Material	Remarks
-1401	47.7	32.0	5.5	Utilized Flake	Chalcedony	Unifacial marginal retouch
-1402	25.4	18.5	3.4	Utilized Flake	Chalcedony	Unifacial retouch on bulbar portion of flake
-1414	(22.2)	12.5	4.0	Biface	Fused Shale	Utilized fragment of shattered point

Table 11. (continued).

stylistic, and executed on a cortex flake, is a large recurved "spoke shave" tool (Figure 30:1614). Well controlled, unifacial pressure retouch defined the cutting edge. Seven additional utilized flakes carrying retouch on at least one edge (Figure 30:1008, 1181, 1042, 1404, 1359; 32:1025, 2747) constitute the remainder of the flake knives-utilized flake catagory.

One broken preform of variegated chalcedony (Appendix I, Figure 7) was recovered in the northern unit of the bone bed. Its presence in the bone bed suggests its use as a butchering tool, while being transported as a preform. Three segments of this tool were recovered, as recognized by the characteristic stone however, its original dimensions are uncertain.

Three scrapers were recovered from the bone bed. One is a high keeled side scraper which may have had an end scraper component (Figure 31:1024), though this has been damaged. The third specimen might be classed as a composite (Figure 32:1041), in that both sides and one end are unifacially retouched; it also has a segment of the dorsal ridge which exhibits a heavy polish. This polish was defined as an obtuse angle scraper (Crabtree, personal communication). The use of the obtuse angle and its function is best described in Crabtree's (1973) article.

Lithologic preference in butchering and processing tools is, again, Knife River Flint. Many of the flake knives appear to have been made from trim flakes of this material, from the manufacture of other tools.

A cumulative graph for Alberta tools (Figure 34), based on Table 12, after the method of Irwin and Wormington (1970) on the Hudson-Meng tool kit, does not fit the expectations one would gain from the graphs of other Paleo-Indian tool kits. Using the data presented for Clovis, Folsom, Midland, Hell Gap, Agate Basin, Cody and Frederick (Irwin and Wormington, *ibid.*), one would anticipate the plot for Alberta tool kits to be an intermediate curve, between Clovis and Frederick. The Hudson-Meng tool kit was plotted alone, and with Alberta material from the only other excavated Alberta sites, Fletcher (Forbis, 1968), and Hell Gap (Irwin, 1968). The Alberta curves are very similar, yet are a closer match with Clovis than with any other Paleo-Indian culture. The MacHaffie assemblage (Knudson, 1973) comes closer to the expected model than does the Alberta assemblage, with fewer tools.

A greater number of projectile points from the Alberta localities is probably due to the nature of the sites, both of which are apparently butchering localities. The tool kit for Hudson-Meng is derived completely from the butchering floor. One other factor is that some of the projectile points from this locality show evidence of having been utilized as butchering tools as well. No associated camp-site, hide-processing area, or associated activity area has been found with the butchering floor.

Based solely on the evidence presented by the cummulative graphs and the

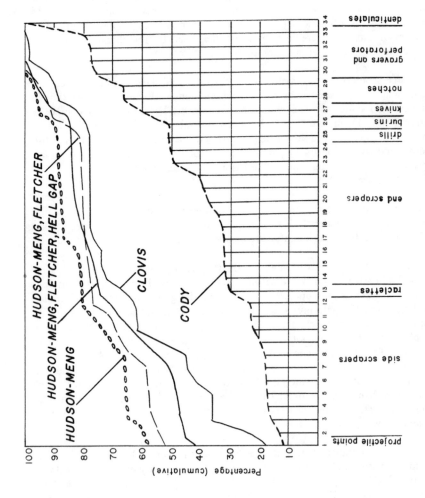

Figure 34. Cummulative Graph: Alberta Tools Compared with Clovis and Cody (after Irwin and Wormington, 1970).

92

Table 12. Irwin-Wormington Classification (1970) Of the Hudson-Meng and Combined Hudson-Meng/Fletcher, Hudson-Meng/Fletcher/Hell Gap Alberta Tool Kits.

Implement Number, type [a,b]	Hudson Meng		Hudson-Meng & Fletcher		Hudson-Meng Fletcher & Hell Gap	
	F	C%	F	C%	F	C%
1. Projectile point	16	57.14	24	53.33	29	42.6
2. SS(S), straight edge	0	57.14	0		1	44.1
3. SS(S), concave edge	0	57.14	0			
4. SS(S), convex edge	2	64.28	2	57.77	2	47.0
5. SS(S), ventral retouch	0		0			
6. SS(S), bifacial retouch	0		0		1	48.5
7. SS(S), transverse retouch	0		0		1	50.0
8. SS(S), thinned back	0	64.28	1	59.99	1	51.5
9. SS(D), convex adjacent edges	1	67.85	2	64.43	2	54.4
10. SS(D), convex + concave edges	1	71.42	2	68.87	4	60.3
11. SS(D), straight or slightly convex edges	0		0			
12. SS(D), completely retouched, no butt	0	71.42	0		2	63.2
13. Raclette	2	78.56	2	73.31	6	72.0
14. ES, pronounced beak or spur	0	78.56	0			
15. ES, pronounced acute bit/side angle	0	78.56	1	75.53	1	73.5
16. ES, ventral retouch on acute bit/side angle	0	78.56	0			
17. ES, extremely large (2-3x normal)	0	78.56	0			

Implement Number, type [a,b]	Hudson Meng		Hudson-Meng & Fletcher		Hudson-Meng Fletcher & Hell Gap	
	F	C%	F	C%	F	C%
18. ES, triangular, fully retouched	2	85.70	2	79.97	2	76.4
19. ES, thinned and retouched	0		0			
20. ES, on large circular flake	0		0			
21. ES, *grattoir à museau*	0		0			
22. ES, markedly asymmetrical bit	0		0			
23. ES, round bit	0		0		1	79.4
24. ES, slightly pointed or ogival bit	0		0			
25. Drill	0		0			
26. Burin	0		0			
27. b, large bipointed form	1	92.84	4	88.85	7	89.7
27. d, Cody Knife	1		0			
28. N, minimal retouch	0		0			
29. N, steep retouch, large concavity	1	99.98	1	91.07	1	91.2
30. G, single-spurred			4	99.95	5	98.5
31. G, multiple-spurred	0				1	100.0
32. G, chisel graver (elongate)	0					
33. Beak	0					
34. Denticulate	0					
TOTAL	28	99.98	45	99.95	67	100.0

Table 12. (continued).

94

similarity to the Clovis graph, one can make a tentative suggestion that Alberta people did not derive, through time, from Clovis Ancestors. The model calls for the Clovis-Folsom-Midland grouping giving rise to the Hell Gap-Agate Basin grouping, which gave rise to the Alberta-Cody grouping based on tool kits. Instead of that continuum, the close similarity of Alberta and Clovis graphs suggests an alternatve explanation for Alberta: the influx of a new group of people, with a lifeway and culture, reflected by the tool kit, very similar to the mammoth hunting Clovis people.

I do not favor postulated "invasions" of cultural groups through time. Based strictly on cummulative graph data, however, the evidence for Alberta is a big game hunting economy, using a variety of tools similar to the Clovis culture. The similarity is to Clovis, rather than postulated Clovis antecedents with more temporal affinity, such as Hell Gap or Cody cultures.

The presence of a Cody Knife in this Alberta assemblage indicates there is a relationship between Alberta and Cody industrial assemblages. The lithic technology of the Alberta and Scottsbluff points also reflects this relationship. If the foregoing assumptions are reasonable, it may also indicate less cultural affinity of Alberta tools for Hell Gap-Agate Basin tool kits as compared to Cody materials. It is probable that the disparity is due to the comparison of tools from butcher sites only as contrasted to tools from a variety of work/activity areas.

Another assumption is that the cumulative graph does not validly represent the cultures in question. The original presentation of each High Plains culture's cummulative graph of tool kit data from the Hell Gap site, with the omission of Alberta material, does suggest a continuum with technologic change through time. The Alberta material from three stratified sites (Hell Gap included) does not fit the model.

PRODUCTION TOOLS

"Production tools" are represented by sandstone abraders. Three partial and three complete abraders (Figure 35 have been recovered. Their use in manufacture of other tools, rather than the butchering process, also indicates knapping and tool manufacture at the site. These implements vary from extremely simple to complex, varying from one groove per specimen to as many as thirteen with some exhibiting patterned placement. All specimens were of a fine grained, carbonate cemented, iron oxide stained sandstone. No source area has been determined. Metric attributes are included in Table 13.

The small size of most of the grooves indicates other than wood working functions. It is possible that these tools were used in the manufacture of lithic tools, for edge grinding and preparation of striking platforms.

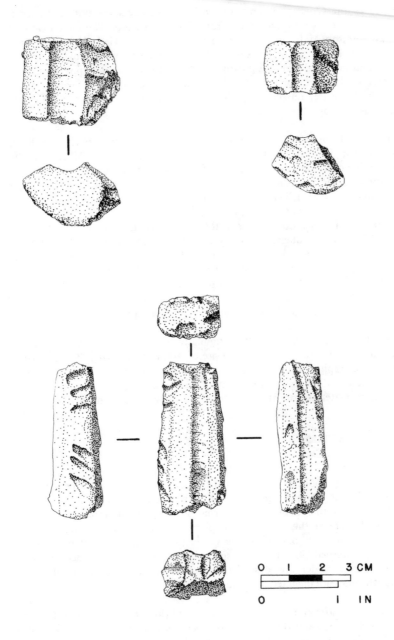

Figure 35. Production Tools (Abraders) from the Hudson-Meng Site.

SPECIMEN	LENGTH	WIDTH	THICKNESS	NUMBER OF GROOVES	X-SECT.	GROOVE WIDTH	GROOVE DEPTH	REMARKS	MATERIAL
HM-945	49.3	17.4-22.9	15.9	13	rectangular	7.9-3.2	1.1-1.7	en chevron design w/6 grooves	red sandst.
-1384	27.2	33.6	22.0	1	concave/ convex	11.6	2.6	complete	red sandst.
-1411	17.6	24.2	17.8	1	concave/ convex	7.6	1	complete	red sandst.
-1392	--	--	--	1	---	12.3	1.2	frag- mentary	red sandst.
-2110	14.6	18.8	11.1	0	plano/ convex	--	--	2 planes	red sandst.
-1391	Fragment of red sandstone abrader. (Probable fragment of 1392)								red sandst.

Table 13. Metric Attributes of Sandstone Abraders.
(Measurements in Milimeters)

WASTE FLAKES

More than 3,500 waste flakes have been collected in the excavation of the site. Many are in tight clusters with respect to lithologic and spatial provenience. Plots of waste flakes delineate workshop or retouch areas for manufacture or resharpening of butchering tools. Waste flakes which fit on the basal, flake scars of the discovery point suggest its manufacture at the site, within the bone bed, prior to its loss. Analysis of the waste flakes, their distribution and the lithic technology of the Hudson-Meng artifacts are discussed in Appendix I (Huckell, this volume).

ANOMALOUS LITHICS

Four anomalous rocks were recovered in the excavated portion of the bone bed. Three of these specimens (Figure 36) are from the west trench of the 1974 season. They are silicified fragments of a satin spar gypsum sheet deposit, such as the fill of a fault zone in the Oligocene badlands. Such material, or chalcedony, often occur as fill material in the fault and fissure planes in the badlands. The occurrence of these specimens in association with the bone bed is anomalous, especially when the sedimentary material in which they are incorporated is in the range of 1/16 to 2 mm. in diameter. Their angular nature precludes stream deposition, and they are interpreted as having been brought to the bone bed, by the hunters or members of the hunting group.

These specimens are harder than normal gypsum and are at least partially replaced by chalcedony. The fibrous to splintery texture of the satin spar is still apparent, though the material will not separate. Upon wetting, the specimens take on a greenish, transluscent character. There is no evidence of battering or any form of modification. They were not used as hammerstones, abraders, etc. Since their occurrence is anomalous and there is no evidence of use, they were evidently brought to the site as curiosities or as desired material for some unknown purpose.

One specimen was found within a meter of the Cody Knife and associated butchering tools near grid point 26S + 26W. Two other specimens were located seven meters west. No other material of this nature was encountered in the excavations.

A fourth specimen (Figure 37) is a large "butte rock" cobble, characteristic of the Miocene Formations which form the high ground south of the site. This cobble was incorporated in the bone bed, with bone beneath, and on top of the specimen. Upon cleaning it in the laboratory and examining it under the microscope, we noted no abrading marks. The conclusion is that this specimen is a hammerstone, used in the butchering process to break bone or aid in separation of joints, etc. It is the only specimen of this nature found in the excavations. No fragments of such material were encountered, which is unusual if there was a

Figure 36. Anomalous Lithics (silicified gypsum) from
The Hudson-Meng Bone Bed.

Figure 37. Butte Rock Hammerstone from
The Hudson-Meng Bone Bed.

major usage of these cobbles, due to their friable nature. Its position in the bone bed precludes emplacement by other than human means.

CHAPTER 9

GEOLOGY OF THE HUDSON-MENG BISON KILL

REGIONAL GEOLOGIC SETTING

The Hudson-Meng site is located on the north slope of the Pine Ridge Escarpment, on a northward protuberance known locally as the Round Top Divide (Witzel, 1974). The escarpment enters Sioux County, Nebraska, from Wyoming, on the west (Figure 38). It reaches its southernmost point along the White River, south of the site, and then proceeds northeasterly through Dawes and Sheridan Counties to enter South Dakota.

Average physiographic relief along the ridge is approximately four hundred feet, with a maximum of seven hundred to eight hundred feet near Crawford, Nebraska. The relief and configuration of the ridge are largely due to erosional dissection of the escarpment by the White River and its tributaries and the Hat Creek drainage network which is tributary to the Cheyenne River. Erosional outliers such as Crow Butte, Sugarloaf, Wayside Butte, Trunk Butte and others give evidence of the southward retreat of this topographic feature.

The escarpment divides this portion of the Great Plains into two physiographic subdivisions. To the south of the ridge the table land is known as the High Plains, spreading discontinuously, as far south as Texas. North of the Pine Ridge is the "unglaciated Missouri Plateau" (Fenneman, 1931) extending north into Canada (Figure 2).

Lithologic units, in the area of the site, vary in age from Cretaceous to Recent. The major units are the Cretaceous Pierre Shale; Oligocene Chadron and Brule Formations; and the Miocene Gering and Monroe Creek Formations. The Tertiary units are continental in origin, predominantly fluvial, characterized by siltstones and sandstones. Oligocene units are interpreted as channel and flood plain deposits. As one rises in the section, eolian components are recognized, as silts, clays and volcanic ash.

Miocene deposits are more coarse grained, especially when contrasted with the Brule Formation, which varies from claystone to siltstone. This geologic texture difference is a major control of the hydrology in the area and is important to the origin of springs such as the one located at the Hudson-Meng Bison Kill.

Figure 38. Satellite Photo of the Pine Ridge Escarpment.

Darton (1903, p. 48) was the first to recognize this spring control, at Round Top. The Oligocene-Miocene contact can often be determined by the occurrence of springs, where the more permeable Gering or Monroe Creek Formation rests on the impermeable Brule. A large spring of this nature still provides the perennial effluent and drainage channel for the modern wash, as well as the paleo-drainage channel which served as the kill site.

It is probable that the spring served not only to provide the drainage which gave the geomorphic nature of the jump, but may have also been the watering spot which attracted the animals and therefore the hunters. The Hudson-Meng site may, in fact, be the result of the coincidence of a natural trap, animals, and hunters, which was not repeated again in time.

The view from the summit makes Round Top a natural lookout for any group of pedestrian hunters. The presence of the large spring and abundant grass would certainly attract grazing bison. A steep banked meander bend in coincidence with natural drive lanes and gathering area provided the trap. It is evident from the analysis of the bone bed and the sediments covering it that the course of the effluent changed, probably choked by combined eolian-colluvial deposits derived from the ridge to the west, and possibly the bone bed, acting as a check dam. As the site was buried, the drainage pattern moved up, over the bone bed, and eastward to its present entrenched position (Figure 39). The same ridge is still actively deflating and filling the drainage system, above the spring, to the south of the kill site.

A reconnaisance map of the local geology of the site is given in Figure 40. The Miocene-Oligocene contact is based on the presence of ephemeral and perennial springs. The Tertiary-Quaternary contacts are based on change in slope, vegetation change and lithologic change. It can be noted that the fill within this local drainage covers a larger area than one might expect on the basis of modern conditions. The prior stream channels have been more extensive laterally and vertically than the present system indicates.

The arroyo just east of the kill site is still actively downcutting and migrating headward. The presence of old, abandoned roads and their previous crossing of the wash help to estimate the rate of headcutting. The oldest road (northern) was used in 1934-1935 (Albert and Bill Meng, personal communication). With progressive headcutting, this was abandoned for the position nearly due east of the homestead. This location was later abandoned in favor of the current crossing at the spring head, an up gradient migration of one-half mile, by the headcut, in 35 years. Headcutting has progressed another hundred yards up slope since the road crossing at the spring head was established.

Alluvial Fill

Auger drilling provided a cross section of the alluvial fill in an east-west

103

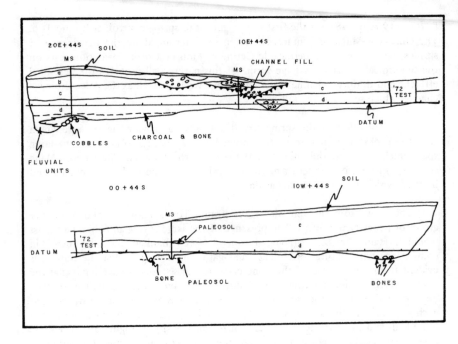

Figure 39. Geologic Section of the Test Trench at 44S.

profile through the site, from the western ridge to the bedrock exposures east of the wash described in the preceeding pragraph. There are two main drainage channels derived from two spring heads separated by an Oligocene high. Alluvium is thickest in the former stream channels and near the western slope, from which much of it was derived.

Exposure of the northwall of the excavations displayed at least three cut and fill sequences, post-bone deposition. Bison bone exposed at the base of this wall is just below an old channel fill (Figure 41). This channel was cut in alluvium heavily impregnated with calcium carbonate (I), it is the unit covering most of the bone bed, throughout the site. That channel was filled with a unit, moderately carbonate rich, which was left as terrace remnants (II) on the side of the channel which cut through it. This channel was filled with a loose brown alluvium (III), which was moderately incised and covered by the modern soil producing zone (IV). Gophers and other burrowing animals have selectively remained in the upper two units which are not carbonate rich.

In the attempt to delineate the west boundary of the site and the configuration of the old land surface which formed the trap, the west test trench was extended in the 1975 field season. It was hoped we would also be able to locate the missing skull caps of more than four hundred bison. It was presumed that the

104

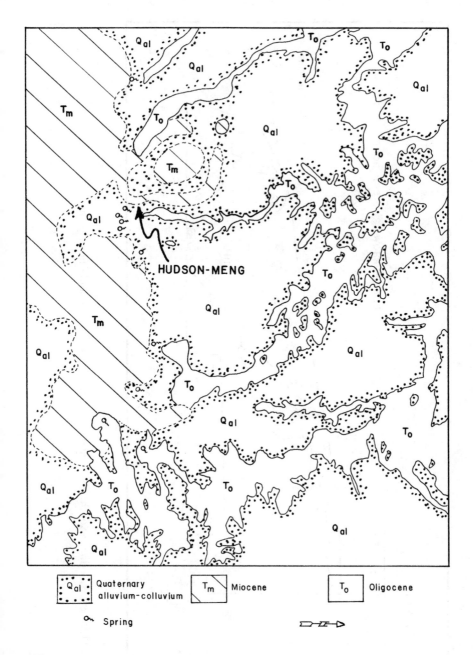

Figure 40. Reconnaisance Geologic Map in the Vicinity of the Hudson-Meng Site.

105

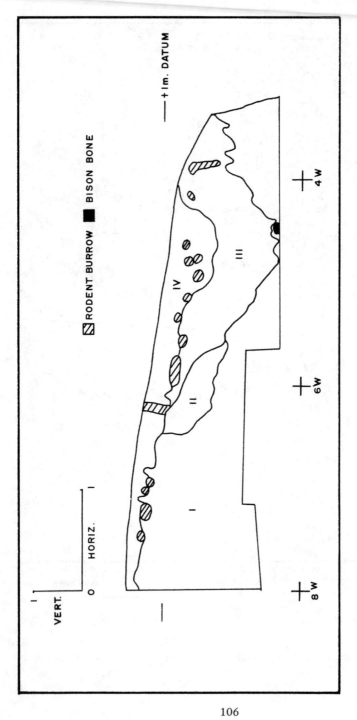

Figure 41. North Wall (line 2-South) Showing the Stratigraphy and the Cut and Fill Sequence.

skull caps had been discarded at the kill site, where rough butchering took place. Water table was encountered, under twenty-seven feet (8.2 m.) of fill, which prevented further exploratory excavation at depth.

The bone bed was exposed in this trench, at twenty-four feet (7.3 m.) below modern surface. Sediments in this fill are predominantly (80%) silt and very fine sand (1/128 to 1/32 mm. in diameter). Clay and very fine silt comprise the remaining 20% (-1/128 mm.). Directly beneath the bone bed horizon, graded stream sediments (Figures 42, 43, 44) were encountered. These sorted sediments were in fluviatile depositional patterns, grading downward to cobbles of the Miocene "butte rock." The new information led to the current interpretation of the surface on which the bone was deposited being a point bar, built up where the drainage had cut a meander bend into Oligocene bedrock on the west. A geomorphic form of this sort would produce a high, steep bank for the jump site, with the kill and rough butchering taking place on the floor of the wash, with carcasses, or portions thereof, spread on the grassy terrace surface to await further butchering and processing.

The alluvial fill above the bone bed is dominantly eolian, with minor slope wash elements. The absence of fluvial features such as cross beds, ripple marks and lag gravels, plus the massive character of the fine grain sediments, supports the model of wind deposition. Two major eolian units are distinguished on the basis of carbonate content, color and the presence of paleosols. The lower unit, I, (Figure 44) lies above the stream deposits and is gradational with them. It is this lower unit that contains and covers the bone bed. A faint to pronounced organic horizon indicates a paleosol, which reflect a period of stability during the accumulation of this unit. The lower unit also contains a great deal of calcium carbonate, allowing it to dry hard and white. It is resistant to trowelling and is more compact than the overlying unit.

The upper eolian unit, III, (Figure 44) is relatively loose and brown. It is much less compact and lacks the carbonate cementation of the lower unit. The contact with the lower unit is sharp, suggesting a partial erosion of that unit prior to emplacement of the latter. Unit IV is a soil, built up after an erosion surface developed on unit III.

A contour map (Figure 45) gives the present topographic surface at the site. A geologic profile (Figure 44) shows the fluvial and eolian units with respect to this surface and the paleo-surface represented by the bone bed. The geologic section of the south trench (Figure 39) shows more modern effluent channels emplaced and abandoned within the eolian units, as the drainage migrated eastward. This eastward shift of the effluent channel is interpreted as being due to the filling of the older channel by increased sedimentation from the ridge to the west.

The geologic profiles taken in the west trench in the summer of 1974 and 1975 provide the geologic sequence in the pre- and post- bone fill. It is from these

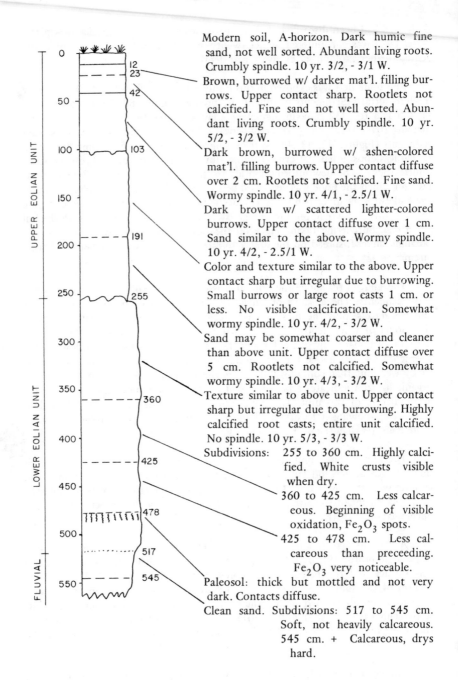

Modern soil, A-horizon. Dark humic fine sand, not well sorted. Abundant living roots. Crumbly spindle. 10 yr. 3/2, - 3/1 W.

Brown, burrowed w/ darker mat'l. filling burrows. Upper contact sharp. Rootlets not calcified. Fine sand not well sorted. Abundant living roots. Crumbly spindle. 10 yr. 5/2, - 3/2 W.

Dark brown, burrowed w/ ashen-colored mat'l. filling burrows. Upper contact diffuse over 2 cm. Rootlets not calcified. Fine sand. Wormy spindle. 10 yr. 4/1, - 2.5/1 W.

Dark brown w/ scattered lighter-colored burrows. Upper contact diffuse over 1 cm. Sand similar to the above. Wormy spindle. 10 yr. 4/2, - 2.5/1 W.

Color and texture similar to the above. Upper contact sharp but irregular due to burrowing. Small burrows or large root casts 1 cm. or less. No visible calcification. Somewhat wormy spindle. 10 yr. 4/2, - 3/2 W.

Sand may be somewhat coarser and cleaner than above unit. Upper contact diffuse over 5 cm. Rootlets not calcified. Somewhat wormy spindle. 10 yr. 4/3, - 3/2 W.

Texture similar to above unit. Upper contact sharp but irregular due to burrowing. Highly calcified root casts; entire unit calcified. No spindle. 10 yr. 5/3, - 3/3 W.

Subdivisions: 255 to 360 cm. Highly calcified. White crusts visible when dry.

360 to 425 cm. Less calcareous. Beginning of visible oxidation, Fe_2O_3 spots.

425 to 478 cm. Less calcareous than preceeding. Fe_2O_3 very noticeable.

Paleosol: thick but mottled and not very dark. Contacts diffuse.

Clean sand. Subdivisions: 517 to 545 cm. Soft, not heavily calcareous. 545 cm. + Calcareous, drys hard.

Figure 42. Geologic Section at 27S, 30W (Jones and Lewis, 1974).

profiles and the walls of the excavations, plus the evidence from the auger drill program, that the geologic section is constructed. From the analysis of the sediments in the overburden, the non-disturbance of the bone, the lack of a secondary accumulation pattern, and the current geomorphic analogs, it is concluded that the post-bone geologic deposition was primarily due to deflation of the ridge west of the site. Modern deflation of the same ridge, farther south, serves as a model. The overburden is apparently combined colluvium and eolian materials, derived primarily from the western ridge and accumulated over the 9820 years since the operation of the kill. Bone condition does not indicate exposure to the elements, but does suggest quick burial of the butchering and processing floor, shortly after deposition of the discarded bone. Eolian deposition, aided by slope wash, would be the most likely explanation, on the basis of all evidence, for such covering.

The model suggested in the second season of excavation has been expanded, refined, and substantiated by four added field seasons and the extension of the trench to the westward. The diagram (Figure 44) shows such a reconstruction, with a steep bank west of the spring effluent, where the drainage had cut against the Oligocene bluffs at the outside of a meander bend. The east bank is a gently sloping point-bar grading into a terrace. Post-bone bed, the unit is covered with a great deal of alluvium-colluvium and a stable period occurs, creating a paleosol that is still apparent over most of the site. Conditions changed giving a major erosional period followed again by aggradation and another degradation-aggradation cycle. The latter cycle was sufficient to bury the site to the modern depth, or greater. This surface was in turn eroded, with minor aggradation giving the present surface and soil.

Haynes (1968) describes the alluvial chronology of the southwestern United States by correlating 135 radiocarbon dates within stratigraphic sequences from more than sixty sites in the western states. Briefly stated, the portions of his sequence which correlate to the Hudson-Meng deposits begin with the upper part of unit B (I at Hudson-Meng). This unit contains, "younger Paleo-Indian artifacts with bones of extinct bison and camel," and, "is composed of alluvial-eolian silt terminated by an eroded paleosol." Unit C (II at Hudson-Meng) is considered Altithermal arroyo fill. It contains Archaic cultural material and terminates with a paleosol which merges, locally, with the unit B paleosol and is often referred to as the "Altithermal soil." His unit D (III at Hudson-Meng) is considered as flood plain and slope-wash alluvium containing modern fauna and pre-ceramic and ceramic cultural remains. This is followed by unit E (IV at Hudson-Meng) which is lithologically similar to D, with ceramic cultural remains.

The major contrast in the Hudson-Meng stratigraphy is the increased eolian materials in units II-IV. This is a local phenomena at Hudson-Meng, resulting from the continued deflation of the ridge on the western periphery of the site. Correlating the alluvial chronology of Haynes (*ibid.*) with the work of Stout, *et al.* (1965) and the stratigraphic, palynologic and chronologic evidence from the Hudson-Meng, a diagramatic cross section, showing the stratigraphic sequence,

109

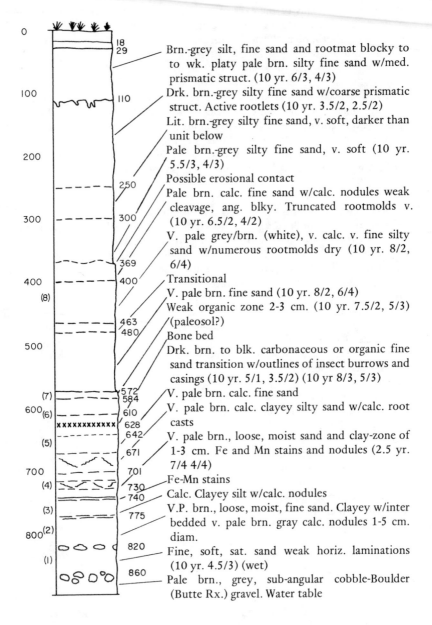

Brn.-grey silt, fine sand and rootmat blocky to to wk. platy pale brn. silty fine sand w/med. prismatic struct. (10 yr. 6/3, 4/3)

Drk. brn.-grey silty fine sand w/coarse prismatic struct. Active rootlets (10 yr. 3.5/2, 2.5/2)

Lit. brn.-grey silty fine sand, v. soft, darker than unit below

Pale brn.-grey silty fine sand, v. soft (10 yr. 5.5/3, 4/3)

Possible erosional contact

Pale brn. calc. fine sand w/calc. nodules weak cleavage, ang. blky. Truncated rootmolds v. (10 yr. 6.5/2, 4/2)

V. pale grey/brn. (white), v. calc. v. fine silty sand w/numerous rootmolds dry (10 yr. 8/2, 6/4)

Transitional

V. pale brn. fine sand (10 yr. 8/2, 6/4)

Weak organic zone 2-3 cm. (10 yr. 7.5/2, 5/3) (paleosol?)

Bone bed

Drk. brn. to blk. carbonaceous or organic fine sand transition w/outlines of insect burrows and casings (10 yr. 5/1, 3.5/2) (10 yr 8/3, 5/3)

V. pale brn. calc. fine sand

V. pale brn. calc. clayey silty sand w/calc. root casts

V. pale brn., loose, moist sand and clay-zone of 1-3 cm. Fe and Mn stains and nodules (2.5 yr. 7/4 4/4)

Fe-Mn stains

Calc. Clayey silt w/calc. nodules

V.P. brn., loose, moist, fine sand. Clayey w/inter bedded v. pale brn. gray calc. nodules 1-5 cm. diam.

Fine, soft, sat. sand weak horiz. laminations (10 yr. 4.5/3) (wet)

Pale brn., grey, sub-angular cobble-Boulder (Butte Rx.) gravel. Water table

Figure 43. Geologic Section at 27S, 50W.
(Haynes and Mead, 1975)

110

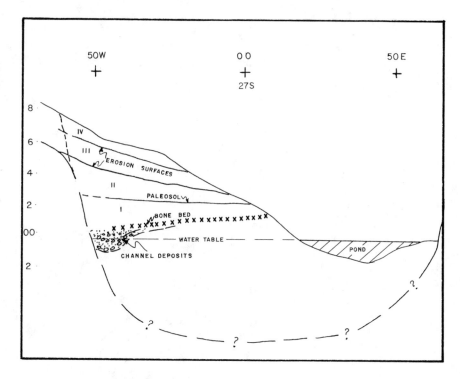

Figure 44. Geologic Cross-section of the Alluvial Fill along the 27S Line.

with age assignments is given in Figure 46.

Unit I is the material containing and burying the bone bed. Its upper limit masked by a distinctive paleosol. Lithologically, it is comprised of alluvial sand and silt with some "butte rock" gravels ranging to cobble size. The upper portion of the unit is increasingly represented by eolian silt with some colluvial components. The high degree of calicification of this unit suggests decreasing soil moisture, indicative of desiccation associated with the increasing temperatures and aridity of the Altithermal.

The Altithermal arroyo cut and fill sequence is represented by unit II. This unit is lithologically similar to I, containing more eolian components and little or no alluvial material, except in the arroyo channel fill. Colluvial materials comprise a minor portion of this unit. Calcification is not as pronounced as in the underlying unit, yet it is greater than with either of the overlying units. Again, this suggests desiccation. It is possible that the paleosol is a compound soil built up in both unit I and unit II time intervals. It is tentatively interpreted as the "Altithermal soil," dated from 4800 ± 900 B.P. (Morrison, 1967) to 4200 B.P. (Haynes, *ibid.*).

111

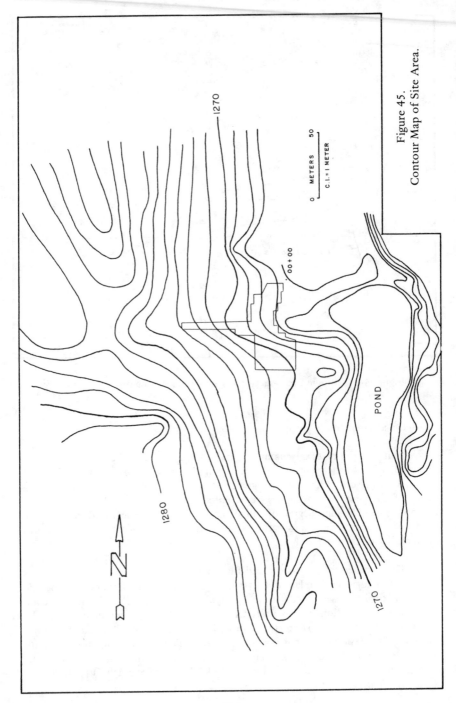

Figure 45.
Contour Map of Site Area.

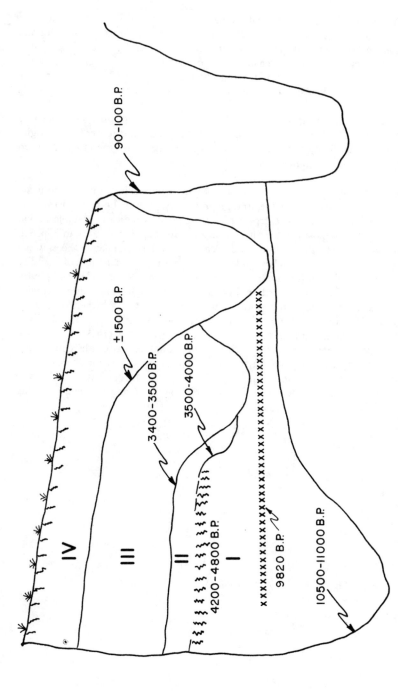

Figure 46. Diagrammatic East-West Cross Section of the Hudson-Meng Site Showing the Relationship of Depositional Units. The vertical wriggley lines indicate soil zones. The "X" horizon is the bone bed. No scale.

90-100 B.P.

±1500 B.P.

3400-3500 B.P.

3500-4000 B.P.

4200-4800 B.P.

9820 B.P.

10500-11000 B.P.

IV

III

II

I

An erosional contact with unit III marks a textural and color change, as well. This unit lacks the calcification of the lower units, is brown to grey in color and is a "cleaner" silt and sand than the lower units. The latter description is probably due to the lack of carbonate cement and root cast fill of the lower units, rather than a sorting or source material differentation. It is considered a relatively young (-3500 B.P.) eolian deposit with minor slope wash components.

The youngest unit, IV, is a grey-brown silt with abundant rodent burrows and a recent soil horizon. Again, it is considered to be dominantly eolian in origin. This unit forms the modern surface and has been incised by the modern arroyo cutting cycle, thought to have begun about A.D. 1880.

Using the data from Figures 42 and 43 some approximations can be made for the rate of deposition of the stratigraphic units. It must be realized that the erosional breaks indicate lost deposits and the paleosol indicates a stable period with little or no deposition making calculations for deposition rates an approximation, at best. Of the four units described, unit I accumulated the slowest, with rates as low as .03 inches (.08 cm.) per century. The period of stability marked by the paleosol is of unknown duration, however. What pollen and phytolith evidence we have for the site indicates this period to be relatively moist with good grass cover, which deteriorated with time, as the Altithermal aridity increased. The initial conditions would suggest slow sedimentation rates. Units II and III reflect the maximum depositional rates of 5.7 inches (14.5 cm.) and 5.1 inches (13.0 cm.) per century, respectively. This would be reasonable, considering the current understanding of Altithermal climatic and vegetational conditions. Unit IV represents a rate of 2.9 inches (7.3 cm.) per century. Considering a post-Altithermal climatic amelioration and the re-establishment of vegetation, this relative rate is again within reason.

CHAPTER 10

CHRONOLOGY AND PALEO-ENVIRONMENTAL INTERPRETATIONS

CHRONOLOGY

Neuman's (1967) summary of radiocarbon dated sites on the northern and central Plains gives no data on Alberta points, but gives a range for Scottsbluff points from 7930 to 4201 B.C. (9880-6151 B.P.) from the sites he records. The dates for sites other than Lime Creek site yield dates of less than 6890 B.C. (8840 B.P.) for this point style.

Radiocarbon dates on Alberta point horizons are rare in site reports or in summary literature. Hell Gap, Wyoming, (Irwin-Williams, *et al.*, 1973) provides maximum and minimum temporal boundaries, although it yields no date from the Alberta Horizon itself. The overlying cultural unit contains Cody Complex (Scottsbluff and Eden points) materials dated at 6650 B.C. (8600 B.P.). The underlying Hell Gap horizon yields dates of 7700-8300 B.C. (9650-10,250 B.P.). Therefore, the Alberta material is in a time interval of 6650-7700 B.C. (8600-9650 B.P.) at this site. The only other excavated, stratified Alberta site in North America is the Fletcher site (Forbis, 1968). Age determinations at this site are geologic estimates, of 7000 to 11,000 B.P.

Although the Hudson-Meng hearth areas containing burned bone, charred and stained ground were present from the first season, charcoal was nearly non-existent. As larger hearth areas appeared, charcoal was still absent, except in exceedingly small fragments, about the size of the tip of a match. The absence of charcoal in the presence of hearth areas called for an explanation. This was best answered by the use of buffalo chips for fuel. Anyone who has had the opportunity to burn chips is aware that the residue is a very fine, powdery ash which would be gone with the first breeze.

Phytolith studies were undertaken at the site in the 1975 season. Although phytoliths were present in all samples taken, their abundance in the hearth areas was several times that of any other portion of the site. It was noted that the abundance in the hearth areas compared favorably to freshly burned dung samples, in abundance of phytoliths (Lewis, Appendix III, this volume). This information lends further credence to the use of chips as fuel in the fires burning at the time of butchering and meat processing at the Hudson-Meng site.

115

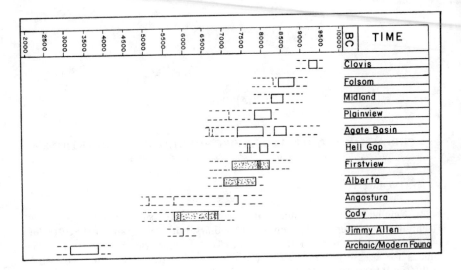

Figure 47. Comparative Plains Paleo-Indian Chronologies
(after Wheat, 1972)

All charcoal encountered in the bone bed was collected and accumulated. In the absence of sufficient charcoal for radiocarbon dates, bone was analyzed. Bone apatite samples, raw and calcined bone were collected for processing. An initial date, on bone apatite of 8990 ± 190 B.P. (SMU-52), was supplemented by a bone collagen date of 9380 ± 100 B.P. (SMU-102). Four years of charcoal flecks were hand picked to give a datable sample. The resultant date of 9820 ± 160 B.P. (SMU-224) is considered the most reliable date for the site (Haynes, personal communication).

It appears that, in the absence of specific dates for Alberta horizons, the information from Hell Gap and other Plains locations give a time bracket of 6650-7700 B.C. (8600-9650 B.P.) for that projectile style. The dates of 8990-9820 B.P. for the Hudson-Meng site fit well with and increase that interval.

Wheat (1972, p. 157) gives a graphic summary of comparative Paleo-Indian chronologies of the Northern and Southern Plains. His plot has a position for Alberta chronology, but no data. I have borrowed Wheat's plot and inserted Clovis data, Hell Gap material from the Casper site, and the Alberta dates from Hudson-Meng, plus the Alberta interval from the Hell Gap site (Figure 47). The result is most significant in the three shaded areas (two by Wheat, one by myself). There is a great deal of duplication of the Firstview chronology, by the Alberta data. Both of these are earlier than the Cody chronology, though they tend to overlap it, on the younger end.

116

PALEO-ENVIRONMENTAL DATA

Combined information from palynology, malacology, and phytolith analysis tend to support the geologic model proposed in the preceding chapter. Wu and Jones (Appendix II, this volume) present an interpretation of the site, based on the study of the snails. Their conclusion is that the conditions at the Hudson-Meng site 9820 years ago were "considerably wetter" than they are at present.

With respect to pollen—it should be noted that the only successful pollen recovery was in the south geologic trench. Pollen samples were taken at numerous other sample sites, especially to correspond with the measured sections. No pollen was recovered from the eolian component of fill, by either of two independent pollen laboratory analyses. Palynological evidence (Kelso, 1977, personal communication) is summarized in Table 14 and Figure 48. Though the pollen yield from the alluvium was not great, nor were dates available from horizons other than the bone bed, a model of the paleoenvironment is suggested. Prior to, and at the time of the kill, the site area was a grassland, probably somewhat more moist than it is currently. Post-kill, the area became increasingly arid, with desert shrubs replacing the grasses, until a semi-arid desert was produced. More recently, this trend was reversed, producing the modern grassland with pine forests in the uplands.

The presence of *Zea mays* at a level below the modern surface is not surprising, in that the Hat Creek Drainage Archaeological Survey, initiated in conjunction with the excavation of the Hudson-Meng site, yielded a burial (Gill and Lewis, 1977) dating 750 ± 90 B.P. (NWU-61), believed to be representative of Woodland occupation of the perenial streams of the region.

Phytolith analysis (Lewis, Appendix III, this volume) tends to support a similar model, i.e., a moist grassland at the time of the kill, followed by change to more arid grassland species.

Table 14. Pollen Count, South Trench Profile, Hudson-Meng (Kelso, 1977).

SAMPLE LOCATION	Pinus	Juniperus	Quercus	Ulmus	Juglans	Carya	Betula	Celtis	Populus	Salix	Artemisia	Ambrosia-type	Cichoreae	Cheno-ams	Sarcobatus	Gramineae	Triglochin	Zea mays
(Surface) 0 cm.	94	2								1	27	18		16		16		
–30 cm.	41		2			2	2				42	34		34		20		9
–60 cm.	10	7		3			1	1		2	21	28	3	19		55		
–230 cm.	2	2	10	4	1				2	2	90	34	2	11		18		
–250 cm.			4	15						3	90	28	7	15		17		
–255 cm. (Bone bed)	3	4		1					2	3	58	58	4	19	1	24	2	
–260 cm.	1		3	12						3	29	30		7		5		
–270 cm.	3	4	3	3						2	6	45		17		23		

SAMPLE LOCATION	cf. Cleome	Umbelliferae	Solanaceae	Leguminosae	Malvaceae	Eriogonum	Polygonaceae	Plantago	Urtica	Rosaceae	Ephedra (nevadensis)	Ephedra (torryana)	Cyperaceae	Typha-tetrad	Typha-monad	Undetermined	Undeterminable	Raw Count	Abs. Count per gram
0		4											12	3		7	1	200	
-30	21	1	2	1	1						1	1	11	1		4	8	200	
-60													3	1		4	18	200	
-230							8		3				1			6	44	200	
-250		4					6		1							10	61	200	118
-255						1	10	3	2	1			1		1	7	68	200	65
-260							6	1					1			3	35	100	137
-270													6			2	83	115	

Table 14. (continued).

119

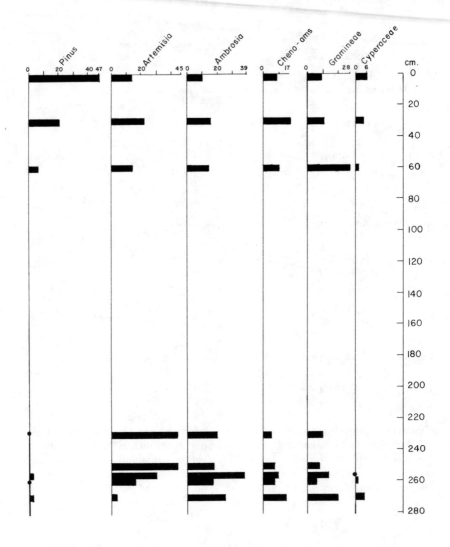

Figure 48. Selected pollen spectra from Table 14. Interval from -60 to -230 cm. devoid of pollen. Extrapolation from surface to bone bed equates approximately 38.5 yrs./cm. -60 cm. = 2310 B.P.; -230 cm. = 8858 B.P. Altithermal interval suggested by increase in drought tolerant vegetation and depletion of water loving plants, by 8858 B.P., with reverse trend post 2310 B.P.

CHAPTER 11

THE CODY COMPLEX IN PLAINS PREHISTORY:

A REASSESSMENT

GENERAL ARCHAEOLOGICAL FRAMEWORK

New World Prehistory was divided into a series of stages by Willey and
Phillips (1958). In their sequence, from Lithic to Post-Classic, they have divided
prehistoric cultures on the basis of a historical-developmental approach. The earliest of these subdivisions, the Lithic, has had a variety of names applied to it,
i.e., Big Game Hunting Tradition (Willey, 1966); Paleo-Indian (Kreiger, 1964);
Early Prehistoric (Mulloy, 1958).

In general, regardless of the title given or the specific substage discussed, we
refer to a time period embracing $\pm$ 20,000 B.C. to as late as 4,000 B.C. The cultures within this time span are usually characterized by distinctive, lanceolate
projectile points. The earliest types are the fluted varieties notably Clovis, Sandia,
and the younger Folsom and its unfluted equivalent, the Midland point.
Following the Folsom substage, we enter a cultural time period characterized by
a variety of projectile points and generally referred to as the Plano (Jennings,
1955). Within the Plano substage, diagnostic point types such as Plainview, Jimmy
Allen, Hell Gap, Agate Basin, Angostura, Alberta, Scottsbluff, Eden, Firstview,
and others replace the catchall term "Yuma." The variety of artifacts apparently
indicate differing cultural groups, or a continuum of cultural change for the
exploitation of the same, though changing, environment and game base.

The association of these projectile points with Pleistocene megafauna of
extinct and modern forms provides the concept of big game hunting traditions.
Repeated associations of Clovis points and mammoth remains from geographically
scattered sites give conclusive proof of this culture-game animal relationship.
Evidence from Murray Springs in southern Arizona (Hemmings 1970) indicates
that bison and possibly horse were also taken by Clovis hunters. Post-Clovis evidence indicates the hunting of bison, of extinct and modern forms, in the latter
portions of the Lithic stage. The majority of the evidence for all the Lithic cultures is derived from "kill," or "butchering" locations.

Perhaps that most important single site in the High Plains, in terms of providing a dated cultural sequence, is Hell Gap, Wyoming (Irwin 1968, Irwin-Williams, *et al.*, 1973). The cultural sequence (Table 15) is reproduced here in reverse order of the original publication. This sequence shows a succession of points called the "Parallel Flaked Projectile Points" (Bryan, 1962) above the Folsom-Midland horizons.

Beginning with Agate Basin points and continuing throughout the Plano substage, point types are characterized by long, lanceolate forms displaying excellent workmanship and well controlled flaking patterns in horizontal and oblique, parallel flake scars. Most of these points have bases defined by basal grinding. Earlier forms have bases which differ little from the overall shape of the point. With the Alberta, and the younger Scottsbluff and Eden points, we have the development of definite shoulders, giving a somewhat squared base and long slender blade to these point types.

THE CODY COMPLEX

Excavations at the Horner site near Cody, Wyoming (Jepsen 1951, 1953) yielded Scottsbluff and Eden points in association with the Cody Knife. The latter artifacts described as "one distinctive artifact which can serve as a diagnostic for the Cody Complex even thought it is unaccompanied by the characteristic projectile points," (Wormington, 1957, p. 128). It was the association of the Scottsbluff and Eden projectile points and associated artifacts that caused Jepsen (*ibid.*) to propose the name Cody Complex. Wormington (*ibid.*) formalized the designation and included the Cody Knife as a marker, or index type, even without the association of projectile points.

Russell Johnston, a collector in Alberta, Canada, was the first person to recognize that Eden and Scottsbluff points and stemmed knives with oblique blades belonged to a single complex (Wormington and Forbis, 1965). He gave the name "Little Gem" to this association found in a series of sites near Cereal, Alberta, in the 1930's. Prior publication, by Jepsen (1953), of the Horner material gave the name Cody Complex to the same association noted by Johnston.

Canadian collectors including Johnston, Hugh Bower, and James Mac Gregor had also discovered another distinctive projectile point type. Commonly found with Scottsbluff points and physically resembling them, implying a relationship, the new points were larger, with larger stems and slightly convex bases. Wormington (*ibid.*) proposed a new type, the Alberta point.

There are only two excavated, stratified Alberta sites in North America. One is the Fletcher site (Forbis, 1968) in Alberta, Canada. Age determinations at this site are geologic estimates, of 7,000 to 11,000 B.P. The other locality is the Hudson-Meng site.

The importance of the Cody Knife is that it can serve as a diagnostic for the

122

Culture	Approximate Radiocarbon Date–BC
Lusk	6000 – 5500
Frederick	6400 – 6000
Cody Complex	6800 – 6400
Alberta	7500 – 7000
Hell Gap	8000 – 7500
Agate Basin	8500 – 8000
Midland	8700 – 8400
Folsom	8800 – 8600
Goshen	9000 – 8800

Table 15. Sequence of Paleo-Indian Cultures at Hell Gap, Wyoming (Irwin-Williams, *et al.* 1973).

Cody Complex. It is distinctive as compared to other High Plains knives in that it is a stemmed knife with the stem at an angle up to 46 degrees from the cutting edge of its transverse blade. Although Cody Knives are known from sites in the High Plains from Canada to New Mexico (Figure 33), the Hudson-Meng site is the first association of this artifact with the Alberta Culture.

There is dated, stratigraphic evidence for the greater antiquity of Alberta artifacts, compared to the classic Cody Complex. Radiocarbon dates on bone and charcoal from the Hudson-Meng site yield earlier values than normally assigned to Scottsbluff and Eden material, yet fit within the range assigned to the Alberta horizon at Hell Gap. Technological criteria also indicate the ancestoral position of the Hudson-Meng Alberta points to younger Scottsbluff and Eden types (Huckell, Appendix, I, this volume).

The artifacts from the Hudson-Meng bison kill call for a revision of the Cody Complex as previously defined for the High Plains, or a reassessment of the diagnostic artifacts which comprise this complex. The discovery of a Cody Knive (Figure 29) in the butchering floor faunal remains associated with artifacts of Alberta type give, not only the oldest dated specimen of this distinctive knife, but associate it with a chronologically earlier projectile point type than any previous association. The implications of this association are that the Alberta point is the prototype of the Scottsbluff and Eden points, and Alberta is also the earliest culture to produce the Cody Knife.

In the light of this new information, the Cody Complex must be expanded to include Alberta points and the implied developmental sequence to the younger Scottsbluff and Eden varieties, or the Alberta designation must be considered an early variant of the younger Scottsbluff points. Radiocarbon dates of bone and charcoal from the Hudson-Meng site yield earlier values than normally assigned to the Alberta horizon at Hell Gap. Technological criteria also indicate the ancestral position of the Hudson-Meng Alberta points to younger Scottsbluff types.

123

It is hereby proposed that Alberta artifacts are directly ancestral to the Cody Complex, that the Cody knife- Alberta association at $9820^{\pm}$ 160 B.P. ($7870^{\pm}$ 160 B.C.) at Hudson-Meng is justification for the inclusion of Alberta points in the Cody Complex. I prefer to use the established complex, rather than propose a new cultural entity. However, the Cody Complex must be expanded to include the ancestoral Alberta material.

CHAPTER 12

MICROBUCKS, MEGAFAUNA AND PALEO-INDIANS

GENERAL STRATEGY AND RESEARCH FRAMEWORK

I believe it was in an introductory course to North American prehistory that I first became aware of what we do not know about Paleo-Indian (+6000 B.P.) archaeology on this continent. This course, plus one in the geology of early man sites and a paper by Haynes (1964) suggesting the presence of a central Canadian corridor for migration of men and fauna into the geography of the present United States led me to consider the states of Montana, North Dakota, and Minnesota as the "threshold" for early man into the High Plains and Central Plains of the continental interior. Assuming this concept was correct, and knowing that the physiographic province known as the High Plains, just east of the Rockies, had produced the largest number of stratified early man sites (Figure 49) in the country, I concluded that the states of Montana, Wyoming, Colorado, North and South Dakota, and Nebraska should produce evidence of their presence. Also puzzling to me was the fact that there were no reported large scale bison kill sites, or buffalo jumps, in the states of North and South Dakota, Nebraska, and Kansas (an area containing the greatest concentration of historic bison). Montana and Wyoming were areas of concentration of such features, with lesser frequency in Colorado and adjacent states. There also was a paucity of professional archaeological investigations of Paleo-Indian sites in the rather large and promising area within a 200-mile radius of Rapid City, South Dakota. The only notable exceptions to that statement are the Long (Angostura) site, South Dakota; Hell Gap and Agate Basin, Wyoming; and the Lime Creek and Scottsbluff sites in Nebraska. Many of these investigations were undertaking during the 1930's and 40's. The results were quite dated, or scantily represented in publications.

With this general setting, it seemed to me that the region might be very productive for early man investigations. Local artifact collections appeared to verify this conclusion, and field work has further proven this. Not only the Hudson-Meng site but the partially completed Hat Creek Survey indicate a rather intense Plano occupation of the area. In addition, Folsom and Clovis artifacts ocur within the study area in sufficient frequency to promote interest in the area at an earlier time depth. The abundance of fossil remains of bison and mammoth, elk and mountain sheep indicates a larger magafaunal population than previously suspected on the basis of historic accounts. Mammoth remains plus non-associated Clovis artifacts, indicate that the faunal base and the specialized

125

1 Hudson-Meng
2 Angostura
3 Agate Basin
4 Hell Gap
5 Scottsbluff
6 Claypool
7 Jones-Miller
8 Lindenmeier
9 Jurgens
10 Dent
11 Olsen-Chubbuck
12 Folsom
13 San Jon
14 Clovis
15 Plainview
16 Domebo
17 Lubbock
18 Scharbaur
19 Bonfire
20 Murray Springs
21 Lehner Ranch
22 Naco
23 Casper
24 Eden
25 Colby
26 Hanson
27 Horner
28 Wasden
29 Anzick
30 McHaffie
31 Fletcher
32 Simonsen
33 Cherokee
34 Lime Creek

Figure 49. Some Important High Plains and Prairie Paleo-Indian Sites.
See numerical tabulation on the facing page for site identity.

hunters were present in the area (Agenbroad, 1973). Recent investigations (Agenbroad and Jones, 1975, Agenbroad, 1976, 1977) indicate large populations of mammoth and associated fauna in the area, prior to the advent of human predation. The Colby site (Frison, 1976) in North-central Wyoming supports the Clovis predation model and time periods of the more southern sites.

The method of excavation of the Hudson-Meng site was aided by the techniques used at Murray Springs, Arizona (Hemmings, 1970; Hemmings and Haynes, 1968; Kelso, Agenbroad, and Haynes, 1972). The methods of excavating the site are discussed in the chapter on archaeology. The final methodology was based on the examples of other, well excavated and reported sites, plus advice of numerous other investigators. Added to this were the unique circumstances of the Hudson-Meng kill site and the fact that, due to minor funding, we carried out the work over several years with laboratory analyses in the intervening time periods, which allowed us to sort and sift and settle on a methodology that not only fit our severe (initial three seasons) budget limitations, but also adapted itself to the site conditions.

I would greatly encourage anyone interested in methodology for excavation of a Paleo-Indian bone bed, to consult Dennis Stanford of the Smithsonian Institution. The techniques and methodology that he and his crew developed and utilized at the Jones-Miller excavations near Wray, Colorado, are exemplary and might be considered as the ultimate in refinement of such techniques. On a much more austere budget, however, I feel the Hudson-Meng methodology produced highly satisfactory results.

The excavation and analysis of the Hudson-Meng bison kill produced an approach to the archaeology of Paleo-Indian sites which may serve as a guide for similar studies by other investigators. The problems and the methods of their solution at this site are hereby discussed—not to point to ourselves and say, "See what we did," but rather to say, "Here is how we did it, and why," so that others can benefit from our results and our mistakes.

CONTRAST IN PALEO-INDIAN VERSUS NEO-INDIAN ARCHAEOLOGY

Initially, it can be accepted that the greater the antiquity of a culture being studied, the less material remains will survive. It is easier to approach a Mexican Classic-Post Classic site, for example, than to systematically undertake a Paleo-Indian kill site. To pursue that statement further: there are almost too many types of data available from an urban location. Cultural remains include a variety of forms, materials, processes, and cultural utilization. In addition, there is the analysis of form, function and structure of not only material such as ceramics, but of the entire site itself. Usually, the mere size of the site and the abundance of all types of cultural remains and their analysis make such a site a "natural" for the "new archaeology" of statistical sampling and analysis, computer data storage and analysis, theorization and testing of multiple hypotheses, and

128

interpretations of the resulting sample data. Such a site can, in fact, serve generations of scholarly investigation and still remain relatively undisturbed, simply due to the size, complexity, and quantity of materials, problems, interpretations and raw data available.

Perhaps the greatest contrast in the archaeology of Paleo-Indian sites is the smaller number and variety of material culture artifacts. Paleo-Indian sites are usually impoverished in cultural remains, as compared or contrasted with Neo-Indian sites. As previously indicated, the majority of these sites, as evidenced by the reported excavations, are relatively small, sparce in the amount of cultural inventory produced, and specific in the cultural function carried out, i.e., kill/butcher sites.

Regretably, most Paleo-Indian sites are represented by kill sites. Therefore, the cultural activity, the tool inventory, etc., are somewhat predictable, even as the site is recognized. The formation of hypotheses to be tested, etc., are rather limited, at the onset of the investigation.

It should not be inferred here that I am saying paleo-archaeology does not allow the use of "new archaeological" methodology. In fact, certain procedures and concepts have been applied, with good results, to just such problems (Kelso, Agenbroad, and Haynes, 1972; Agenbroad, 1970), on sites older and younger in prehistory than the Hudson-Meng site. The point I am attempting to make is that most Paleo-Indian sites present a microcosm of artifactual material for description, analysis, and intepretation, especially when contrasted to Formative and later sites. Ceramic cultures, as an example, create an infinite number of artifacts (potsherds) which can be counted, classified, analyzed, studied as to type of manufacture, raw materials, temper analysis, firing temperatures, oxidation/reduction environments, size, shape, form, decoration, and function. Added to that, one can study the distribution and association of certain "types," with other cultural attributes such as room types, non-ceramic artifact associations, lineage or clan affiliation, etc. Again, this serves only to illustrate the complexity of one class of cultural items (ceramics) common in younger archaeological sites.

The only items corresponding to the frequency of ceramics in formative and later sites, in Paleo-Indian investigations, are faunal, or lithic. Usually, there is not even a high return (for hours of labor expended) in the lithic tools recovered. Waste flakes from tool sharpening or manufacture more closely represent the ceramic frequency of younger sites. Lithic tools may represent the only cultural "artifacts" of the paleo-site, . . . which in itself can be considered a cultural artifact.

The discovery of one "tool" in an entire season (such as the initial season at Hudson-Meng) does not ignite a hot flame of research and investigation in other than a Paleo-Indian specialist. To have a total artifactual inventory of fewer than 50 specimens at a close of six years of field work is equally unexciting to many. Yet it is just such endeavors that have produced what we know, and what we are

129

still finding out, about the antiquity of man in the Americas.

One other element is usually abundant in paleo-sites: faunal remains. Since the majority of these sites are kill and/or butchering sites, as previously stated, this is a logical conclusion. The analysis of faunal remains has been ignored too long, however. Major exception to this are the Bonfire Shelter (Dibble and Lorrain , 1968), Casper Site (Frison, *et al.*, 1974), Jones-Miller (Stanford, in press), to name a few recent studies.

Most sites are preserved and exposed by a sequence of geological phenomena and events. The fact that any paleo-sites remain is an anomaly. Recent land modification, such as reclamation, irrigation, mining, etc., further reduce the recognition and research of those sites which have been preserved. The geological framework provides another dimension in the investigation of paleo-sites and the interpretation of the geologic, palynologic, palenotologic evidence that remains.

The foregoing is meant simply to point out the differences found in the sites themselves, their archaeology, and the methods of analysis and, therefore, suggest a somewhat different approach to Paleo-Indian archaeology and Neo-Indian archaeology.

HUDSON-MENG: ITS UNIQUE ASPECTS

In the example of the Hudson-Meng site, several other factors are present: 1) the presence of an unproven site which several major institutions had rejected, or ignored, over a 34-year period; 2) the investigation of a large Paleo-Indian site by a newly formed department of a minor institution; 3) the lack of funding and related support by that institution (initially); 4) the lack of adequate (major) funding from any source for several seasons; 5) the utilization of untrained volunteers (first season) and inexperienced undergraduates as a field crew; 6) use of short-term, inexperienced personnel provided by Educational Expeditions International; 7) laboratory analysis and the training of inexperienced undergraduate laboratory personnel; and 8) production of professional papers by undergraduate students.

The inconclusive results of two seasons of testing are described elsewhere in this text. The concentrated efforts, under the initial permit, proved the site to be archaeological and important; and, as stated, it began after the commencement of an academic semester, in a geographic area famous for unpredictable fall and winter weather.

After we had established the importance of the site, excavation began, immediately, in spare time, with a volunteer crew. The majority of the volunteers had never had any experience in field excavation, and most had no academic background in archaeology. Enthusiasm and willingness to learn quickly compensated for those deficiencies.

130

It was here that some of the other problems with a major excavation at a small, isolated institution began to appear. Of immediate concern was the supply of tools and equipment for the field work. A person living in an urban area with multiple sources for a needed item cannot imagine the frustration of being unable to secure the basic pieces of equipment necessary for excavation. As a case in point, we bought every whisk broom, paint brush, and trowel in town—without supplying half the work force. To complicate matters more, since the trowels were all inexpensive, foreign-made products with welded shanks, many did not last for one day. At that time, Marshall-Towne trowels were unknown in our local stores. The crew literally used pie spatulas and tablespoons for part of the first season. Added to equipment problems were the twins of time and finance. As indicated previously, it was a new department in a small college. This means operation on a budget which is essentially non-existent, and a teaching load nearly double that of a major university professor.

Another dimension, one which added intrigue, was the reaction of certain members of the "big" institution in the state. Local landowners began to inform me of phone calls asking them to keep me off their property, to reserve such rights for the representatives from "big U." I learned of remarks concerning my competence and credentials, that were passed within and without the "professional" community in the state.

Nature, too, played its role in the frustration and rewards. The site was located in a sparsely populated portion of the county. Isolation of the site can best be illustrated by the fact that when the field crew was in camp, we were the second largest community in Sioux county, an area of approximately 2,200 square miles. Access was approximately five miles of paved roads, followed by twelve miles of gravel road, followed by four miles of graded, ungravelled road and a mile of unimproved road. This gave no problems (other than dust) during dry weather; however, rain made travel on the latter three segments of road next to impossible. One storm so sufficiently dampened the roads that it took 3½ hours to travel seventeen miles, to the pavement. For three seasons the roads were of this nature. Rain, especially the spectacular, violent, thunderstorms, also showed us the faults of "bargain" tents purchased from non-existent budgets. These events dropped as much as three inches of rain in as many hours. Add the unbelievable lightning displays and you have spectacular weather conditions, wet duffle and crew members, to say the least.

Our first season drew to a close on November 16, 1971. We backfilled the site at 4 p.m. The first major blizzard and deep freeze arrived at 6 p.m. the same day. Of the fall and winter seasons since, only 1976 would have allowed the field work period we enjoyed in 1971.

An aspect unique to small, non-research oriented institutions is that of lack of facilities, funding, encouragement, philosophy, or even a concept of field research. Research funds and release time were unknown. In fact, it was from such frustration that the initiation of the state college research institute was begun.

A research institute (Chadron State College Research Institute) was initiated, from legislative funding, prior to the first field season. Having no precedent, locally, the modest funding was divided equally among the five academic divisions on campus. No funding remained at the time the Hudson-Meng site was initiated. The second season (first summer field season) saw us with a funding of less than $2,500 for a six-week excavation financed in part by the crew, as participants in a field school. Private and "bargain" tents gave us a modest camp at the site, in the shelter of the Nance homestead windbreaks. Our camp kitchen consisted of two Coleman stoves, two ice chests and a Dutch oven. During the second season, we were donated a gas stove and a gas refrigerator. Some of the visiting scientists from larger institutions made such heartening comments as "I wouldn't even consider such an excavation, on your budget." Our problem was simply this: we had to prove that the site was significant enough to promote funding by any of the granting agencies.

Grant requests were written, submitted, and denied multiple times and to multiple sources. They were denied for various reasons: "too much," "too little," "site insignifiance," etc. In this same period of frustration due to lack of funding, I listened to a colleague complaining about having up to four projects funded, at plus $60,000, for the upcoming field season. His concern was that he might have to reject one of the grants!

The first two seasons were volunteer and field school operations. At the conclusion of the second field season, we had proven the worth of the site, the fact that it was much more extensive than anyone suspected and that it was yielding Alberta culture artifacts in and among the remains of a large population of extinct bison. At this point in time (1972), a former student, on an expedition to Africa with the newly organized Educational Expeditions International (E. E. I.), wrote suggesting I contact that organization for funding. The contact was made and the result was funding (for 1974) in return for incorporating inexperienced participants of all ages, from all occupations and geographic areas as my crew. The National Science Foundation (N. S. F.) also awarded funding for 1973-75 seasons, and we emerged from "rags to (comparative) riches," even though our modest budgets brought exclamations of dismay, shock, contempt, and humor from other investigators.

With expanded funding and larger crews, we were able to: 1) do more machine work in testing and removing overburden; 2) do more hand excavation; 3) open several sections of the site simultaneously; 4) have enough experienced crew members to supervise the inexperienced crew members and participants; 5) add needed items to our field equipment inventory; and 6) provide work study compensation for laboratory analysis.

The 1975 field season saw the addition of an appropriation by the Nebraska State Legislature, which could be spent on non-salary items. This allowed the

the purchase of a second hand backhoe, giving us unlimited on-site machine capability instead of the 1-2 day per season machine work previously done on a contract basis. The funding also greatly contributed to the preparation of maps, plates, diagrams for seasonal reports and papers as well as this publication, plus the replenishment of wornout tools, tents, and other equipment.

CREWS

Having participated in a number of excavations over a period of years, I was used to crews made up primarily of graduate students and upperclassmen who were usually majoring in archaeology, geology, or some other related discipline. I had also experienced several methods of crew selection based on grade point average, experience, letters of recommendation, and personal knowledge.

All these methods were made ineffectual in the operation of the Hudson-Meng site. As previously described, the first (1971) season was entirely volunteer. Many of those persons would last only a short period of time, from ½ day to 2-3 days. Others became the core of the following season's crew. All were inexperienced, most were undergraduates, and all were unpaid for their efforts.

The 1972 season, operated as a field school, was subsidized by a small grant from the Chadron State College Research Institute, and by the crew itself, with numerous volunteers. Late in this season, we were donated gas appliances for our field kitchen. Nineteen hundred seventy-three saw a much enlarged field school operation, financed by the National Science Foundation, with an enlarged staff on modest compensation. We remained rather local (Wyoming, South Dakota, Nebraska) in make up, with several students from Utah.

The funding by N. S. F. and E. E. I. in 1974 made our crew rather cosmopolitan, with participants from as far away as Hawaii, Panama, South Africa, Ethiopia, and nearly all regions of the United States as well as several Canadian provinces. It also gave us age spreads from 14 to over 60 and all ranges of background and experience. The range of feeling of the incoming "unknowns" was from severe cultural shock to outstanding enthusiasm. Without exception, the experience was rewarding.

Renewed funding by the supporting agencies allowed a repeat performance of the 1974 season, in 1975, with an even larger E. E. I. component. In return for the time taken in training new excavators, twice each season, we gained greatly in the amount of work done and the added insight into the analysis of the cultural and faunal remains of the site. Less tangible and assessable are the human relationships developed with participants and their new appreciation of field science, to the point of new career goals for some.

The use of non-trained, limited background participants in a major scientific endeavor has been extremely rewarding (with the exception of two individuals

133

in more than 160 total). This is a higher success ratio than which I had experienced in other crews, with different size and makeup. I personally endorse the concept which E. E. I. promotes, and the participants which it has supplied to my field research. Without the financial and participant support of E. E. I. and the financial support by N. S. F., allowing experienced field and laboratory crews, the Hudson-Meng site could not have been excavated in the manner which it has been; nor do I think the results would have been the same. The extended period of excavation allowed a seasonal analysis and promoted the direction of the following field period, based on this analysis.

RESULTS

One of the aspects of any field operation is the training of people, not just the excavation crew, but the general public, including those persons who visited the excavations (some came every season for five years), but also those who heard or read about the activities. It was not uncommon to have as many as 300 visitors per day at the site. This tally probably represents approximately one half of those who attempted to find us and got lost once they left improved roads. To handle the visitors, two members of the excavation team were rotated to "tour guide" status each working day. This allowed the remainder of the crew to go about their work uninterrupted and gave each crew member, in turn, the chance to deal with the public on a "first-hand encounter" basis.

Added to the tourists were field schools and dig crews from other institutions such as the Smithsonian Institution, University of Wyoming, Colorado State University, South Dakota State Archaeological crew, University of Nebraska field school, Webb School, and numerous high school and grade school groups. Many of these visitations allowed transfer of ideas, mutual problems, etc., in both formal and informal manner. They also produced some outstanding prairie and plains volleyball teams!

During the several field seasons, 55 crew members received college credit for their participation. An additional 46 persons ranging from teenagers and professional people to retired persons gained new insight, appreciation for and experience in field archaeology, as participants from Educational Expeditions International.

Laboratory studies of the faunal remains and lithic materials trained new persons, or gave added depth to members of the excavation teams. These studies also called for solution of new problems in metric analysis, methodology, etc., and promoted numerous research projects of individual and group nature. A total of 21 professional papers were presented on various aspects of the investigation of the Hudson-Meng materials. Of this total, 10 papers were published in scientific journals. In addition, numerous articles appeared in local, state, and out-of-state newspapers. Several periodicals such as *National Geographic, Nebraskaland, Popular Archaeology*, and *Earth Science* also carried articles featuring the excavations.

134

This type of exposure, in person and through the press, publicized the site, the college, and the state to the rest of the area, nation, and world. It focussed attention to Paleo-Indian archaeology in the High Plains, particularly in Nebraska and the contiguous states.

CHAPTER 13

SUMMARY AND CONCLUSIONS

The Hudson-Meng excavations have given us a rather detailed look at Alberta culture bison procurement and processing. Approximately sixty percent of the site, as known from test pits, trenches and bone bed trend, was excavated. Of that sixty percent, approximately half (30%) of the faunal remains were left *in situ* with the anticipation of future development as an exhibit of a Paleo-Indian kill site.

Among the contributions and conclusions gained from the excavation and analysis of the bone bed are:

1) The first stratified, absolute dated Alberta site in the New World. (Fletcher was stratified but lacked absolute dates; Hell Gap was stratified but had no absolute dates from the Alberta horizon, though it produced an age bracket with dates from cultures older and younger than Alberta.);

2) An absolute date of 9820 $\pm$ 120 B.P. for a stratified Alberta culture site. The date is on a composite sample of charcoal collected from the bone bed. It is supported by bone-apatite and bone-collagen dates;

3) The oldest (dated) occurrence of the Cody Knife in the New World;

4) Indications as to the ancestral nature of Alberta points to the younger Scottsbluff and Eden materials. A re-evaluation of the Cody Complex, to include Alberta points;

5) Analysis of a large scale, single event kill; or several smaller kills over a short time interval (approximately one month);

6) Added information on bison evolution on the High Plains. The lack of skulls with horn cores necessitated extensive post-cranial studies and comparisons, indicating the Hudson-Meng bison are an intermediate form, as compared with modern forms and the common extinct forms;

7) Added information on the methods of bison procurement and processing by pedestrian hunters at a time depth of 9820 B.P.;

137

8) Non-use of bison elements as butchering tools, in contrast to such evidence found at the Casper site, and the Jones-Miller site;

9) Identification of butchering taking place at or near identifiable hearth/ activity areas with bone discard in a somewhat random, radial pattern from these centers;

10) The feasibility of processing some 600 animals by a relatively small group, *ca.* 75 persons, as contrasted to the 150-200 person group postulated for the Olsen-Chubbuck site (Wheat, 1972);

11) The necessity for some type of storage system for the impressive quantities of jerked meat produced from the mass kill and butchering operation;

12) The non-utilization of some 4500 pounds (1980 kg.) of bone-marrow resources;

13) Palynological, depositional, and phytolith analysis support of an Altithermal dessication (drought), as suggested by Anteus (1955);

14) An intensive study of Alberta culture lithic technology;

15) The initiation of the Hat Creek Archaeological Survey, which has produced information and evidence of the prehistoric utilization of N. Sioux and Dawes County;

16) A paleo-site which has been only partially excavated (60%) with most of the faunal material in the excavated portion left *in situ*. The land is controlled by the U. S. D. A.-Forest Service. The site has been included on the National Registry of Historic Places and has the added potential of future development as an *in situ* exhibit of a Paleo-Indian kill site;

17) This monograph and its effect on the interpretation of Plains Prehistory;

18) Formulation of and field testing of methodology, interpretations, conclusions and research models which are explained in this report and are thereby made available to others who wish to use, modify, or reject them.

Fletcher (Forbis, 1968) is the only other major, reported Alberta site occurring in a stratified situation. No comparisons with other large scale Alberta kill sites are possible.

As outlined by Wheat (1972), most earlier Paleo-Indian kills reflect small group activity with small numbers of animals collected in favorable natural trap environments. Though mass kills are evidenced, the number of animals taken in each site, or at least in each kill at a given site, was relatively small. Data from the Hell Gap culture sites at Casper (Frison, 1974) and Wray (Stanford, in press)

138

indicate mass kills in natural traps such as sand dunes (Casper) and snowdrifts (Wray) as alternates to "wet ground" models, or the classic "drop" or "fall" as evidenced at Hudson-Meng.

A kill, in Paleo-Indian horizons of the magnitude of the Hudson-Meng site is unreported. Table 16 gives an estimated tally of the number of animals taken and the number of drives in which they were accumulated, as indicated by the published reports. From the recorded data, single kills of more than 100 animals were rare in Paleo-Indian times, the Olsen-Chubbuck site being one of the few recorded single-event kills of a large quantity of bison.

All evidence at Hudson-Meng, whether geological, cultural, or faunal, supports the conclusion of a single event. I have allowed for the possibility of several small drives over a thirty to forty-day period, but in the 9820 years since the event, that still suffices for a single event. There is no evidence to support multiple seasons of accumulation on the Hudson-Meng butchering floor. Should that have been the case, I would expect to find stratigraphic separation of the bone accumulations. I would also expect to find evidence suggesting butchering in the bone-free areas (hearth centers) of previous operations. The bone bed supports the single-event model. The bone bed is a continuous, thin-layer phenomenon, spread over at least 2000 square meters of a former point bar-terrace on the inside curve of a meander bend. The bone bed contains at least six, large, rather uniformly spaced hearth areas. An analysis of the distribution of faunal elements for the excavated portions of the bone bed indicates that these hearth areas were the centers for butchering activity, with bones discarded randomly and radially from these centers.

To interpret this accumulation, with its consistent patterning, as accumulation over a series of years and multiple bison kills within that time interval is taxing the field evidence with bias, in my opinion. My own interpretation of a single event, whether one kill or several smaller ones in a very short time duration, may also be biased. It is the interpretation most strongly supported by the field evidence, however.

As summarized by Wheat (1972: pp. 159-161), Paleo-Indian bison kill operations began small and grew progressively larger and more refined with time and experience, to sophisticated, formalized, ritualistic techniques in later time periods, lasting to the historic examples. If the interpretation of the single event at Hudson-Meng is correct, it is one of the earliest massive mass kills recorded in the North American archaeological record. It must reflect the contemporaneity of natural and cultural events and circumstances which led to such a large-scale bison harvest, i.e., the formation of a natural trap, a meander bank of sufficient drop, in just the right geographic location; the accumulation of a large herd of bison in the proper grazing area; the contemporaneity of experienced hunters to allow semi-controlled movement and ultimate stampede of the animals over the cut bank; and weather conditions allowing slow meat spoilage (Oct.-Nov.) to permit the degree of intensive butchering reflected in the disarticulated skeletal

SITE	CULTURE	NO. ANIMALS	NO. DRIVES
Folsom, New Mexico	Folsom	23	?-multiple suggested
Lindenmeir, Colorado	Folsom	9	1
Linger, Colorado	Folsom	5	1
Zapata, Colorado	Folsom	5	1
Clovis, New Mexico	Folsom	"hundreds"	?
Lipscomb, Texas	Folsom/Plainview	14	1
Bonfire, Texas	Plainfiew	120	3
Scottsbluff, Nebraska	Scottsbluff	"exeedingly dense"	?
James Allen, Colorado	Jimmy Allen	?	?
Horner, Wyoming	Scottsbluff-Eden	+200	?
Finley, Wyoming	Scottsbluff-Eden	48	"several"
Agate Basin, Wyoming	Folsom/Agate Basin	?	"multiple"
Casper, Wyoming	Hell Gap	74-100	1-6
Jones-Miller, Colorado	Hell Gap	$^{+}_{-}200$	2
Hudson-Meng, Nebraska	Alberta	+600	1
Olsen-Chubbuck, Colorado	Firstview	190	1

Table 16. Paleo-Indian Mass Bison Kills.

140

remains. This latter fact also argues for a conservative practice, even in a mass-kill situation. Virtually all of the animals represented in the Hudson-Meng bone bed indicate complete (heavy) butchering. Of the 438 animals mapped in the area excavated, only six (1.37%) of the animals are in any recognizable degree of articulation. Some skeletal elements such as legs and vertebral columns were still articulated, however, the majority of these units were not portions of a recognizable individual animal, and are thought to indicate butchering units.

The magnitude of the Hudson-Meng kill, its testimony to the completeness of butchering, and the resultant estimates of usable meat resources clearly indicate efficient, skilled utilization of animal resources in the High Plains. It also foreshadows later prehistoric and the historic developments of not only bison utilization, but the modern ranching, feed lot and slaughter operations.

I feel the evidence from Hudson-Meng is a tribute to the efficiency, resourcefulness, and ability of pedestrian Early American big game hunters.

141

REFERENCES

Agenbroad, Larry D.
    1968 The Five Fingers Buffalo Jump, *The Explorer's Journal,* Vol. 46, No. 4, pp. 279-286.
    1970 Clovis Projectile Point Occurrences in Northwestern Nebraska. A paper presented at the 81st Annual Meeting of the Nebraska Academy of Sciences, Lincoln.
    1976 a) Buffalo Jump Complexes in Owyhee County, Idaho. *Tebiwa, Misc. Papers of the Idaho State University Museum of Natural History,* No. 1, Pocatello.
        b) Progress Report: Hot Springs Mammoth Site, South Dakota. A paper presented at the 36th Annual Meeting of the Society of Vertebrate Paleontology, Boulder, Colorado.
    1977 *Mammoth Site of Hot Springs, South Dakota.* Caxton Printers, LTD. Caldwell.
    1978 Cody Knives and the Cody Complex in Plains Prehistory: A Reassessment. *Plains Anthropologist* (in press).

Agenbroad, Larry D., C. Vance Haynes, Jr. and Gerald Kelso
    1972 The Clovis Hunting Camp at Murray Springs, Arizona: An Analysis After Two Seasons. A paper presented at the 37th Annual Meeting of the Society for American Archaeology, Miami, Florida.

Agenbroad, Larry D. and Charles A. Jones
    1975 The Hot Springs Mammoth Site, Hot Springs, South Dakota. A paper presented at the 28th Annual Meeting of the Rocky Mountain Section, Geological Society of America, Boise, Idaho.

Antevs, Ernst
    1955 Geologic-climatic Dating in the West. *American Antiquity,* Vol. 20, No. 4, Pt. 1, pp. 317-335.

Barbour, Erwin H. and C. Bertrand Schultz
    1932 The Scottsbluff Bison Quarry and Its Artifacts. *Bulletin of the Nebraska State Museum,* Vol. 1, No. 34, pp. 283-286, Lincoln.
    1936 Paleontologic and Geologic Consideration of Early Man in Nebraska. *Bulletin of the Nebraska State Museum,* Vol. 1, No. 45, pp. 432-449.

Bedord, Jean M.
1974 Morphological Variation in Bison Metacarpals and Metatarsals in *The Casper Site: A Hell Gap Bison Kill on the High Plains*. George C. Frison (ed.), pp. 199-240. Academic Press, New York.

Bryan, A. L.
1962 Paleo-American Culture History, A New Interpretation. M. S. Thesis, Harvard University, Cambridge.

Butler, B. Robert, Helen Gildersleeve and John Sommers
1971 The Wasden Site Bison: Source of Morphological Variation. In *Aboriginal Man and Environments of the Plateau of Northwest America*. Stryd, Arnoud H. and Rachel A. Smith (eds.). Archaeological Association, University of Calgary, Alberta, pp. 126-152.

Clayton, Lee, W. B. Bickley and W. J. Stone
1970 Knife River Flint. *Plains Anthropologist*. Vol. 15, No. 50, Pt. 1, pp. 282-290.

Crabtree, Don E.
1973 The Obtuse Angle as a Functional Edge. *Tebiwa*, Vol. 16, No. 1. Idaho State University Museum, Pocatello.

Darton, N. H.
1903 Preliminary Report on the Geology and Water Resources of Nebraska West of the One Hundred and Third Meridan. *U.S. Geological Survey Professional Paper*. No. 17. Washington.

Denig, Edwin T.
1930 Indian Tribes of the Upper Missouri. J. N. B. Hewitt (ed.), Bureau of American Ethnology. *Forty-sixth Annual Report*. Washington.

Dibble, David S. and Dessamae Lorrain
1968 Bonfire Shelter: A Stratified Bison Kill Site, Val Verde County Texas. *Texas Memorial Museum Miscellaneous Paper No. 1*. Austin.

Dick, Herbert W. and Bert Mountain
1960 The Claypool Site: A Cody Complex Site in Northeastern Colorado. *American Antiquity*, No. 26, pp. 223-235.

Dorsey, George A.
1900 An Aboriginal Quartzite Quarry in Eastern Wyoming. *Field Columbian Museum Publication 51, Anthropological Series:* Vol. II, No. 4. Chicago.

Duffield, Lathel F.
1973 Aging and Sexing the Post-Cranial Skeleton of Bison. *Plains Anthro-*

pologist. Vol. 18, No. 60, pp. 132-139.

Emple, W. and T. Roskosz
1963 Das Skellett der Gliedmassen des Wisents, *Bison bonasus* (Linnaeus, 1758). *Acta Theriologica.* Vol. 7, No. 13, pp. 259-297.

Farrens, W., D. S. Hoffman, and D. L. McDonald
1972 Preliminary Analysis of the Bison Bones from the Hudson-Meng Site, Sioux County, Nebraska. A paper presented at the 82nd Annual Meeting of the Nebraska Academy of Sciences. Lincoln

Fenneman, N. M.
1931 Physiography of the Western United States. McGraw-Hill. New York.

Forbis, Richard G.
1968 Fletcher: A Paleo-Indian Site in Alberta. *American Antiquity,* Vol. 33, No. 1, pp. 1-10.

Frison, George C.
1970 The Glenrock Buffalo Jump. *Plains Anthropologist,* Memoir 7, Vol. 15, No. 50, Pt. 2.
1976 Cultural Activity Associated with Prehistoric Mammoth Butchering and Processing. *Science,* Vol. 194, pp. 728-730.

Frison, George C. and Charles A. Reher
1970 Age Determination of Buffalo by Teeth Eruption and Wear in the *Glenrock Buffalo Jump,* 48C0304, Memoir 7, by George C. Frison. *Plains Anthropologist,* Vol. 15, No. 50, Pt. 2.

Frison, George C. (editor)
1974 *The Casper Site: A Hell Gap Bison Kill on the High Plains.* Academic Press, New York.

Frison, George C., Michael Wilson and Diane J. Wilson
1976 Fossil Bison and Artifacts from an Early Altithermal Period Arroyo Trap in Wyoming. *American Antiquity,* Vol. 41, No. 1, pp. 28-57.

Gill, G. W. and R. O. Lewis
1977 A Plains Woodland Burial from the Badlands of Western Nebraska. *Plains Anthropologist.* Vol. 22, No. 75, pp. 67-73.

Hartley, John A. and Joe Pokorski
1973 Skull Elements from the Hudson-Meng PaleoIndian Site. A paper presented at the 83rd Annual Meeting of the Nebraska Academy of Sciences, Lincoln.

145

Hartley, John A. and Garry Luoma
1974 The Hat Creek Drainage Archaeological Survey, 1973 Field Season. A paper presented at the 84th Annual Meeting of the Nebraska Academy of Sciences, Lincoln.

Haynes, C. V. , Jr.
1964 Fluted Projectile Points: Their Age and Dispersion. *Science.* Vol. 145, No. 3639, pp. 1408-1413.

1968 Geochronology of Late Quaternary Alluvium in *Means of Correlation of Quaternary Successions.* Morrison, R. B. and H. E. Wright, (ed.), Vol. 8 Proceedings VII Congress, International Association for Quaternary Research, Salt Lake.

Haynes, C. Vance, Jr. and E. Thomas Hemmings
1968 Mammoth-Bone Shaft Wrench from Murray Springs, Arizona. *Science.* Vol. 159, No. 3811, pp. 186-187.

Hemmings, E. Thomas
1970 Early Man in the San Pedro Valley, Arizona. Unpublished Ph.D. Dissertation, University of Arizona, Tucson.

Hillerud, John M.
1966 The Duffield Site and Its Fossil Bison, Alberta, Canada. Masters Thesis, Department of Geology, University of Nebraska, Lincoln.

Holmes, W. H.
1919 Quartzite Quarries, Wyoming. *Bureau of American Ethnology: Handbook of Aboriginal American Antiquities: Part I: Introduction to the Lithic Industries.* Bulletin 60, Pt. 1, pp. 210-213. Washington.

Huckell, Bruce
1978 Hudson-Meng chipped stone in *The Hudson-Meng Site: An Alberta Bison Kill in the Nebraska High Plains.* By Larry D. Agenbroad. Appendix I. University Press of America, Washington.

Irwin, Henry T.
1968 The Itama: Late Pleistocene Inhabitants of the Plains of the United States and Canada and the American Southwest. M.S. Doctoral Dissertation, Harvard University, Cambridge.

Irwin, Henry T. and H. M. Wormington
1970 PaleoIndian Tool Types in the Great Plains. *American Antiquity,* Vol. 35, No. 1, pp. 24-34.

Irwin-Williams, Cynthia, Henry Irwin, George Agogino and C. Vance Haynes, Jr.
    1973 Hell Gap: Paleo-Indian Occupation on the High Plains. *Plains Anthropologist*. Vol. 18, pp. 40-53.

Jennings, Jesse D. and Edward Norbeck
    1955 Great Basin Prehistory: A Review. *American Antiquity*, Vol. 21, pp. 1-11.

Jepsen, Glen L.
    1953 Ancient Buffalo Hunters of Northwestern Wyoming. *Southwestern Lore*. Vol. 19, pp. 19-25. Boulder, Colorado.

Johnson, Willard D.
    1901 The High Plains and their Utilization. *Twenty-first Annual Report of the United States Geological Survey*, Part IV. Government Printing Office, Washington.

Kehoe, Thomas F.
    1967 The Boarding School Bison Drive Site. Memoir 4, *Plains Anthropologist*.

Knudson, Ruthann
    1973 Organizational Variability in Late Paleo-Indian Assemblages. Unpublished Ph.D. Dissertation. Washington State University, Pulman.

Krieger, Alex, D.
    1964 Early Man in the New World in *Prehistoric Man in the New World*, Jesse D. Jennings and Edward Norbeck (eds.), pp. 23-81. University of Chicago Press, Chicago.

Landrey, Cheri Y.
    1974 Selected Post-Cranial Measurements, 1973 Season, Hudson-Meng Site. Paper presented at the 84th Annual Meeting of the Nebraska Academy of Sciences, Lincoln.

Lewis, Rhoda O.
    1978 Use of Opal Phytoliths in Paleoenvironmental Reconstruction at the Hudson-Meng site in *The Hudson-Meng Site: An Alberta Bison Kill in the Nebraska High Plains*. By Larry D. Agenbroad. Appendix III. University Press of America, Washington.

Lorrain, Dessamae
    1968 Analysis of the Bison Bones from Bonfire Shelter in Bonfire Shelter: A Stratified Bison Kill Site, Val Verde County, Texas. By David S. Dibble and Desamae Lorrain. Miscellaneous Paper, No. l, pp. 77-132, Texas Memorial Museum, Austin.

147

Luoma, Garry
1975 The Hat Creek Drainage: Archaeological and Paleontological Survey. A paper presented at the 85th Annual Meeting of the Nebraska Academy of Sciences, Lincoln.

McHugh, Tom
1958 Social Behavior of the American Buffalo *(Bison bison bison)*. *Zoologica,* Vol. 43, pp. 1-40.

Moody, David L.
1974 Distribution of Skull Elements from the Hudson-Meng Site. A paper presented at the 84th Annual Meeting of the Nebraska Academy of Sciences, Lincoln.

Morrison, Roger B.
1967 Principles of Quaternary Soil Stratigraphy in *Quaternary Soils,* Roger. B. Morrison and Herbert E. Wright, Jr. (ed.). Vol. 9, VII Congress, International Association for Quaternary Research. University of Nevada, Reno.

Mulloy, William
1958 A Preliminary Historical Outline for the Northwestern Plains. *University of Wyoming Publications,* Vol. 22, Nos. 1 & 2, Laramie.

Neuman, Robert W.
1967 Radiocarbon-Dated Archaeological Remains on the Northern and Central Great Plains. *American Antiquity,* Vol. 32, No. 4, pp. 471-486.

Reher, Charles A.
1970 Population Dynamics of the Glenrock *Bison bison* Population in *The Glenrock Buffalo Jump 48C0304.* George Frison (ed.). *Plains Anthropologist,* Memoir 7, Appendix II.

1973 The Wardell *Bison bison* Sample: Population Dynamics and Archaeological Interpretation in *The Wardell Buffalo Trap 48 SU 301: Communal Procurement in the Upper Green River Basin, Wyoming.* By George C. Frison. University of Michigan, Anthropological Papers No. 48, Appendix II. Ann Arbor.

1974 Population Study of the Casper Site Bison in *The Casper Site: A Hell Gap Bison Kill on the High Plains.* George C. Frison (ed.), Academic Press, New York.

Renaud, E. B.
1931 Archaeological Survey of Eastern Wyoming. University of Denver, Department of Anthropology.

Russell, Kathleen D.
  1973 An Analysis of Bison Denitition: Hudson-Meng Site, Sioux County
       Nebraska. Paper presented at the 83rd Annual Meeting of the Neb-
       raska Academy of Sciences, Lincoln.

  1974 Further Analysis of the Bison Dentition: Hudson-Meng Paleo-
       Indian Bison Kill, N. W. Nebraska. Paper presented at the 84th
       Annual Meeting of the Nebraska Academy of Sciences, Lincoln.

  1976 An Analysis of Bison Dentition: Hudson-Meng Site, Sioux County,
       Nebraska. *Transactions of the Nebraska Academy of Sciences.*
       Vol. 3, pp. 85-91, Lincoln.

Schultz, C. Bertrand and Loren Eiseley
  1935 Paleontological Evidence for the Antiquity of the Scottsbluff Bison
       Quarry and its Associated Artifacts. *American Anthropologist,* new
       series, Vol. 3, No. 2, pp. 306-319.

Skinner, Morris F. and O. C. Kaisen
  1947 The Fossil Bison of Alaska and a Preliminary Revision of the Genus.
       Bulletin of the American Museum of Natural History. Vol. 89,
       pp. 123-256, New York.

Stout, Mylan T., V. H. Dreeszen, C. B. Schultz, and C. K. Bayne
  1965 Pleistocene Classifications in *Guidebook for Conference D: Central
       Great Plains.* VII Congress, International Association for Quater-
       nary Research. Nebraska Academy of Sciences, Lincoln.

Thornthwaite, C. Warren
  1941 Climate and Settlement in the Great Plains in *Climate and Man:
       Yearbook of Agriculture, 1941.* G. Hambridge (ed.), Department of
       Agriculture, Washington.

Uridil, Sandra Jo
  1972 Preliminary Analysis of Bison Bone Material from the 1972 Field
       Season, Hudson-Meng Site, Northwest Nebraska. A paper presented
       at the 30th Plains Conference, Lincoln.

  1973 Analysis of Faunal Material from the Hudson-Meng Site: 1972
       Session. A paper presented at the 83rd Annual Meeting of the
       Nebraska Academy of Sciences, Lincoln.

Voorhies, Michael R.
  1969 Taphonomy and Population Dynamics of an Early Pliocene Verte-
       brate Fauna, Knox County, Nebraska. *Contributions to Geology:
       Special Paper No. 1.* University of Wyoming, Laramie.

Webb, Walter P.
1931 *The Great Plains.* Blaisdell Publishing Co., Waltham.

Wheat, Joe Ben
1972 The Olsen-Chubbuck Site: A Paleo-Indian Bison Kill. *American Antiquity,* Vol. 37, No. 1, Pt. 2, Memoir 26.

1977 Technology, Typology, and Use Patterns at the Jergens Site in *Paleo-Indian Lifeways,* Eileen Johnson (ed.). The Museum Journal. No. 17. West Texas Museum Association, Lubbock.

White, Theodore E.
1953 Observations on the Butchering Technique of Some Aboriginal Peoples. No. 2, *American Antiquity,* Vol. 19, pp. 160-164.

Willey, Gordon
1966 *An Introduction to American Archaeology. Vol. 1: North and Middle America.* Prentice-Hall, Inc., New Jersey.

Willey, Gordon and Phillip Phillips
1958 *Method and Theory in American Archaeology.* University of Chicago Press, Chicago.

Witzel, Frank
1974 Guidebook and Road Logs for the Geology of Dawes and Northern Sioux Counties, Nebraska. Masters Thesis, Chadron State College, Chadron.

Witzel, Frank and John Hartley
1973 Two Possible Source Areas for the Quartzite Artifacts of the Hudson-Meng Site: A Comparative Study. A paper presented at the 83rd Annual Meeting of the Nebraska Academy of Sciences, Lincoln.

Witzel, Frank and John Hartley
1976 Two Possible Source areas for the Quartzite Artifacts of the Hudson-Meng Site: A Comparative Study. *Transactions of the Nebraska Academy of Sciences.* Vol. 3, pp. 12-19, Lincoln.

Wormington, H. Marie
1957 Ancient Man in North America. *Denver Museum of Natural History Popular Series No. 4,* Denver.

Wormington, H. Marie and Richard G. Forbis
1965 An Introduction to the Archaeology of Alberta, Canada. *Proceedings No. 11, Denver Museum of Natural History,* Denver.

Wu, S. -K., and Charles A. Jones
    1978 Molluscs From the Hudson Meng Site in *The Hudson-Meng Site: An Alberta Bison Kill in the Nebraska High Plains.* By Larry D. Agenbroad. Appendix II. University Press of America, Washington.

Young, Lawrence W. II and Ronald R. Weedon
    1978 Vegetation and Flora of the Hudson-Meng Bison Kill in *The Hudson-Meng Site: An Alberta Bison Kill in the Nebraska High Plains.* By Larry D. Agenbroad. Appendix IV. University Press of America, Washington.

APPENDIX I

HUDSON-MENG CHIPPED STONE

BRUCE HUCKELL
UNIVERSITY OF ARIZONA

INTRODUCTION

Excavations at the Hudson-Meng site resulted in the amassing of a large collection of completed chipped stone artifacts and waste flakes, or debitage. The size of the collection, as well as the fact that it represented the relatively unstudied Alberta industry, offered a chance to significantly augment present knowledge of Paleo-Indian lithic industries. More than this, the Hudson-Meng material presents the first in-depth look at the characteristics which distinguish the Alberta industry and those features which relate it to both earlier and later Paleo-Indian industries on the High Plains.

The analysis of the Hudson-Meng collection began with the debitage recovered from the site. Lithologically and spatially discrete groupings of flakes occured at several loci within the bone bed; it was decided that the debitage could therefore most easily be understood by examining each of these distinct clusters of flakes as a unit. It was assumed that each cluster represents a specific flintknapping operation, and that the general nature of that operation could be defined by the characteristics of the flakes composing that cluster. With these assumptions in mind two major research objectives were established: first, the reconstruction of the sorts of flintknapping activities being pursued by the hunters after the kill, and secondly, the generation of a fuller understanding of some of the specific details of Alberta lithic technology. A technological analysis of the completed artifacts recovered from the site was also carried out in order to complement the data derived from the debitage. For technological studies of this sort, it is most important to have both debitage and completed artifacts in order to obtain the fullest possible picture of the industry they represent.

This report is organized into two major sections. The first of these is a detailed description and discussion of the debitage, including its distribution and composition, the artifacts it represents, and its importance for the site interpretation. The second section is a brief consideration of Alberta lithic technology as expressed at Hudson-Meng, followed by an overview of the Alberta industry and its relationships to other Paleo-Indian industries.

153

DEBITAGE: METHODS OF STUDY

The first problem encountered in the examination of the debitage was the very small size of most of the flakes and flake fragments; an average flake from the Hudson-Meng site would display a maximum dimension of not more than 5 mm. Due to this, as well as their frequently fragmentary condition, it was decided that a qualitative study of the flakes rather than a metric, quantitative one would be attempted. An emphasis was placed on the observation of those attributes which most directly reflect how the flake was produced and from what sort of implement it was derived. Therefore, such attributes as type of striking platform, presence or absence of lipping, use of platform abrasion, size and shape of flake, and character of previous flake scars on the exterior surface were all consistently observed and recorded. All of these technological attributes are suitable to help provide the means to realize the major research objectives presented above.

To begin the analysis it was necessary to separate the debitage into spatial and lithologic clusters. This was accomplished by plotting all flakes on an overall map of the site; the system of one meter grid squares and the care used in the excavation permitted accurate provenience control, and with few exceptions, flakes could easily be assigned to one cluster or another. Plotting revealed four major spatial clusterings of flakes, but each of these knapping loci contained from five to ten lithologically distinct clusters of flakes. For purposes of simplicity each of the four knapping loci was labelled A, B, C, and D, while the different lithologic clusters within them were numbered serially; thus an individual cluster may be designated A-2, B-5, and so forth. Figure 1 presents an overall site map with the various clusters plotted on it.

After the segregation of the flakes into individual clusters had been completed, each cluster was examined separately. A brief series of qualitative observations was made on each flake or flake fragment belonging to a particular cluster; most of these observations dealt with the attributes of the striking platform (when present), specifically those mentioned above. When a given flake was sufficiently complete, an impression of what flake type (hard or soft hammer percussion, or pressure) it represented was recorded; while this could be a difficult judgement to make, it was necessary to help develop a picture of what type of operation the flake cluster as a whole represented. Several years' flintknapping experience was drawn upon to aid in making such determinations. However, due to their fragmentary condition and the fact that there is some degree of overlap between percussion and pressure debitage, most of the flakes in each cluster could not be classified as to the type of operation they represented. Summary statistics for each cluster are presented in Tables 1-5; the following section will briefly discuss each of these clusters in order to amplify and integrate the information in the tables. It should also be noted that the term "flake" will be used in its general sense in these discussions, and is meant to include both complete and fragmentary pieces of debitage.

154

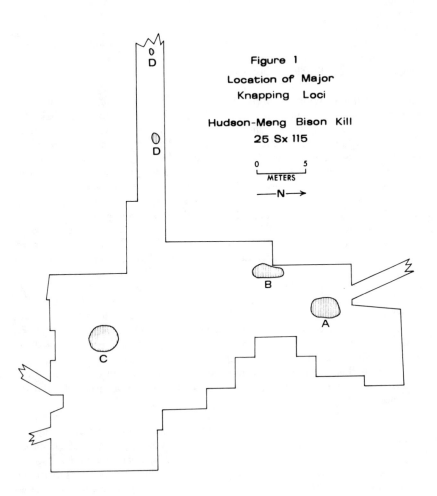

Figure 1

Location of Major
Knapping Loci

Hudson-Meng Bison Kill
25 Sx 115

0   5
METERS

N

Containing ten lithologically distinct groups of flakes and covering an area of some 12 square meters, Knapping Locus A is very large, second only to Knapping Locus C in size and content. It is centered in grids 8S, 7W and 8S, 8W (Figure 1), where a dense cluster of Knife River Flint flakes is present. Spreading out in a scatter to the east of the Knife River Flint concentration are small numbers of flakes of both quartzite and chert; both of these materials can be separated into four lithologic sub-varieties.

The major component of this locus is a central cluster of 695 Knife River Flint flakes and flake fragments, designated Cluster A-1. Summary statistics for this cluster (Table 1) show a high percentage of multiple facetted (prepared), lipped striking platforms; in fact 259 out of the 289 striking platforms examined (89.6%) showed multiple facetting, bespeaking their origin as flakes of bifacial retouch or thinning (Bordes 1961: 6). In this feature the A-1 cluster is representative of all the major clusters from the site, and most of the smaller ones as well. It is also interesting to note the total lack of platform abrasion in this large sample, which includes flakes produced by both pressure and percussion. Pressure flakes outnumber percussion flakes by about a 1.5 : 1 ratio in this cluster; in the remainder of the large clusters this ratio increases in favor of the pressure flakes. Figure 2 illustrates a typical selection of pressure and percussion flakes from this cluster.

It should also be mentioned that the larger number of Knife River Flint flakes in this A-1 cluster seems to invalidate the initial assumption of the analysis, namely, that each cluster represents a single flintknapping operation. However, I would suggest that this cluster probably does indeed represent one operation in the sense that it is the same operation performed on more than one biface of Knife River Flint. There was some slight variation in the texture and translucence of the flakes in this cluster, but not enough to allow consistent recognition of the varieties.

Four varieties of quartzite flakes were found associated with this knapping locus; these were separable on the basis of color. In order of relative abundance a white quartzite (A-2) was most common, followed by a dark purple (A-3) quartzite, a grey-speckled white (A-4) quartzite, and a golden brown (A-5) quartzite. Examination of the summary statistics for these clusters of quartzite flakes shows strong similarities to the patterns already discussed for the Knife River Flint cluster A-1. The predominance of multiple facetted, lipped striking platforms, and the degree of flake breakage or fragmentation are both reflected in the quartzite as they were presented for the Knife River Flint. However, there seems to be more of a tendency for the striking platforms to have been abraded on the quartzite flakes. Whether this reflects a desire for a stronger striking platform when working this tougher, more resistant material cannot be established satisfactorily, for the relative numbers of ground platforms are very low. Pressure versus percussion-

Figure 2. A typical group of flakes from Knapping Locus A, Cluster 1 (Knife River Flint). The group in the upper left corner are all pressure flakes, oriented with their interior surfaces up and striking platforms to the top. The five flakes in the lower left corner are fragmentary percussion flakes. Above the penny are flake fragments without striking platforms, typical of the majority of the debitage from the site.

157

KNAPPING LOCUS A

CLUSTER	MATERIAL	TOTAL N	COMPLETE	FRAGMENTARY	PLATFORM N	PLAIN	MULTIPLE FACETTED	LIPPED	GROUND	CRUSHED	PERCUSSION	PRESSURE
1	KNIFE RIVER FLINT	695	114	581	289	30	259	260	0	68	107	168
2	WHITE QUARTZITE	59	15	44	22	4	18	19	3	13	12	10
3	PURPLE QUARTZITE	35	3	32	11	1	10	10	1	5	12	13
4	GREY SPECKLED QUARTZITE	28	3	25	11	0	11	11	0	3	3	9
5	GOLDEN BROWN QUARTZITE	27	0	27	7	0	7	6	2	3	5	6
6	CHERT #1	42	4	38	15	2	13	15	0	5	3	3
7	CHERT #2	10	0	10	4	0	4	3	1	1	1	4
8	CHERT #3	5	0	5	3	2	1	2	0	1	0	1
9	CHERT #4	17	4	13	11	3	8	9	0	1	6	2

TOTAL FLAKES 918

Table 1. Summary Statistics for Knapping Locus A.

produced flake ratios are nearly 1 : 1 for the white and golden brown quartzites, but pressure flakes are much more common for the grey-speckled white quartzite, while percussion flakes are most abundant for the purple quartzite.

Four small groups of chert flakes (A-6 through A-9) were also present in Knapping Locus A. Three of these amounted to fewer than 20 flakes each, but were examined individually nevertheless since each represents the retouching of a separate, distinct artifact. These varieties are simply labelled Cherts 1 through 4 in Table 1 for ease in discussion; they are more precisely described in Table 6. Once again, the chert flakes are characterized by the presence of multiple facetted, lipped striking platforms which nearly all lack platform abrasion. With the exception of Chert 4 (A-9), pressure flakes are much more common than percussion flakes. The A-9 cluster may represent a different flintknapping operation, however, since three of the flakes in it display attributes of unifacial tool retouch flakes. However, eight more flakes in this cluster displayed multiple facetted striking platforms, implying that this was at least a partially bifacially retouched implement--its exact nature is uncertain, due to the small number of flakes which represent it.

KNAPPING LOCUS B

This second locus is situated eight meters southwest of Knapping Locus A, being centered in grids 14S, 11W and 15S, 11W (Figure 1). It too is dominated by a large concentration of Knife River Flint flakes, and contains much smaller clusters of three varieties of quartzite, four varieties of chert, and a clear chalcedony. Knapping Locus B is spread over approximately three square meters, and is nearly identical to Knapping Locus A in terms of lithologic composition.

The largest member of Knapping Locus B is a concentration of 295 Knife River Flint flakes (Cluster B-1). As evidenced by the figures presented in Table 2, this cluster presents a similar statistical picture to that of the A-1 Knife River Flint flake cluster. Flakes which display multiple facetted, lipped striking platforms are most common (79.5%), but there is a larger percentage of plain (featureless) platforms in this cluster than in A-1. Whether this implies that unifacial tool retouch flakes are present in this cluster is debatable; one large flake with a plain striking platform is certainly a by-product from the repair of a large biface. It seems probable that several of the other flakes with plain striking platforms were the result of this same operation. Pressure flakes are more common in Cluster B-1 than percussion flakes, by nearly a 2 : 1 margin. All in all, the A-1 and B-1 clusters are nearly identical in their attributes; the suggestion of a single operation being performed on more than one biface is probably valid for this cluster as well.

The three varieties of quartzite in Knapping Locus B are also present in Knapping Locus A. Still, the white quartzite (B-2), purple quartzite (B-3), and

KNAPPING LOCUS B

CLUSTER	MATERIAL	TOTAL N	COMPLETE	FRAGMENTARY	PLATFORM N	PLAIN	MULTIPLE FACETTED	LIPPED	GROUND	CRUSHED	PERCUSSION	PRESSURE
1	KNIFE RIVER FLINT	295	78	217	127	27	101	109	2	48	57	99
2	WHITE QUARTZITE	14	2	12	5	1	4	4	2	1	5	2
3	PURPLE QUARTZITE	9	0	9	3	0	3	3	1	0	4	0
4	GOLDEN BROWN QUARTZITE	6	0	6	1	0	1	1	0	0	1	1
5	CHERT #2	14	0	14	4	1	3	4	0	1	2	3
6	CHERT #3	6	0	6	3	1	2	3	0	1	1	1
7	CHERT #1	5	0	5	2	0	2	2	0	0	2	0
8	CHERT #4	2	1	1	1	1	0	0	0	1	1	0
9	CHALCEDONY	5	1	4	3	0	3	2	0	1	0	0
	TOTAL FLAKES	356										

Table 2. Summary Statistics for Knapping Locus B.

golden brown quartzite (B-4) total only 29 flakes, and nearly half of these are of the white quartzite. The small samples of quartzite flakes make it difficult to be certain exactly what sorts of operations are represented. Again, however, they appear to be following the trends evidenced by their counterparts in Knapping Locus A. Multiple facetted, lipped striking platforms, some of them abraded, dominate this small collection of flakes. Percussion flakes seem to be more abundant than pressure flakes, but there is not too much difference from ratios seen for the same three materials in Knapping Locus A.

The four varieties of chert here are also present in Locus A. These four (B-5 through B-8) are like the quartzites in that there are only a small number of flakes for each variety. This makes it difficult to draw any conclusions from the statistics presented in Table 2, except to say that the few figures seem to hold to the general pattern of flakes with multiple facetted, lipped striking platforms probably resulting from bifacial retouch.

The five flakes of translucent chalcedony (B-9) fit into the same general framework. They are the result of biface retouch insofar as can be determined. While no flakes of this material were present in Knapping Locus A, forty-six were present in Knapping Locus C, some fifteen meters to the south.

KNAPPING LOCUS C

This locus is the largest of the four, even though it contains the fewest (5) lithologically separable individual clusters. Centered in the 31S, 5W and 32S, 4W grids (Figure 1), about 22 meters south of Knapping Locus A, Knapping Locus C is composed of different materials than either Locus A or B. Only Knife River Flint is shared among all three loci. Despite the large numbers of flakes, it is tightly concentrated, with over 90% of all the flakes falling in four grid squares.

The largest single member of this locus is a concentration of fine grained red jasper flakes (C-1), the majority of which were tightly clustered in the northwest quarter of grid 32S, 4W. It should be noted, in order to place the large number of flakes of red jasper (866) into perspective, that several hundred flake fragments were no larger than 2 mm in maximum dimension. This is reflected in the complete/fragmentary flake statistics in Table 3 for this cluster, suggesting a relatively high degree of breakage, probably due in part to the extremely fine-grained texture of the jasper. This breakage factor undoubtedly serves to increase the numbers and thus the apparent size of the cluster. The jasper does reflect, however, the same basic trends described for the Knife River Flint Clusters A-1 and B-1, except that pressure flakes are present in a nearly 3:1 ratio to percussion flakes. Striking platforms are overwhelmingly multiple facetted, lipped, and not abraded, indicating that the flakes are the result of biface retouch. Cluster C-1 may also represent the retouching of more than one biface of red jasper.

161

KNAPPING LOCUS
C

CLUSTER	MATERIAL	TOTAL N̄	COMPLETE	FRAGMENTARY	PLATFORM N̄	PLAIN	MULTIPLE FACETTED	LIPPED	GROUND	CRUSHED	PERCUSSION	PRESSURE
1	RED JASPER	866	67	799	184	16	168	154	0	68	55	149
2	BROWN JASPER	236	40	196	99	11	88	90	0	29	38	80
3	KNIFE RIVER FLINT	174	28	146	63	15	48	50	0	20	17	75
4	CHALCEDONY	46	1	45	9	0	9	8	0	6	3	14
5	PURPLE-SPECKLED CHERT	5	2	3	1	0	1	1	0	2	1	1

TOTAL FLAKES 1327

Table 3.   Summary Statistics for Knapping Locus C.

A cluster of over two hundred flakes of a dark brown jasper (C-2) made it the second most common material present in Knapping Locus C. It too is made up of flakes which exhibit a preponderence of multiple facetted, lipped striking platforms, suggesting that they are the result of bifacial retouching. A similarly high ratio of pressure to percussion flakes holds for the brown jasper cluster as well (Table 3). An interesting aspect of the brown jasper cluster is the presence of a chalky white cortex on approximately 15% of the flakes. This cortex is most commonly observed on the distal ends of larger flakes, suggesting that perhaps a patch of cortex had been left toward the midline or center of a biface.

The ubiquitous Knife River Flint was the third most common material in Knapping Locus C. Designated Cluster C-3, this group of flakes exhibited nearly the same attributes as the C-1 and C-2 clusters. It was largely concentrated in grids 30S, 5W and 31S, 5W, and in this overlapped the distribution of the brown jasper cluster. Both these materials were relatively uncommon in grid 32S, 4W, the locus of the high concentration of red jasper.

Cluster C-4 was a group of 46 flakes of translucent to clear chalcedony, the same lithology as that described for Cluster B-9. All but one of these flakes were fragmentary, and most of the fragments lacked striking platforms. Still the pattern suggested by those flakes which could be more completely analyzed is like that of the majority of the assemblage described thus far: typical products of biface retouch.

Finally, five flakes of a purple-speckled orange brown chert were found associated with Knapping Locus C. The small sample size makes it difficult to but no departure from the biface retouching pattern is indicated. This same material is most common in Knapping Locus D, to be discussed next.

KNAPPING LOCUS D

The fourth locus is actually composed of two small loci, one centered in grid 25S, 26W, far to the southwest of Knapping Loci A and B, and some 20 meters west of Knapping Locus C (Figure 1). The second locus lies 8 meters to the west in grid 26S, 33W, and is included with the other because of a thin scatter of flakes between them and for ease in discussion. It contained a concentration of only 8 flakes, discussed below as Cluster D-4. Locus D is the smallest cluster of the four, having only 125 flakes of six different materials in it. Of these six materials, five are the same as those described for Knapping Locus C. Nevertheless, Locus D is an interesting one, for it contains two clusters within its confines which depart from the established patterns observed in the other three knapping loci.

One of the clusters which varies slightly is a group of 52 flakes of a purple-speckled, orange-brown chert (D-1). This cluster is centered in grid 25S, 26W, and

163

shows again a large number of fragmentary flakes (Table 4), as was noted for the red jasper flake cluster C-1. However, unlike the C-1 cluster, this chert concentration has many large flakes, such that an average flake from this cluster would measure nearly 10 mm. in maximum dimension (Figure 3). The striking platforms exhibited by the flakes are still multiple facetted, lipped, and unabraded, but there is nearly a 1 : 1 ratio of percussion to pressure-produced flakes. This represents a significant departure from the 3 : 1 pressure to percussion ratios seen in other clusters, and will be discussed in more detail later.

Red jasper (D-2) and Knife River Flint (D-3) are the next most common materials in Knapping Locus D, although both are relatively poorly represented. These two materials show no differences from the patterns already described for them in previously discussed knapping loci, with the exception of the lower percussion to pressure ratio indicated for the jasper (D-2).

Although it is represented by only nine tiny flakes, the D-4 cluster is an interesting one, for it represents the only consistent group of flakes which may be attributed to the retouch of a unifacial tool. This group came from the vicinity of grid 26S, 33W some 8 m. west of the major portion of Locus D, but is included with it to facilitate description. The material is a very fine-grained quartzite, grey in color. As can be seen from Table 4, the five flakes which retained them exhibited plain striking platforms, a slight but noticeable curvature in the length dimension, and other features such as would result from the retouching of a unifacial tool made on a flake (see Frison 1968: 150, Jelinek 1966: 403). All five of these flakes were lipped, and were probably removed by percussion--the angle formed by the striking platform surface and the exterior of the flake suggests that the flakes were the products of the retouching of a fairly steep edged tool such as a scraper.

The final two materials in Knapping Locus D are a dark brown jasper (D-5) and a translucent chalcedony (D-6), represented by three and four flakes respectively. Due to the small size of these samples, little can be done except to note their presence in this locus and the occurence of these same materials in Knapping Locus C.

MISCELLANEOUS UNPLACED MATERIALS

As seems common with sites which contain evidence for an active chipped stone industry, the Hudson-Meng site yielded several flakes which did not fit lithologically with any of the previously described materials. In many cases these were single flakes representing a unique material, or two or three flakes of the material. Most often they were not associated with any particular knapping locus, nor did they show any evidence of utilization. For this reason they were broken down into two major categories, cherts and quartzites, and each flake was examined in the same fashion as those from the clustered materials. The results of this analysis are presented in Table 5.

164

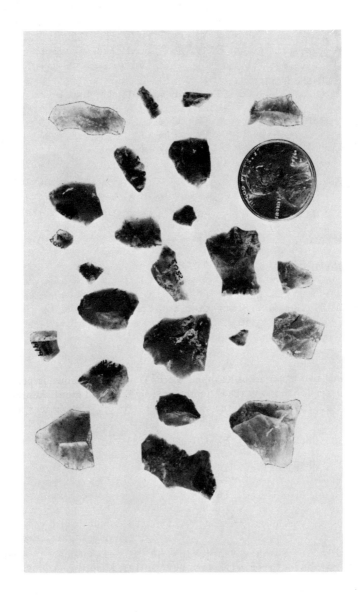

Figure 3. A representative group of flakes from Knapping Locus D, Cluster 1 (purple speckled orange brown chert). These are mixed percussion and pressure flakes, with the striking platforms oriented to the top on those flakes which retain them.

KNAPPING LOCUS D

CLUSTER	MATERIAL	TOTAL N̄	COMPLETE	FRAGMENTARY	PLATFORM N̄	PLAIN	MULTIPLE FACETTED	LIPPED	GROUND	CRUSHED	PERCUSSION	PRESSURE
1	PURPLE-SPECKLED CHERT	53	5	48	14	1	13	14	0	6	16	14
2	RED JASPER	36	4	32	8	1	7	8	0	6	14	14
3	KNIFE RIVER FLINT	20	6	14	8	1	7	8	0	3	5	12
4	GREY QUARTZITE	9	8	1	5	5	0	5	0	3	8	0
5	BROWN JASPER	3	0	3	0	0	0	0	0	1	0	0
6	CHALCEDONY	4	1	3	1	1	0	1	0	0	0	0
	TOTAL FLAKES	125										

Table 4. Summary Statistics for Knapping Locus D.

MATERIAL	TOTAL N̄	COMPLETE	FRAGMENTARY	PLATFORM N̄	PLAIN	MULTIPLE FACETTED	LIPPED	GROUND	CRUSHED	PERCUSSION	PRESSURE
MISC. CHERT	52	13	39	14	3	11	10	0	10	29	0
MISC. QUARTZITE	14	1	13	6	0	6	6	1	1	12	0
TOTAL FLAKES	66										

Table 5. Summary Statistics for Miscellaneous
Flakes not Associated with any Particular Knapping Locus.

The majority of these flakes were fragmentary but large. In addition, every flake could be classified as to its mode of production was found to have all the characteristics of a percussion flake. Further, several of these exhibited prominent bulbs of percusssion, greater relative thickness and less curvature, and often cortical striking platforms, all of which tend to point towards a hard hammer decortication origin for them. One feature not entirely consistent with this proposition is the high number of lipped striking platforms present in the sample. This may be explained by the unquestionable inclusion of some soft hammer biface retouching or thinning flakes in the group, as well as the possible use of "soft" hard hammers of sandstone or quartzite. Since it is made up of a variety of different materials and different flake types, no single process or operation can be cited as the source for these flakes. Still, the large percentage of hard hammer flakes suggests that either basic flake production or the retouching of large pieces of material was responsible for many of the unplaced flakes. The lack of cores and heavy chopping tools prevents further refinement of this idea.

MATERIALS

Some attention should be devoted to the various raw materials which were being used by the Alberta flintknappers at the Hudson-Meng site. Despite the several different, distinguishable materials present in the site, only a few can actually be traced to definite source areas. Table 6 summarizes some basic information concerning the major materials from the knapping loci.

Knife River Flint (actually a silicified lignite) is the most abundant of all the materials, at least in terms of sheer numbers of flakes present (Table 6); it is also the material of which the majority of the projectile points are made. The flakes of this stone from the four knapping loci show a noticeable amount of variation, especially with respect to color. Most of the Knife River Flint flakes from Knapping Loci A and B are a relatively dark brown color, while those from Locus C are a lighter brown, almost ranging into an amber color. The Munsell color values for both these groups are given in Table 6. There seems little doubt that the general source area for this material is the west central portion of North Dakota, approximately 325 miles north-northeast of the Hudson-Meng site. Clayton, Bickley, and Stone (1970: 282) studied Knife River Flint in detail and concluded that, "Most of the Knife River Flint used by Indians was probably quarried from secondary sources in the Knife River valley of Dunn and Mercer Counties, North Dakota." Their Munsell color values agree well with the dark brown variety present at the Hudson-Meng site, and they also note that the range of variation includes lighter brown shades.

In any event, Knife River Flint is a superb knapping material when it is free of fractures and flaws. Normally, however, fractures are developed along bedding planes, although in some cases fractures pass vertically or obliquely across bedding planes. Plant fossils are also apt to be present along these planes. If a thick enough

MATERIAL	N̄	LUSTER	MUNSELL COLOR	FRACTURE	TRANS-LUCENCE	REMARKS
Knife River Flint	1184	Dull-waxy	10YR 2/2 7.5 YR 4/4	Conchoidal	Yes	Darker material from Loci A and B largely
Red Jasper	902	Dull	7.5R 3/4	Conchoidal	Opaque	Some gray (7.5R 6/0) inclusions, coarser texture
Purple Speckled Chert	58	Dull	5YR 3/3	Conchoidal	Slightly	Speckles are dark purplish brown, pin head-sized
White Quartzite	73	Vitreous	N 7/0	Even	Yes	
Gold-brown Quartzite	33	Vitreous	10YR 3/3	Even	Very Slightly	
Gray-speckled Quartzite	28	Vitreous	N 5.5/0	Even	Very Slightly	Black (N 2/0) pin head-sized inclusions
Brown Jasper	239	Dull	10YR 3/2	Conchoidal	Opaque	Some flakes w/ white (5Y 8/1.5) cortex
Gray Quartzite	9	Waxy	N 6/0	Conchoidal	Opaque	Extremely fine-grained, slightly variegated
Chert 1	47	Dull	5YR 6/3 7.5YR 8/2	Conchoidal	Slightly	Variegated mixture of both colors, small vesicles
Chert 2	24	Dull	N 5.5/0	N 5.5/0	Opaque	Slightly burned; some flakes w/ potlids
Chert 4	11	Dull-Waxy	10YR 5/7	Conchoidal	Opaque	Thin, black vein-like inclusions
Chert 5	19	Dull	5YR 4/1	Conchoidal	Yes	
Chalcedony	9	Dull-waxy	-------	Conchoidal	Amost transparent	Occasional slight fractures & yellow (2.5Y 7/6) inclusions

Table 6. Attributes of Major Raw Material Types From Hudson-Meng.

section can be obtained between fracture planes, the flint can be worked with little trouble. It might be noted that three of the points (Figures 4a, b, d) bear traces of either cortex or bedding plane surfaces on one face. It is interesting that Knife River Flint is the most abundant material at the site, in view of the distance of the site from the quarry. Knife River Flint seems to have rated very highly with the Alberta flintknappers at Hudson-Meng.

Following closely behind Knife River Flint in abundance is a very fine grade of red jasper (Table 6). Despite the fact that 902 flakes of this material were found, no completed artifacts of it were recovered. It too is a superior knapping material, being slightly finer in grain size and more conchoidal in fracture than Knife River Flint. A virtually identical jasper comes from the vicinity of Shell, Wyoming, on the west side of the Bighorn Mountains. Comparative samples of this material, also known as "phosphoria" for formation in which it occurs, were provided by Bruce Bradley. More detailed analysis will be needed to determine if this area is indeed the source for the Hudson-Meng jasper. Due to the fact that it is so plentiful at the site it too must have been a preferred material, though it may outcrop as much as 200 miles northwest of the site.

Although represented by only 187 total flakes, the several varieties of quartzites are important materials in the assemblage. Represented by both debitage and completed artifacts, these quartzites may have originated from more than one source area. A petrographic and microscopic study of them was undertaken by Witzel and Hartley (1973). The quartzite artifacts and debitage from Hudson-Meng were compared with samples from the well-known Spanish Diggings quarries in southeastern Wyoming and from the Flint Hill quarries in the southwestern corner of South Dakota. They concluded, based on the textural and color attributes of the quartzites, that the golden brown flakes most closely resembled the Flint Hill material, but that the purple (red in their paper) flakes may have come from either quarry, though texturally they matched Flint Hill material more closely. One point (Figure 5d) was tentatively assigned a Spanish Diggings origin, based on its relatively fine grained texture. Witzel and Hartley cautioned that there were other possible quarries which they had not studied--thus the Flint Hill and Spanish Diggings assignments should be regarded as tentative ones. The study also indicated possible breakdowns within each color category of quartzite, again based on texture. Some of these varieties were recognized in this study, but were generally assigned to the miscellaneous quartzite flakes since they were unique or poorly represented (Table 5). This additional category serves to reinforce the probability of multiple origins for the quartzites. Thus, while firm assignments to source areas cannot be made for this group of materials, there is nevertheless a strong suggestion that some may have come from the Flint Hill quarries of South Dakota, with a hint of some material from Spanish Diggings in southeastern Wyoming. Local quartzites found as cobbles in the White River drainage may also have been utilized.

The several varieties of cherts and the chalcedony are even more difficult to pin down to specific or even general source areas. Chert of variable quality, color, and texture is available throughout the area around the Hudson-Meng site, as are quartzites (Agenbroad, personal communication). Often these occur in lag gravels in the White River drainage, and certainly similar situations prevail in parts of eastern Wyoming, western South Dakota, and southern North Dakota. The Alberta flintknappers apparently used materials from this wide geographic range, and therefore had ample opportunity to pick and choose from a variety of sources, both primary and secondary, in the course of their movements. Some cherts may have come from specific localized quarries, but none of these were identified in this analysis. It may be safely said that the continual search for high quality lithic raw materials led these people to sample a wide variety of cherts, and that these sources were capitalized upon whenever and wherever they were found.

DISCUSSION

The debitage offers some insight into the activities being pursued after the bison kill, but also raises a few questions. The most salient feature of the debitage is the overwhelming preponderance of bifacial retouch operations. Flakes resulting from the sharpening or manufacture of unifacially retouched tools are rare. This is in marked contrast to most Paleo-Indian bison kill sites; Casper site (Frison 1974: 95-99), for example, yielded only 308 flakes, about a third of which could be positively identified as having resulted from the retouching of unifacial tools. Apparently no biface retouching was done at the kill site; the only flakes obviously derived from bifaces could be explained as impact flakes from projectile points. While the sharpening or manufacture of bifaces is not unknown from Paleo-Indian sites, it is not a commonly reported activity. Still, the presence of biface thinning flakes to the near exclusion of other flake types does seem unusual. To my knowledge only the Murray Springs Clovis site (Hemmings 1970) displays such an overwhelming concentration of biface retouch operations in a kill, rather than a camp, situation.

From what type or types of bifacial tools were these flakes derived? Given the types of implements known to have been used by the Alberta hunters at Hudson-Meng, as well as the types of bifacial flakes recovered, four possible explanations must be considered:

1. The flakes resulted from the repair of projectile points.

2. The flakes resulted from the manufacture or sharpening of Cody knives.

3. The flakes resulted from the retouching of generalized bifaces (or "blanks" or "preforms").

4. The flakes resulted from the manufacture of projectile points.

170

Each of these alternatives has some value in accounting for the observed types of bifacial retouch flakes. The first alternative, the repair of projectile points, is an attractive one. Figures 4-6 illustrate the Alberta points and fragments recovered from the bone bed; Figures 5 and 6 especially serve to demonstrate the sorts of damage suffered during use. It is logical that repair of those points not too badly damaged must have been carried out, and that replacement of those broken beyond salvage had to occur. In fact, a single large flake of purple quartzite from cluster A-3 is in all probability derived from the first stage of projectile point repair, namely the removal of a vertical edge created by a snapped tip. The exterior surface of the flake exhibits a flake scar pattern nearly identical to that seen on the finished points from the site; however, one lateral margin is a 5 mm-thick vertical edge. The abraded striking platform is bifacial and shows somewhat excessive removal of the opposite surface lipping. I would suggest that this flake was one of the first to be removed during the repair of this projectile point.

Normally one might expect that this sort of activity should be carried out at the campsite, not at the place of the kill. Still, other flake clusters (besides A-3) suggest that projectile point repair was being done, especially at Knapping Locus A and Locus B. Two lines of evidence can be used to support this inference; first, at both these knapping loci a wide variety of materials is present, and secondly, aside from the numerous flakes of Knife River Flint in both clusters, the other materials are represented by small numbers of flakes (see Tables 1 and 2). Cluster A-2, a white quartzite, is represented by 59 flakes, and it is the most common material in that knapping locus, after Knife River Flint. The average number of flakes for each of the non-Knife River Flint material types is just under 25 in Knapping Locus A, and averages 7.5 flakes for Knapping Locus B. The flake types vary in proportion from material to material, but it is clear that both pressure and percussion flakes are represented for most materials. Unhappily none of the flakes from these clusters can be fitted onto any of the points recovered, and in fact, only three materials (gold-brown quartzite, purple quartzite, and chert 1) from the clusters match the projectile point materials. Still a diversity of material is also seen in those points recovered from the bone bed. This diversity of material types, the generally small numbers of flakes, and the use of both pressure and percussion techniques are three characteristics which would be consistent with projectile point repair activities. Small numbers of flakes, perhaps from 10 to 20, might be expected if only simple repointing of the projectile were required, while progressively larger numbers of flakes (up to 60 or so?) would reflect more major repairs which might include thinning, reshaping, or constructing a new base. The Knife River Flint flakes, numerous as they are, may reflect the repair of several points of this material, although other flintknapping activities are likely represented in this debitage as well.

The second hypothesis, the origin of some of the debitage due to the manufacture or resharpening of Cody knives, became a necessary consideration after the discovery of a Cody knife at the site in 1974. The solitary specimen (Figure 7a) exhibits both pressure and percussion scars, and could have served as a

171

tool with which to butcher the bison. The degree of steepness of the working edge and the narrowness of the blade indicate that this Cody knife was considered used up by its owner and discarded. It seems likely that more were in use at the site, and since the portion of the site excavated is a kill/butchering area, evidence for their use should occur here.

While there does seem to be some latitude in terms of technique for Cody knife manufacture, pressure flaking does seem to be important in maintaining a sharp working edge. The configuration of the cutting edge on the Hudson-Meng knife shows unifacial resharpening, common at Plains sites. As the steepness of the edge angle increases, distinctive retouch flakes will be produced, resembling those derived from unifacial tools except that the platform will usually be facetted rather than plain. Such flakes were noted in clusters A-1 and B-1 but were very rare. Either this pattern of retouching was not carried out often at Hudson-Meng or there were not that many Cody knives being sharpened. Still the large numbers of pressure flakes seen in clusters such as A-1, B-1, and C-1 could conceivably have been derived from Cody knife manufacture or resharpening. Until the manufacturing and use patterns of this specialized tool become better known it will be difficult to evaluate its representation in the Hudson-Meng debitage.

The retouching of generalized bifaces or "preforms", the third alternative, is the easiest of the three to document and support. The presence of occasional large percussion flakes or flake fragments with good bifacial, multiple facetted, lipped striking platforms indicates that bifaces were present and being reduced. The discovery of the base of a variegated chert or chalcedony biface (Figure 7b) gives one indication of the shape and size of the bifaces being worked at the site. This particular specimen exhibits a marked perverse fracture (Crabtree 1972: 82-83), a common manufacture break.

Certain clusters of debitage seem to represent just simple biface reduction, and among these are included clusters A-l, B-1, C-l, C-2, and D-1. A group of flakes from the A-1 and D-1 clusters are illustrated in Figures 2 and 3 as examples of debitage from the reduction of generalized bifaces. While similar in number to the flakes of cluster A-2 mentioned earlier, the flakes from the D-1 cluster are much larger, and include percussion flakes four to six times the size of the A-2 flakes. The D-1 flakes are definitely derived from a large biface, but may be the products of a slightly different biface reduction operation as discussed later. The flakes composing the C-2 cluster are smaller than those in cluster D-1 but exhibit a relatively large percentage of cortex, more so than on any point, or in any other flake cluster. Also, large percussion flakes clearly derived from large bifaces are present in the A-1, B-1, and C-1 clusters, indicating the presence of generalized bifaces of Knife River Flint and red jasper.

Why should a great amount of debitage from larger bifaces be present at a kill site? Two possibilities come to mind. First, since this is a kill site, some type of implements must have been used in the butchering process. The artifacts from

172

the site include a few utilized flakes, a very few unifacial tools, and only a single bone butchering tool; it seems unlikely that these would have sufficed by themselves for the skinning and dismemberment of over 600 bison carcasses. It is possible that projective points themselves served as butchering tools, but not one shows wear patterns suggestive of such use; neither is the frequent need for resharpening reflected in the extant patterns of flake scars on the points. The use of generalized bifaces as butchering tools is therefore a definite possibility, and with the small numbers of flake tools and bone tools, seems to be a logical one. The relative amounts of pressure and percussion could also be accounted for by this hypothesis. Sharpening of the bifaces could be accomplished by pressure flaking, thus generating a sharp, even cutting edge. If the continued use of pressure flaking led to what was deemed too great a thickness relative to width, it would be a simple matter to construct suitable striking platforms to permit the removal of percussion thinning flakes. This would reduce the thickness to width ratio of the biface, and permit its continued use for butchering, and also its eventual modification into a completed projectile point, if desired. In addition, because Knife River Flint is the most common material type at the site, and since the site is 325 miles away from the quarries for this material, a great quantity of it must have been transported by the Alberta hunters. One way to transport a large quantity of raw material is to reduce it at the quarry into the form of large bifacial blanks or preforms. This serves to reduce excess weight, and permits utilization of such generalized forms for a multiplicity of purposes. Given the rarity of cortex on the Knife River Flint flakes from Hudson-Meng, it appears that the implements from which the flakes came had already been fairly well modified, again suggesting some generalized form of biface.

The fourth alternative to account for the numbers of bifacial retouch flakes is to view them as resulting from the finishing of bifacial preforms into projectile points. Thus instead of the debitage representing the sharpening of bifaces used for butchering, it would represent the manufacture of new projectile points. The manufacturing techniques used to produce the Alberta points at Hudson-Meng are discussed in the following section, but it should be noted here that none of the major flake clusters (A-1, B-2, C-1) contain the proper sizes and numbers of flakes which might be expected to result from projectile point manufacture. The final retouch pattern of flake scars seen on most of the Hudson-Meng points should result in the production of a specific type of flake in fairly specific numbers; only the D-1 cluster exhibits this "proper" flake type in expected numbers. The vast majority of flakes from the major clusters are pressure flakes, too narrow and too short to be derived from the final flake series scars seen on the Hudson-Meng points. Further, if this explanation is accepted, it is difficult to see how and with what tools the bison were butchered.

By way of summary, three of the four alternative explanations presented earlier seem to have merit in accounting for the preponderance of bifacial retouch flakes. The repair of projectile points, as represented by the numerically smaller clusters of cherts and quartzites, is believed to have occured in Knapping Locus A and Locus B. However, most of the debitage present in the large clusters of A-1, B-1, and B-2 and in Knapping Locus C and Locus D is interpreted as the result of the retouching of generalized bifaces. Projectile point manufacture does not seem to be indicated by the debitage from most of the clusters, though this explanation may best explain the D-1 flake cluster. Finally, the presence or absence of Cody knives and flakes derived from their resharpening cannot be evaluated at present, due to a lack of knowledge of the uses and patterns of retouching for this tool.

Some mention should be made of the few examples of unifacial tool retouch flakes which were recovered from the site. As described earlier, the D-4 cluster of nine grey quartzite flakes represents the only tightly associated group of unifacial tool retouch flakes thus far located at the site. All of them are small, and exhibit a steep (approx. 70°) striking platform/exterior flake surface angle, suggesting their removal from a steep-edged tool such as a scraper. A single "classic" snub-nosed end scraper of grey brown chert (Figure 31) exhibits such an edge angle and in fact some of the Chert 4 flakes from Knapping Locus A may well have come from this tool; two of these are certainly from such a unifacial tool. In any case, it is suggested that the tool represented by the D-4 cluster may also have been of a similar size and type as this endscraper. Although occasional flakes with plain striking platforms were present in many flake clusters in all four knapping loci, they did not necessarily come from unifacial tools. Such flakes can easily result from the retouching or removal of transverse, vertical-edged breaks through a biface or point, excessively large section of striking platform collapse, or from a portion of a biface which has a large, featureless area caused by a large flake scar or a fracture plane. Flakes which seemed to be the result of unifacial tool retouch were carefully examined when encountered, but always seemed isolated, not associated with other similar flakes (Tables 1-4). In short, unless such flakes occured in close proximity with one another or were of a distinctive material type, they were viewed with caution in this analysis. When they were present in clusters of flakes which otherwise appeared to be derived from biface retouching operations it was deemed probable that they too were the result of this operation.

As presented in Table 5, a number of scattered flakes of various materials were found which bore no obvious traces of use. Many of these were hard hammer decortication flakes, which may represent either the testing of local materials, the sharpening of large chopping tools, simple flake manufacture, or the removal of one or two flakes from a biface. No choppers were located in the bone bed, nor were any large cobbles or cores, so what process the larger flakes represent remains uncertain.

It is interesting to note the lithological similarities shared by Knapping Locus A with Locus B, and those shared by Knapping Locus C and Locus D. Not only are these pairs united by similar material types, they also share spatial proximity as indicated by Figure 1. Several lines of reason might be presented to account for this phenomenon; while it is certain that no conclusive explanation can be advanced at this time, I feel that a temporal one has a good deal of merit.

174

At the most basic level, each knapping locus can be viewed as representing a separate center for flintknapping activities. It seems probable that loci A and B represent the retouching/resharpening of many of the same implements, possibly with some slight degree of temporal separation--the same hypothesis may be advanced to account for the similarities between loci C and D. If this idea is combined with the suggested activities represented by the knapping loci (projectile point repair and biface retouching), it is possible to propose that more than a single kill event is represented at Hudson-Meng.

I would suggest that two kills are represented, based upon the numbers of knapping loci presently known and the types of activities indicated at each of them. As mentioned above, the smaller clusters of flakes present in Knapping Locus A (A-2 through A-9) and Knapping Locus B (B-2 through B-9) may be interpreted as resulting from the repair of projectile points. If such is assumed to be the case, two episodes of projectile point repair involving several of the same points are indicated, one episode for each knapping locus. The A-1 and B-1 clusters, representing biface retouching (and possibly some projectile point repair), may also be interpreted as two episodes of resharpening the same generalized biface or bifaces. Similarly, Knapping Locus C and Knapping Locus D involve no projectile point repair but rather biface retouching; again the similarity of material types in each of these loci can be cited as evidence for two separate times of retouching the same bifaces. Two separate kill events closely spaced in time may thus be postulated, each kill having its associated centers of animal processing and weaponry maintenance, represented by the knapping loci. If such is the case the kills must be quite closely spaced in time, perhaps only days or a week or two apart.

Unfortunately, the bone bed contains no stratigraphic evidence for more than one kill, so no support for the idea of two separate kills may be found in that quarter. It is also possible that the separate knapping loci represent the movements of flintknappers from one place to another during the butchering of a large single-event kill. If such were the case it seems odd that so few loci would result, and that these four would represent the moving of two major centers of flintworking once each. Therefore, it is proposed that the four knapping loci resulted from activities associated with two distinct bison kills separated by a short interval of time. This explanation seems to me to best account for the observed distribution of material types and the spatial arrangement of the knapping loci, but it must be viewed as tentative at best.

LITHIC TECHNOLOGY AT HUDSON-MENG

The debitage discussed in the first section of this appendix has aided in shedding some light on the sorts of lithic activities being pursued at Hudson-Meng. When coupled with the completed artifacts from the site, it can also be of use in formulating a partial picture of Alberta lithic technology, at least as it is expressed at this site. "Partial picture" is a necessary phrase for as has already been shown,

Figure 4. Complete and nearly complete Knife River Flint Alberta projectile points from the Hudson-Meng site. Length of a is 124.7 mm.

d   e

Figure 4.(continued).

Figure 5. Quartzite, chert, and silicified shale Alberta projectile points from the Hudson-Meng site. Not the concave-based points (a & b) probably made from fragments of Alberta points. Length of c is 67 mm.

Figure 6. Basal (a & b) and Tip (c-g) Fragments of Alberta Points from the Hudson-Meng site. Length of g is 66 mm.

b

a

Figure 7. Cody Knife and Biface Basal Fragment from the Hudson-Meng site. Maximum length of the biface fragment is 48.5 mm.

180

only a limited number of flintknapping operations are represented. Because these operations centered around the working of bifaces, and because projectile points are the most abundant form of chipped stone artifacts from the site, it will be this facet of Alberta lithic technology which will be emphasized in this discussion. Even this description of biface technology must be limited, for the earlier stages of reduction of bifaces are not present in this assemblage.

Perhaps the most striking aspect of the projectile points from Hudson-Meng is the uniformity of shape and finishing technique. This is especially true of the Knife River Flint points (Figure 4) whose flake scars are especially pronounced, but also applies to the other points made of quartzite, chert, or silicified shale (Figures 5 and 6). All are relatively long and slender unless reworked (such as Figure 5c, e, and f), and all have been finished by well-controlled direct percussion, which produced very regular collateral flake scar patterns. In fact the first few points recovered from the site seemed typologically intermediate between Alberta and Scottsbluff, based on these attributes. What combination of manufacturing techniques led to this particular configuration of projectile point?

It is presently impossible to generate an exact manufacture sequence for a Hudson-Meng style Alberta point, for there are no preforms or earlier stages of biface reduction with which to work. Figure 8 is a suggested reduction sequence, based upon inferences derived from the completed points, flintknapping experimentation, and limited knowledge of the mode of occurence of some of the raw materials from the site.

The sequence begins with either a large flake (Figure 8a) or a tabular piece of material derived from the natural fracturing of the source deposit (i.e. Knife River Flint). A thin nodule would also suffice. Initial modification of the piece of raw material could be accomplished using either a hammerstone or large antler baton. This work was probably devoted to removing the striking platform and bulb (if any), eliminating any gross irregularities, minor fractures, or excessive areas of cortex, and in general help create a bifacially flaked margin (Figure 8b). No bifaces at this hypothetical stage of reduction were present at Hudson-Meng, nor was there any debitage such as might be expected to result from the working of a biface of this size and condition.

A biface of this type could then be subjected to more extensive thinning with an antler hammer, creating what might be termed a preform or blank (Figure 8c). It is at this stage of reduction that the Hudson-Meng material begins. The major flake clusters A-1, B-1, C-1 and C-2 reflect in part the retouching of bifaces at this stage. It seems that this work was accomplished almost entirely without striking platform abrasion, as evidenced by the extremely low incidence of this practice among the flakes of these clusters (Tables 1-5). It is probably not entirely correct to conceive of these bifaces simply as "preforms;" it is more likely, as suggested earlier, that they were being used as butchering implements. While functioning in this role they were likely retouched or sharpened only sparingly as the necessity arose, and then perhaps only by pressure or very light

181

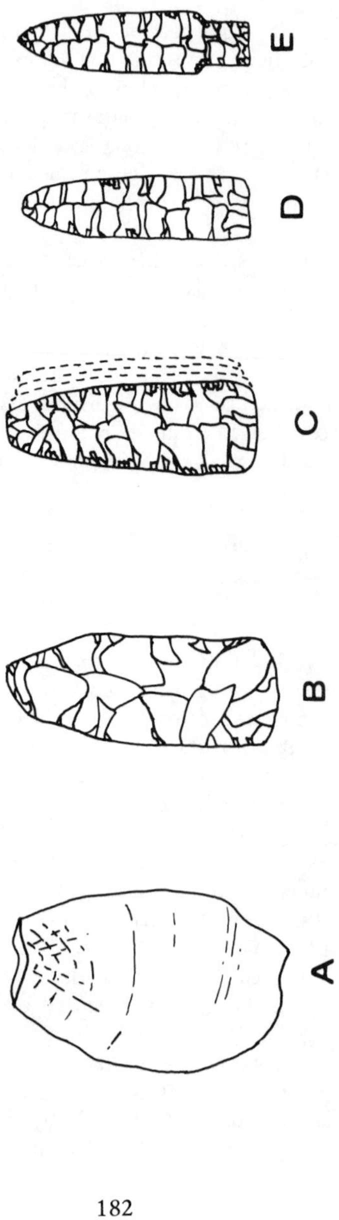

Figure 8. Generalized Manufacturing Sequence for Hudson-Meng Alberta Points.

182

percussion. Major thinning flakes may thus have been removed only at intervals, when the thickness of the biface relative to its width became excessive. Such a pattern is suggested at Hudson-Meng by the low numbers of large biface thinning flakes and the contrastingly high numbers of small percussion and pressure flakes. Thus, rather than simply representing an intermediate stage of reduction in a projectile point manufacturing sequence, these bifaces are truly implements in their own right. As with any tool they must continually be resharpened, and therefore continually decrease in size (Figure 8c); in contrast to many other implements, they can be modified after reaching a given size into projectile points. The reduction sequence being proposed here really produced two distinct implements from one piece of material, and may cover a considerable amount of time before the final product is completed.

It is the final flake series that gives the Hudson-Meng style Alberta point its distinctive appearance (Figure 8d, Figure 9). This last operation is accomplished by the serial removal of a number of percussion flakes at spaced intervals along the margins of the preform; the D-1 flake cluster probably represents flakes derived during this process. It is possible that a somewhat smaller antler baton was used in this operation. Individual striking platforms, perhaps up to 12, were prepared at fairly regular intervals along one margin; the construction of these platforms may have been done by pressure to establish more precise angles and stronger, better isolated platforms. Beginning at one end of the preform, the flint-knapper would remove a small, controlled percussion flake from the first prepared striking platform, and then proceed to work down the margin refining and utilizing the successive platforms. An average spacing of approximately 11 mm from the center of one scar to the center of the next scar seems to characterize the larger Knife River Flint points; this permitted each successive flake to be guided in part by the edge of the previous flake scar, generating a fairly regular collateral pattern. Each of these flakes normally carry just beyond the midline of the projectile point, where they feather terminate. Naturally, the striking platforms could be adjusted or moved depending upon the results obtained from previous blows to maintain the desired spacing interval. If a blow was mis-struck or a particular section of margin would not support a proper platform or yield the desired flake type, it was passed over. On occasion after work on the opposite face of the point had changed the configuration of that part of the margin, another striking platform was constructed and the flake removed out of sequence. This can be seen on two examples especially (Figure 9). Some of these patterned scars removed out of sequence appear to be pressure flakes, and it is certainly possible that they are. The final finishing of the base, the creation of the shoulders and stem, and the final shaping of the margins of the blade was done by pressure. The stem was then abraded and the point was complete.

This proposed reduction sequence could be described as highly efficient in that it permits maximum utilization of a given piece of material. A system of this sort may be more characteristic of a group which expected to be away from its favored material sources for a long period of time, for it would permit them to consume the small stock of material they carried with them at a much slower

Figure 9. Detail of Flake Scar Patterns on Two Alberta
Points probably made by same artisan.

rate than would be possible if the intermediate stage biface (Figure 8c) was not employed in a functional capacity.

Efforts towards material conservation can be observed in other quarters as well; the two concave-based points (Figure 5a and b) recovered from the site are interesting examples of this idea. Both, when examined at the extreme end of their basal corners, exhibit vertical or slightly concave, featureless breaks--these seem to be the remnants of bend breaks or transverse snaps. It is suggested that these points are the result of the reworking of larger tip fragments from broken Alberta points. This modification could be accomplished relatively easily by simply taking a broken tip fragment of an Alberta point and, by use of laterally and longitudinally directed pressure techniques, thin and remove the vertical face of the broken edge. This would simultaneously taper the sides of the fragment (lateral pressure flaking) and thin the base, leaving a concavity (longitudinal pressure flaking). Since lateral pressure flaking would help thin the base as well, there might be no need to remove longitudinally directed flakes from the extreme corners of the base; thus the original vertical break would be preserved there. These two points might serve as a caution against equating a single style of projectile point with a single culture. Based upon their morphological attributes both of these points could be termed Plainview; yet both contextual and technological information indicates that they are the products of the same people who produced the long, stemmed Alberta points.

A second, though indirect, line of evidence for material conservation is represented by the fact that none of the basal fragments of the tips illustrated in Figure 6c-g were recovered from the site. It seems probable that they were salvaged and re-pointed or perhaps even modified into Cody knives, though this operation is a guess at present. By the same token, no other portions of the points represented by the basal fragments in Figure 6a-b were located; they too were apparently salvaged. A probable sequence of breakage and reworking is presented in the form of a flow diagram in Figure 10.

A final technological aspect of the Hudson-Meng collection should receive attention, and that is the possible existence of flintknapping specialists in Alberta society. Based upon consistencies of technique and execution, and to a lesser degree on shape, it is possible to propose that at least five and as many as seven of the Hudson-Meng points had their origins in the hands of the same craftsman. These five specimens (Figures 4a, b, c, e, Figure 6e), and possibly two additional ones (Figures 4d, 6f), I would suggest were produced by a single individual who was highly skilled in their manufacture. His skill left a tangible mark on these points, especially in the consistency of size and patterning of flake scars of the final retouch series. While the shapes of these points do show noticeable variation, this may be explained in part by the vagaries and restrictions present in the original piece of material from which each was fashioned, as well as by subsequent repair and re-pointing work (Figure 4c, for example). It is difficult to judge the significance of the presence of such a number of projectile points which all appear to be the products of one artisan. It can be suggested that this is due to sampling

185

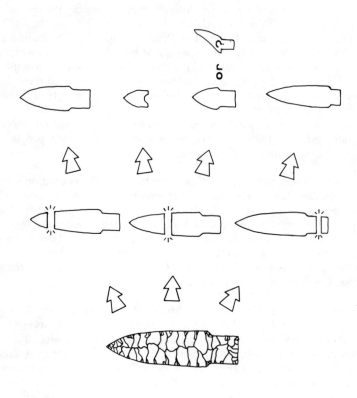

Figure 10. Suggested Patterns of Breakage and Repair of Alberta Points.

error, and that the points of this one individual are over-represented in the recovered sample. Or one can postulate that because of a demonstrated skill at flintknapping, he may have produced projectile points as a specialty, for use by others. Whether he, in turn, received full or partial societal support to enable him to practice his trade on a full-time basis is impossible to establish. Still, the presence of several points which may be attributed to a single individual is thought-provoking, and hints at possible occupational specialization in Alberta society.

How representative of Alberta lithic technology as a whole is the Hudson-Meng assemblage? To date so few Alberta sites have been investigated that our knowledge of this industry is relatively meager in contrast to the work done with other Paleo-Indian industries. In fact the only published material dealing with the excavation of Alberta sites is that of Forbis (1968), which describes the material from the Fletcher site in extreme southern Alberta, and the brief report on the Hell Gap site (Irwin-Williams, et al., 1973). The Fletcher site assemblage is unusual in that both Alberta and Scottsbluff points were present at the site according to Forbis' typological assessment. Although the Scottsbluff points were not recovered *in situ* in the bone bed along with the Alberta points, Forbis sees the two types as coeval and in all probability associated with one another. After viewing the illustration of the points which accompanies the report (Forbis 1968: 4, Figure 1), I would question whether the typological separation of these two groups of points is necessary. Certainly the "Scottsbluff Type 1" (Forbis 1968: Figure 1, i) fits well within the range of variation shown by the Hudson-Meng Alberta specimens. With the exception of an apparently crushed tip it is virtually identical to the red quartzite point from Hudson-Meng (Figure 5d). Admittedly the remaining three Fletcher specimens (Forbis 1968: Figure 1j, k, l) do not share the same formal attributes with "normal" Alberta points. However, outside of the fact that the specimens designated as Scottsbluff display slightly shorter stems and less convex blade margins, there seems no reason to separate them from the Alberta points. Such formal characteristics can easily be changed through reworking damaged points, and none of the four shows the even collateral pressure flaking patterns normally considered typical of Scottsbluff. It thus seems possible that the other Scottsbluff specimens at Fletcher are in fact Alberta. Insofar as I am able to determine from the illustration, all of the Fletcher projectiles seem to be technologically identical. It appears that all were flaked by direct percussion with varying but generally slight amounts of selective pressure flaking. The only obvious difference in manufacturing technique from the Hudson-Meng material is that the percussion flaking is not as carefully controlled, so no collateral flake scar pattern is developed. This difference, however, may be more reflective of the idiosyncracies and abilities of individual flintknappers than of differences at a higher level of sociocultural or temporal significance. All in all the points from both sites display a noteworthy similarity to one another both in terms of manufacturing technique and, to a lesser degree, in shape.

Aside from a single occupation level at Hell Gap (Irwin-Williams, et al., 1973: 45, 48) the Alberta industry is known largely from surface finds of points.

187

I have not seen the Alberta material from Hell Gap, and thus cannot offer any comparisons of it with the Hudson-Meng material. Wormington and Forbis (1965) present several specimens from various private collections which came from the plains of Alberta. Many of the Alberta points they illustrate are very similar to Hudson-Meng specimens, both in shape and apparent manufacturing technique. It thus seems safe to conclude that the Hudson-Meng projectiles are typical products of the Alberta industry, although the degree to which several show patterned collateral percussion flaking is unusual.

It is also interesting to compare the lithic technology of the Hudson-Meng projectile points with that of the earlier Hell Gap industry and the later Cody Complex. It has been postulated that there exists a developmental continuum of projectile point running from Agate Basin to Hell Gap to Alberta to Cody (Irwin-Williams, *ibid.*, 47-49), basically revolving around the development and refinement of the stemmed projectile point. If such a stylistic continuum is present, one could also expect certain regularities in technological development. This is odd, since the trend runs from pressure finished points (Agate Basin) to percussion finished ones (Hell Gap and Alberta) then back to pressure finished points (Cody). Agate Basin points are finished by fairly well controlled pressure flaking, which generally removes all traces of previous percussion work. Hell Gap points, at least those from the Casper site (Frison 1974: 71-85; Bradley 1974: 192-194), seem to show a trend away from pressure flaking as a finishing technique. That is, pressure flaking was used in conjunction with stem production, edge straightening and sharpening, and re-pointing, but direct percussion was generally employed for both preforming and finishing. At any rate, more dependence on percussion flaking seems to develop in Hell Gap times, a trend which continues into the Alberta industry. Alberta points seem to display slightly less pressure work than the Casper—style Hell Gap points, but when employed, pressure is used in the same fashion as outlined for Hell Gap. Alberta points thus display manufacturing techniques most similar to those practiced by Hell Gap flint-knappers, but shapes more like those seen in Scottsbluff, or other Cody Complex points. The final flaking of Cody Complex points is normally done by pressure in a patterned collateral fashion; when the Hudson-Meng points are compared to with them the resemblance is even more striking due to the patterned collateral flake scar pattern present on the Hudson-Meng specimens. This, coupled with the presence of a Cody knife make it possible to propose that the Hudson-Meng Alberta industry is not simply ancestral to but actually the basal member of the Cody Complex. If the collateral flake scar pattern seen on these points reflects more than a single individual's work it may be that the Hudson-Meng material stands near the beginning of a long trend which ultimately culminates in the fine collateral pressure flaking seen on Cody points from the Claypool and Finley sites (Dick and Mountain 1960; Satterthwaite 1957).

SUMMARY

The study of the nearly 3000 pieces of debitage from the Hudson-Meng site

188

aids greatly in clarifying the technological processes and activities being pursued at the site, after the kill. Evidence was found to suggest that bifaces were almost the only implements being flaked, much in contrast to the usual predominance at Paleo-Indian sites of unifacial tool retouch operations. It is more difficult to specify the nature of the bifacial implements being worked, but projectile point repair and possibly some manufacture, as well as the simple retouching of generalized bifaces seems to be represented in the debitage. The paucity of unifacial tool retouch flakes and the near absence of bone tools imply that these generalized bifaces were employed in the butchering process. Based on the distribution and composition of the four knapping loci, it is possible to tentatively suggest that two kill events occured at the site, separated by a short interval of time.

The completed artifacts from the site have contributed significantly to the understanding of the Alberta industry. It has been possible, using completed artifacts and debitage, to reconstruct a generalized reduction sequence for Alberta point manufacture and to relate the artifact assemblage to other Alberta specimens and sites. The Hudson-Meng assemblage can also be at least roughly positioned along the proposed continuum leading from the Agate Basin industry to the Cody industry. Further, it can be shown to contain certain technological and stylistic features of both the earlier Hell Gap and later Cody industries.

This particular research has been carried out at a rather high level of generality and with a good deal of simple non-metric data. However, it is hoped that it can aid in demonstrating that a good deal of potentially useful information can be obtained from detailed technological studies of both finished artifacts and the debitage left by their manufacture and use.

REFERENCES

Bordes, Francois
    1961 *Typologie du Paleolithique ancien et moyen.* Two volumes.
            Bordeaux.

Bradley, Bruce
    1974 Comments on the Lithic Technology of the Casper Site Materials
           in *The Casper Site: A Hell Gap Bison Kill on the High Plains.*
           George C. Frison (ed.). pp. 191-197. Academic Press, New York.

Clayton, Lee, W. Bi ckley, Jr. and W. J. Stone
    1970 Knife River Flint. *Plains Anthropologist.* Vol. 15, No. 50, pt. 1,
           pp. 282-290 .

Crabtree, Don
    1972 An Introduction to Flint Working. *Occasional Papers of the Idaho
           State University Museum.* No. 28, Pocatello.

Dick, Herbert W. and Bert Mountain
    1960 The Claypool Site: A Cody Complex Site in Northeastern Colorado.
           American Antiquity. Vol. 26, No. 2, pp. 223-235.

Forbis, Richard D.
    1968 Fletcher: A Paleo-Indian Site in Alberta. *American Antiquity.*
           Vol. 33, No. 1, pp. 1-10.

Frison, George
    1968 A Functional Analysis of Certain Chipped Stone Tools. *American
           Antiquity.* Vol. 33, No. 2, pp. 149-155.
    1974 *The Casper Site: A Hell Gap Bison Kill on the High Plains.* (ed.).
           Academic Press, New York.

Haynes, C. Vance, Jr.
    1967 Carbon-14 Dates and Early Man in the New World in *Pleistocene
           Extinctions: The Search for a Cause.* P.S. Martin (ed.). Yale Univer-
           sity Press, New Haven.

Hemmings, E. Thomas
    1970 *Early Man in the San Pedro Valley, Arizona.* Unpublished Ph.D.

thesis, University of Arizona, Tucson.

Irwin, Henry T. and H. Marie Wormington
1970 Paleo-Indian Tool Types in the Great Plains. *American Antiquity.* Vol. 35, No. l, pp. 24-34.

Irwin-Williams, Cynthia, Henry Irwin, George Agogino and C. Vance Haynes, Jr.
1973 Hell Gap : Paleo-Indian Occupation on the High Plains. *Plains Anthropologist.* Vol. 18, No. 59, pp. 40-53.

Jelinek, Arthur J.
1966 Some Distinctive Flakes and Flake Tools from the Llano Estacado. Papers of the *Michigan Academy of Science, Arts and Letters.* Vol. II, pp. 399-405.

Satterthwaite, Linton
1957 Stone Artifacts at and near the Finley Site near Eden, Wyoming. *Museum Monographs.* The University Museum, University of Pennsylvania, Philadelphia.

Witzel, Frank and John Hartley
1973 Two Possible Source Areas for the Quartzite Artifacts of the Hudson-Meng site: A Comparative Study. A paper presented at the 83rd Annual Meeting of the Nebraska Academy of Sciences, Lincoln.

Wormington, H. Marie and Richard G. Forbis
1965 An Introduction to the Archaeology at Alberta, Canada. *Proceedings of the Denver Museum of Natural History*, No. 11, Denver.

APPENDIX II

MOLLUSCS FROM THE HUDSON-MENG SITE

SHI-KUEI WU
UNIVERSITY OF COLORADO

CHARLES A. JONES
BENDIX FIELD ENGR. CORP.

INTRODUCTION

Shells of nonmarine gastropods were first found in the bone bed during the 1972 field season. More shells were found in 1973. In order to recover additional shells, a fine-screening project was conducted during the 1974 field season. Fine-screening produced a surprisingly large number of very small specimens that account for most of the species diversity in the combined sample of large and small shells. The total number of identifiable shells recovered by screening or hand picking was 1211. These represent 11 species of nonmarine gastropods and 1 species of sphaeriid clam (Table 1).

METHOD

Sediment was removed from the bone bed in meter squares 25 to 28 S. and 20 to 28 W. Care was taken to sample only sediment from the bone bed; sediment from above or below the bone bed was carefully excluded. Approximately 80 liters of sediment was screened in 2 to 6 liter batches. (Subsequent sampling has shown the sediments above and below the bone bed to be completely barren of mollusc shells.)

Screening was a two-step operation. The sediment disaggregated easily in water and was then screened through screen boxes. The boxes consisted of wooden frames with ordinary window screen stretched across the bottom. Openings in window screen are approximately 1 to 1½ mm. in diameter. Large shells were hand picked from the residue caught on this screen.

Sediment and shells passing through the window screen boxes were fine-screened using an 8-inch brass sieve (U. S. Standard Sieve No. 40) with openings 0.4 mm. in diameter. No complete or nearly complete shells were observed to pass through this finer screen. The residue of shells and sand caught on the fine screen along with the larger hand-picked shells were taken to the laboratory at Chadron State College for sorting and initial identification. Final identifications were made by the senior author at the University of Colorado Museum.

PREVIOUS WORK

The most important study of High Plains molluscan paleoecology is the oft-cited work of Taylor (1960). Taylor considered the ecologic significance of nine fossil molluscan faunas from the Pliocene and Pleistocene--all older than Hudson-Meng--and compared them with living molluscan faunas at 18 localities in northern Nebraska. The Hudson-Meng molluscs will be considered in light of Taylor's work.

Taylor does not, in general, give diagnostic data for the identification of shells. Rather, Pilsbry (1939, 1940, 1946, and 1948), Leonard (1959), La Rocque (1966, 1967, 1968, and 1970), and Burch (1962) should be consulted for shell identification. All of the above, with the exception of Burch (1962), give ecologic data.

ECOLOGIC INTERPRETATION

There are several elements in the bone layer at Hudson-Meng that may be useful in reconstruction of environmental conditions at the time of the kill. These are the vertebrates, the sediments, the flora, and the molluscs.

The macro-vertebrates themselves are not particularily useful for paleo-environmental reconstruction. Both bison and man were extremely mobile, capable of migrating hundreds of miles each year. According to historic accounts of the last modern bison herds, the herds passed through several degrees of latitude during their seasonal migrations. Small mammals, such as rodents, rabbits, squirrels, and small carnivores, are more restricted in their power of dispersal, and show a high degree of endemism to specific habitats. Unfortunately, Hudson-Meng has been surprisingly barren of small mammal remains.

Deprived of useful environmental data from small mammal remains, the sediments, flora, and molluscs remain as the key to the environmental conditions in the immediate vicinity of the bone bed. Description of the flora, the sediments, and the stratigraphic interpretation is given elsewhere in this volume. Briefly, sediments beneath the bone bed are fluvial sands deposited by a stream. Sediments above the bone layer are fine sands and silts deposited in part by streams and slope wash, but probably deposited by wind.

These sediments from above and below the bone bed are barren of mollusc shells. The absence of shells suggests that sedimentation either before or after the kill may have been rapid or not conducive to molluscan preservation. Sedimentation rates are generally difficult to determine, but the greater they are, the less time for a molluscan fauna to colonize an area or for their shells to accumulate.

194

The alternative is that the shells may have been subsequently destroyed by disso-lution.

MOLLUSCAN PALEOECOLOGY

Paleoecologic interpretations are based on the uniformitarian principle that the ecologic factors limiting the distribution of a species today are the same as limited the distribution of that species in the past. For late Cenozoic molluscs from the High Plains, Taylor found no significant exceptions to invalidate this assumption (Taylor, 1960, p. 4). Therefore it is reasonable the molluscs from the bone bed had habitat preferences and requirements similar to those observed for the same species living today. Table 1 lists the molluscan species from the bone bed and their possible habitats, by using Taylor's (1960) observation for the same species living today in northern Nebraska, a few hundred miles to the east of Hudson-Meng.

The largest number of individual shells, *Gastrocopta holzingeri, G. armifera, Vallonia costata, Cionella lubrica, Discus cronkhitei, Retinella electrina,* and *Euconulus fulvus,* represent a damp habitat on slightly damp leaves or on soil under timber or rocks not necessarily close to a lake or stream. Several of these species were found by Taylor in damp areas that were also wooded. It is quite possible that with climate somewhat cooler and more moist 9,000+ years ago, forests and wooded areas were extensive in the hills or along the creeks around the site.

One species of *Pisidium casertanum* represents an aquatic habitat and four

Molluscan Species From the Hudson-Meng Site	Water Body Quiet	Water Body Flowing	Terrestrial (marginal)	Damp Seep	Ground Woods
Pisidium casertanum	X	X			
Succinea avara					
Cochlicopa lubrica					X
Vallonia costata					X
Helicodiscus singleyanus					
Gastrocopta armifera				X	
Gastrocopta holzingeri				X	
Gastrocopta tappaniana			X	X	
Vertigo ovata			X		
Retinella electrina					X
Discus cronkhitei					X
Euconulus fulvus					X

Table 1. Possible Habitat for Hudson-Meng Species in Northern Nebr.

gastropods, *Succinea avara, Vertigo ovata, Gastrocopta tappaniana,* and *Discus cronkhitei* represent a marginal habitat. The distribution of this small fresh-water clam is widespread. It frequents quiet rivers, streams and ponds. A flood could easily have carried *Pisidium* from the stream to the sampling site within the bone bed either before or after the butchering. Aquatic and terrestrial molluscs are often mixed in low-lying areas adjacent to streams. The presence of the marginal habitat species *S. avara, G. tappaniana, V. ovata* and *D. cronkhitei* may also be explained in this way. Normally these two species would have probably lived closer to permanent water than the sampling site 8 meters away from the creek. *G. tappaniana,* of course, may be found away from permanent water just as long as the ground is wet, such as around seeps where the water table intersects the topography.

SYSTEMATIC ACCOUNTS

Class Gastropoda

Family Succineidae

Succinea avara (Say)

Figure 1.

Description

The shell is opaque white and rather solid. The whorls are convex. The suture is deep. The number of whorls is 3 1/8; body whorl is large, about 9/19 of the shell length. The aperture is oval in shape, its length is 6/10 of the shell length.

Measurement

A single shell measures 13 mm. in shell length, 7.9 mm. in shell width and 8 mm. in aperture width.

Distribution

Newfoundland; Ontario north to James and Hudson Bays; north to Lat. 62° on the Mackenzie River; British Columbia; south to Florida in the east and to northern Mexico in the west. (Pilsbry, 1948).

Habitats

Pilsbry (1948) reported that *Succinea avara* is usually found on vegetable debris thrown up on muddy shores, or crawling on the muddy banks of ditches, often exposed to the sun; also in swampy places in pastures, as I have found it in Essex County, N. Y. But it is an upland species as well, to be seen understone with Pupillidae, or occasionally after rains crawling up the trunks of trees.

Remarks

Burch and Patterson (1965) considered that *Succinea avara* is probably none other than *Catinella vermeta*.

Family Cochlicopidae

Cochlicopa lubrica (Müller)

Description

The shell is oblong, smooth and glossy, thin and translucent. Outer edge of aperture is sharp and columella is slightly sinuated. The number of whorls is 4 1/4.

Measurements

Among four specimens examined, one has the aperture missing, two have only a part of the spire and one is a complete specimen. The latter one measures 6 mm. in shell length, 2.4 mm. in shell width.

Distribution

United States except Georgia, Florida, Texas and California (Burch, 1962).

Habitats

This species lives among the damp under-leaves in densely shaded places; under wood, such as old board sidewalks; and in chinks of stone walls and under stones (Pilsbry, 1948). It generally occurs in moister and more sheltered habitats than *Cochlicopa lubricella* (Evans, 1972).

197

Family Vallonidae

Vallonia costata (Müller)

Figures 2-4

Description

The shell is minute with 1.45-2.8 mm. shell diameter, depressed and moderately thick. Surfaces of shell (Figures 2-4) are sculptured with radial ribs, about 30 to 50 on the last whorl. The minute ridges are seen irregularly between the ribs. Embryonic shell is smooth and is 1 4/8 to 1 7/8 whorls. The number of whorls is 3 to 3 5/8. Spire is low and slightly convex (Figure 2). Suture is well impressed. Abapical side of shell (Figure 3) is widely umbilicated; the umbilicus is round and deep, its diameter is one-third of shell diameter. Aperture is almost circular and oblique; its edge is expanded and slightly reflected.

Measurements

Measurements of 46 specimens selected randomly from 300 collected are:

	Range	Mean and Standard Deviation
Height (H)	0.75 – 1.2 mm.	0.95 ± 0.07 mm.
Diameter (D)	1.45 – 2.8 mm.	1.92 ± 0.14 mm.
Ratio H/D	0.44 – 0.59	0.49 ± 0.03

Distribution

North America.

Habitats

Wu's observation in the vicinity of Boulder, Colorado is that *Vallonia costata* occurs under the surface of rough rocks on sand-gravel substrate. According to Evans (1972), *V. costata* can live in woodland in small numbers, thrives in abundance on stone walls--in both cases as a rupestral species, probably browsing on unicellular algae--lives in short-turfed grassland, again frequently in vast numbers,

198

and is characteristic of the fauna of rubbish dumps, in association with synanthropic species such as *Oxychilus draparnaldi* and *Hygromia striolata,* scavenging on semi-decomposed organic matter. This species is climatically very tolerant.

Remarks

Vallonia parvula, V. gracilicosta, V. perspectiva, V. albula and *V. sonorana* are considered here as synonyms of *V. costata.*

Family Vertiginidae

Gastrocopta armifera (Say)

Figure 8.

Description

The shell is elongate-oval shape, perforate, white and glossy. Whorls are moderately convex, with indistinct oblique growth lines. Number of whorls is 6 1/8 to 6 7/8. Aperture is square to irregular round and its edge is slightly reflected. Angular and parietal lamellae of aperture united, columellar lamella and lower palatal fold are located far interior to the aperture.

Measurements

Measurements of seven collected specimens are:

	Range	Mean
Shell length (L)	3.6 – 4.1 mm.	3.85 mm.
Shell width (W)	2.0 – 2.1 mm.	2.08 mm.
Ratio W/L	0.51 – 0.58	0.54

Distribution

Maine to Florida, west to North Dakota, Colorado and New Mexico (Burch, 1962), Eastern United States and Canada (Pilsbry, 1948).

Habitats

This species prefers limestone districts (Pilsbry, 1948). Usually occurs in calcareous areas under limestone rocks, leaf litter or rotting logs. It may be found in moist situations or on dry sparsely-wooded hillsides (Cheatum and Fullington, 1973).

Gastrocopta holzingeri (Sterki)

Figures 9-10.

Description

The shell (Figure 9) is elongate-oval, smooth and white. Whorls are moderately convex, the last whorl has an oblique ridge some distance behind the outer edge of the aperture (Figure 10). Number of whorls is 4 1/2 to 5 1/4. The apertural edge reflects slightly outwardly. Parietal and angular lamellae resemble a mirror image of letter "y"; lower palatal fold projects inwardly; upper palatal fold is short and suprapalatal fold is present.

Measurements

Measurements of 50 specimens selected randomly from 349 collected are:

	Range	Mean and Standard Deviation
Shell length (L)	1.4 – 1.9 mm.	1.62 ± 0.1 mm.
Shell width (W)	0.85 – 1 mm.	0.9 ± 0.04 mm.
Ratio W/L	0.5 – 0.64	0.56 ± 0.03

Distribution

Ontario, Canada and western New York to Montana, south to Illinois, Kansas and New Mexico (Pilsbry, 1948).

Habitats

Found on timbered slopes under leaf mold (Franzen and Leonard, 1947).

Gastrocopta tappaniana (Adams)

Figures 11-12.

Description

The shell (Figure 11) is oblong-conic in shape and its apex is obtuse. Whorls

200

are convex; the last whorl has a low ridge close to the outer edge of the aperture (Figure 12). Number of whorls is 4 1/2 to 5 1/8. Parietal lamella of aperture is simple; columellar and subcolumellar lamellae present. The palatal folds are five in number (Figure 11).

Measurements

Measurements of 37 specimens collected are:

	Range	Mean and Standard Deviation
Shell length (L)	1.7 - 2.2 mm.	1.95 $\pm$ 0.12 mm.
Shell width (W)	1.05 - 1.3 mm.	1.22 $\pm$ 0.06 mm.
Ratio W/L	0.57 - 0.68	0.63 $\pm$ 0.03

Distribution

Maine to Georgia, west to South Dakota, Kansas and Arizona (Burch, 1962). Ontario and Maine to Virginia and Alabama, west to South Dakota and Kansas, southwest to Arizona (Pilsbry, 1948).

Habitats

This species is found in low, moist places, under wood, often with *Vertigo ovata* (Pilsbry, 1948). It occurs in low wetlands, marshes and floodplains; usually under wood or plant litter (Camp, 1974). Its preferred habitat seems to be on woodland slopes adjacent to streams or other bodies of water. Unlike *Gastrocopta pentodon* it is usually associated with moist areas. This species is sometimes associated with *Vertigo ovata* (Cheatum and Fullington, 1973).

Vertigo ovata (Say)

Figures 13-14.

Description

The shell (Figure 13) is oblong-conic in shape and its apex is obtuse. Whorls are convex; the last whorl has an opaque ridge close to the outder edge of the aperture (Figure 14). A groove (Figure 14) runs from the middle point of the outer apertural edge and passes through the ridge. Number of whorls is 4 3/8 to 5. The parietal lamella is strong; angular lamella is small; a minute infraparietal lamella is present. Columellar lamella is strong. Basal, lower and upper palatal folds are strong and on the ridge; suprapalatal fold present (Figure 13).

201

Measurements

Measurements of 12 collected specimens are:

	Range	Mean
Shell length (L)	1.6 – 2.1 mm.	1.8 mm.
Shell width (W)	0.95 – 1.4 mm.	1.15 mm.
Ratio W/L	0.59 – 0.7	0.64

Distribution

Maine to Florida, west to Oregon and California (Burch, 1962).

Habitats

Usually associated with considerable moisture; under humus, rocks, logs, near springs, creeks and marshy area (Cheatum and Fullington, 1973).

Family Endodontidae

Discus cronkhitei (Newcomb)

Description

A broken shell measures 5 mm. in diameter and 1.5 mm. in umbilicus. The spire of shell is missing and the body is round at periphery. The riblets of the shell surface continue over the abapical side of the shell. The aperture of the shell is round in shape.

Distribution

Maine to Maryland, west to Washington and California (Burch, 1962).

Habitats

In the east it lives in humid forests, under dead wood, and among rotting leaves or grass in rather wet situations (Pilsbry, 1948). In northern Nebraska it occurs under sticks and logs on moist leaf mold, always close to running water (Taylor, 1960). It usually lives in damp woodland under dead wood or in leaf litter (La Rocque, 1970). Cheatum and Allen (1965) stated that *Discus cronkhitei* requires humid surroundings and usually occurs along stream beds or in well-shaded areas where moisture is retained. Wu's observation in Colorado is that *D. cronkhitei* occurs with *Oxyloma retusa, Catinella vermeta, Vallonia purchella* and *V. costata* along the edge of river banks, under the shade of grass *(Pholaris arundiacea),* the bullrush *(Scirpus sp.),* the spike rush *(Eleocharis sp.)* and the willow *(Salix interior).*

Helicodiscus singleyanus (Pilsbry)

Figures 5-7.

Description

The shell is minute size (1.6-2.4 mm. in shell diameter), strongly depressed and thin. Surface of the shell is smooth or weakly marked by irregular ripples. Whorls are expanding regularly (Figure 7) and its number is 3 1/8 to 3 7/8. The spire is slightly convex and the suture is well impressed (Figure 5). The abapical side of the shell (Figure 6) is widely umbilicated; the umbilicus is deep, its diameter is one-third of its shell diameter. The aperture is lunate shape and its edge is thin and simple (Figure 5).

Measurements

Measurements of 50 specimens selected randomly from 400 collected are:

	Range	Mean and Standard Deviation
Shell diameter (D)	1.6 - 2.4 mm.	1.87 ± 0.15 mm.
Shell height (H)	0.8 - 1.15 mm.	0.97 ± 0.09 mm.
Ratio H/D	0.45 - 0.57	0.51 ± 0.02

Distribution

New Jersey to Florida, west to South Dakota and California (Burch, 1962).

Habitats

Helicodiscus singleyanus collected by Allyn G. Smith, October 24, 1937, from roots and bulbs of iris, daffodils, etc. (Baker, 1929).

Family Zonitidae

Retinella electrina (Gould)

Figures 15-17.

Description

The shell is medium size (3.4-5.5 mm. in shell diameter), moderately depressed and thin. The surface of the shell is white opaque, glossy and smooth or with very weak radial grooves. Whorls are not expanding rapidly (Figure 17) and its number is 3 to 4. The spire is low conic and the suture is not well impressed (Figure 15). The abapical side of shell (Figure 16) is narrowly umbilicated; umbilicus is deep and its diameter is about one-sixth of its shell diameter. Body whorl is round at its periphery (Figure 15). The aperture (Figure 15) is rotund-lunate shape and its edge is thin and simple.

Measurements

Measurements of 38 specimens collected are:

	Range	Mean and Standard Deviation
Shell diameter (D)	3.4 – 5.5 mm.	4.2 $\pm$ 0.49 mm.
Shell height (H)	1.7 – 3.0 mm.	2.2 $\pm$ 0.3 mm.
Ratio H/D	0.49 – 0.6	0.53 $\pm$ 0.03

Distribution

Vermont to Virginia, west to Washington and Arizona (Burch, 1962).

Habitats

Under sticks and bark (Clapp, vide Pilsbry, 1946, p. 259).

204

Class Bivalvia

Family Sphaeriidae

Pisidium casertanum (Poli)

Figures 18-19.

Description

Shell is small, solid and medium inflated (with W/H 0.71). Surface of shell is dull to slightly glossy and sculptured with fine striae. Lateral view shell is suboval with the posterior end truncated (Figures 18-19). Beak is located far posterior to the mid-length line of the shell and is raised distinctly from the upper hinge line. Hinge plate is wide and ligament is short. Upper hinge line is not parallel to lower hinge line. Cardinal tooth of right valve (C3) is curved and somewhat enlarged at its posterior end. The inner laterals (AI, PI) of right valve (Figure 18) are distinct but not much elevated while the outer laterals (AIII, PIII) are small and not elevated either. The upper cardinal tooth (C4) of left valve is thin lamella and slightly curved; the lower cardinal (C2) is either triangular, or diamond, or round and not placed immediately above the lower hinge line. Laterals of left valve (AII, PII) are strong and short with blunt central cusps. The cardinal teeth are located closer to the cusps of the anterior lateral teeth than to the cusps of the posterior lateral teeth.

Measurements

Measurements of 5 specimens collected are:

Length (L)	Height (H)	Width (W)	H/L	W/H
5.6 mm.	4.8 mm.	3.6 mm.	.86	.75
3.6	3.1	2.0	.86	.64
3.5	3.1	2.1	.89	.68
2.4	2.1	1.6	.88	.76
2.2	1.7	1.2	.77	.71
			Mean = .85	Mean = .71

Distribution

Nearly cosmopolitan in distribution. It has been reliably recorded from all of the United States except Hawaii and Kentucky (Burch, 1975; Cvancara, *et al.*, 1972).

Habitats

Pisidium casertanum has succeeded in adapting itself to a wide variety of habitats. One finds it in bog ponds, ponds, swamps that dry up for several months during the year, swamp-creeks with considerable current, rivers and lakes, including the Great Lakes (Herrington, 1962). This species mainly inhabits muddy environments with rich organics, or decaying plant mat in a clear, calm water (Wu, 1978).

KEY TO THE LETTERINGS OF FIGURES 1-19.

AI, anterior inner lateral tooth; AII, anterior lateral tooth; AIII, anterior outer lateral tooth; A, anterior; al, angular lamella; apl, anguloparietal lamellae; B, beak; bf, basal fold; C2, lower cardinal tooth; C3, cardinal tooth; C4, upper cardinal tooth; cl, columellar lamella; G, groove; HP, hinge plate; LIG, ligament; lpf, lower palatal fold; PI, posterior inner lateral tooth; PII, posterior lateral tooth; PIII, posterior outer lateral tooth; P, posterior; pl, parietal lamella; R, ridge; scl, subcolumellar lamella; spf, suprapalatal fold; upf, upper palatal fold.

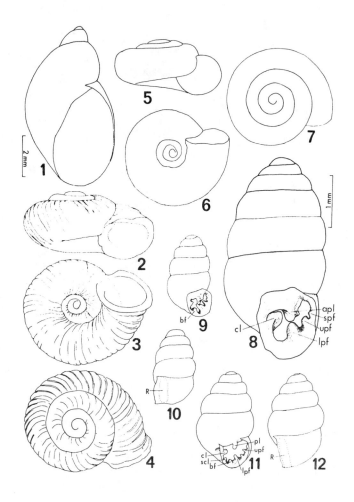

Figure 1. *Succinea avara* (Say), apertural view; Figures 2-4. *Vallonia costata* (Muller): 2, apertural view; 3, abapical view; 4, apical view; Figures 5-7. *Helicodiscus singleyanus* (Pilsbry): 5, apertural view; 6, abapical view; 7, apical view; Figure 8. *Gastrocopta armifera* (Say), apertural view; Figures 9-10. *G. holzingeri* (Sterki): 9, apertural view; 10, lateral view; Figures 11-12. *G. tappaniana* (Adams): 11, apertural view; 12, lateral view;

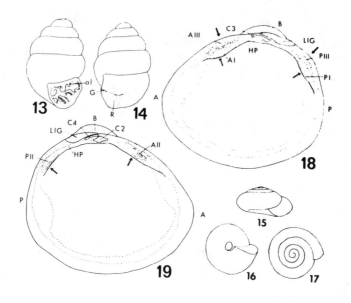

Figures 13-14. *Virtigo ovata* (Say): 13, apertural view; 14, lateral view; Figures 15-17. *Retinella electrina* (Gould): 15, apertural view; 16, abapical view; 17, apical view; Figures 18-19. *Pisidium casertanum* (Poli): 18, medial view of the right valve; 19, medial view of the left valve. (The apertures of Figures 8, 9, 11 and 13 are stippled to show the details of the lamellae and folds. Arrows at Figures 18-19 indicate the position of cusps. The scales of Figures 1, 15-17 are at 1 and the scales of Figures 2-14, 18-19 are at 8.)

REFERENCES

Baker, H. B.
    1929 Pseudohyaline American Land Snails. *Proceedings of The Academy of Natural Sciences of Philadelphia.* Vol. 81, pp. 251-266.

Burch, J. B.
    1962 *How to Know the Eastern Land Snails.* W. C. Brown Co., Dubuque, Iowa.

    1975 *Freshwater Sphaeriacean Clams (Mollusca: Pelecypoda) of North America.* Revised edition. Malacological Publication, Hamburg, Michigan.

Burch, J. B. and C. M. Patterson
    1965 A Land Snail for Demonstrating Mitosis and Meiosis. *American Biology Teacher.* Vol. 27, pp. 203-207.

Camp, M. J.
    1974 Pleistocene Mollusca of three Southeastern Michigan Marl Deposits. *Sterkiana.* No. 56, pp. 21-64.

Cheatum, E. P. and D. Allen
    1965 Pleistocene Land and Freshwater Mollusks from North Texas. *Sterkiana.* No. 18, pp. 1-16.

Cheatum, E. P. and R. W. Fullington
    1973 The Aquatic and Land Mollusca of Texas. Part 2. The Recent and Pleistocene Members of the Pupillidae and Urocoptidae (Gastropoda) in Texas. *Bulletin of the Dallas Museum of Natural History.* Vol. 1, pt. 2, pp. 1-67.

Cvancara, A. M., J. M. Erickson and J. J. Delimata
    1972 Present and Past Mollusks of the Forest River, North Dakota. *Proceedings of the North Dakota Academy of Sciences.* Vol. 25, pp. 55-65.

Evans, J. G.
    1972 *Land Snails in Archaeology.* Seminar Press, London and New York.

Franzen, D. S. and A. B. Leonard
    1947   Fossil and Living Pupillidae (Gastropoda: Pulmonata) in Kansas. *Kansas University Science Bulletin,* Vol. 31, pp. 311-411.

French, P. S., S. -K. Wu and C. A. Jones
    1975   Land Snails from the Hudson-Meng Site, A Preliminary Report. A paper presented at the 85th Annual Meeting of the Nebraska Academy of Sciences, Lincoln.

Herrington, H. B.
    1962   A Revision of the Sphaeriidae of North America (Mollusca: Pelecypoda). *Miscellaneous Publications of the Museum of Zoology.* University of Michigan. No. 118: 1-74.

La Rocque, A.
  1966-1970 Pleistocene Mollusca of Ohio. Parts I-IV. *Bulletin of the Ohio Division of Geologic Survey,* Vol. 62, pp. 1-800.

Leonard, A. B.
    1959   Handbook of Gastropods in Kansas. *University of Kansas Museum of Natural History, Miscellaneous Publications,* No. 20: 1-224.

Pilsbry, H. A.
  1939-1948 Land Mollusca of North America (North of Mexico). *Academy of Natural Sciences of Philadelphia. Monograph 3,*1: 1-944, 2:1113.

Taylor, D. W.
    1960   Late Cenozoic Molluscan Faunas from the High Plains. *U. S. Geological Survey Professional Paper.,* No. 337, pp. 1-94.

Wu, S. -K.
    1978   The Bivalvia of Colorado. Pt. 1. The Fingernail and Pill Clams (Family Sphaeriidae). *Natural History Inventory of Colorado,* No. 2, pp. 1-39.

APPENDIX III

USE OF OPAL PHYTOLITHS IN
PALEO-ENVIRONMENTAL RECONSTRUCTION
AT THE HUDSON-MENG SITE

RHODA OWEN LEWIS
UNIVERSITY OF WYOMING

One of the goals in recent archaeological excavations has been the attempt to reconstruct the paleo-environment. Palynology has been the best known and widest used method for this research. However, soil and climate conditions in the Wyoming-Nebraska-Colorado area of the High Plains are not conducive to pollen preservation. In an attempt to find a viable alternative to pollen studies in paleo-environmental reconstruction, the Department of Anthropology, University of Wyoming has been conducting opal phytolith research.

Phytolith studies can provide data about types of grasses growing on the site area and on nearby grazing areas, changes in vegetational types, and changes in moisture levels. We may be able to determine use of buffalo chips for fuel, rough dressing areas of game animals, sleeping areas with grass pads, and types of grasses ground on metates. Humid grass phytoliths may indicate a previous water source and phytoliths in fill material can give some information about vegetation from areas draining into the site.

Opal phytolith studies can provide information concerning not only the climate in a particular area during the time a site was actually deposited, but can also show changes that have occured in that area over a period of time. Changes in vegetation are shown by the changes in class types of phytoliths. Phytolith size is also indicative of changes in moisture (Yeck and Gray 1972: 639). Rovner (1971: 343-344) lists three criteria which must be met for any fossil system to be useful to the archaeologist: 1) the material must be able to withstand decomposition; 2) have sufficient taxonomically significant, morpholgic differences; 3) be of sufficient quantity to reflect the parent assemblage. Although phytoliths may not meet all three criteria in all situations, they are able to provide us with valuable insight and their contribution to the archaeological record must be considered.

Opal phytoliths form as plants take up soluble silica in the form of monosilic acid. The soluble silica forms around and in plant cells producing distinctive shapes (Yeck and Gray, *ibid.*). When the plants decay, the resistant silican forms are deposited in the soil. Work done by Twiss, Suess, and Smith (1969: 111-112) produced a morphological classification of grass phytoliths into four classes: Chloridoid (short grass), Panicoid (tall grass), Festucoid (humid grass), and Elongate which appears in all grasses. Phytoliths are not indestructible; they can be fused by fires, eroded by soil action, and are susceptable to soil chemistry and moisture patterns. Amounts of opal phytoliths available in samples differ from site to site depending on the variables present. By running a percentage count of phytolith types appearing in each slide, we are able to ascertain with some degree of reliability the grasses predominent in the site area.

Several methods have been used by researchers in sample preparation. With the laboratory facilities available through the Anthropology Department at the University of Wyoming, I have found the following method for sample preparation the most practical. The soil sample to be examined was first ground with a mortar and pestle. Fifty grams were weighed from the sample and placed in a beaker with distilled water and ten milliliters of 30 percent hydrogen peroxide to destroy any organic materials present. After sitting for 24 hours, the sample was agitated with ten milliliters of Calgon to disperse the soil particles. When the sand had settled to the bottom of the beaker, the clay and silt portion was poured off through a U.S.A. Standard Testing Sieve number 270 (53 micron openings) and saved. The clay particles were separated by centrifuging the sample with distilled water. The sample was centrifuged for five minutes at 750 r.p.m., the clay portion was then poured off, retaining the silts. This procedure was repeated until the silt sample was free of clay. The silt portion was then dried. In order to separate the phytoliths from one gram of dried silt, a mixture of bromoform and bromobenzene with a specific gravity of 2.30 was added to the silt and centrifuged at 3000 r.p.m. The phytoliths and other light minerals were decanted, filtered through a Watman 1 filter paper, washed several times with acetone, then mounted permanently on slides for examination. The amount of phytoliths in each class was counted and percentages calculated to determine the major class or classes of grasses found in the site area.

One of the sites examined during this study was the Hudson-Meng Bison Kill located in the northwestern corner of Nebraska. Soil samples were taken at Hudson-Meng during the 1975 field season from eight levels in the trench (Figure 43); from a hearth in square 26S, 12W; and from the bone bed, in the southeast quadrant of square 18S, 14W.

Slides were prepared and transects of the slides were studied. The number of phytoliths in the majority of the samples made a complete count infeasible. Silt samples used in the final preparation of the trench slides each weighed one gram. The silt sample from the hearth area weighed .25 grams and the sample from the bone bed weighed .3 grams. In order to compare all the samples, actual phytolith counts from the hearth and bone bed were increased proportionally (Table 1). Since Elongated phytoliths are present in all classes and were abundant in the samples, no count was made of them. Diatom counts are included since they may indicate a difference in moisture. Under ponded or poorly drained conditions, 1/3 to 1/2 of the opal isolate may be composed of diatoms (Wilding and Drees 1971: 1008).

Tables 1 and 2 show actual identifiable phytolith counts in each class and give a percentage determination. Unknown and unidentifiable opal fragments were present but not included in the total count from each sample. The high percentage of Festucoid class phytoliths in all the trench samples indicates the constant presence of humid grass, possibly a micro-environment created by the spring or stream area. Trench samples 1, 3, and 4 (in the stream cross-section) imply a time of increased moisture when tall grass prairies would be present. Trench samples 6 and 7 show reversal of this trend with short grass phytoliths being more common. Samples 2 and 5 were essentially void of phytoliths which may indicate an extremely dry period, or failure of accumulation and preservation of phytoliths.

Extrapolated figures from the bone bed and hearth area and figures from sample 6, the Alberta bone bed level in the trench, are compared in Figure 1. Sample 6 was taken from outside the butchering area; the high percentage of Festucoid phytoliths indicates a nearby water source. The phytolith counts of Festucoid and Panicoid classes in the bone bed sample are consistent with Sample 6. The contents of the bison visera deposited during butchering account for the significant increase in Chloridoid class phytoliths. The evidence in the bone bed sample implies that the bison had been grazing on short grass prairie just prior to the kill. Examination of slides made from ashed down coprolites show an extremely high concentration of phytoliths. The increased phytolith count from the hearth area, the high percentage of Chloridoid class phytoliths, and the lack of charcoal strongly suggests the use of dried feces for fuel.

Changes in vegetation through time can be shown, butchering procedures may be verified, vegetation at the site itself as well as surrounding grazing areas can be identified, and certain geological aspects may be substantiated. Opal phytolith studies cannot be considered the definitive answer in vegetational reconstruction of paleoenvironments. They are, however, an important link and cross-check for other methods currently being used. Although opal silicon studies have been conducted for over 100 years, their use in archaeological reconstruction is in its infancy. The potential for opal phytolith studies in archaeology is barely tapped and its limits unknown.

	FESTUCOID		CHLORIDOID		PANICOID		DIATOMS
	N	%	N	%	N	%	N
Bone Bed SE¼, 18S, 14W (.3 gm. x 3)	15	42	18	50	3	8	--
Hearth 26S, 12W (.25 gm. x 4)	20	25	40	50	20	25	8

	FESTUCOID		CHLORIDOID		PANICOID		DIATOMS
	N	%	N	%	N	%	N
Sample 8	14	30	13	28	20	43	27
Sample 7	13	45	15	52	1	3	41
Sample 6	13	59	6	27	3	14	7
Sample 5	3	75	--		1	25	--
Sample 4	13	46	2	7	13	46	78
Sample 3	22	28	1	1	55	71	29
Sample 2	--		--		--		--
Sample 1	21	42	8	16	21	42	12

Tables 1,2. Location, Count and Percentages for Phytoliths, plus Diatoms from the Hudson-Meng Bone Bed; Hearth, and Trench samples. See Figure 43, this volume, for sample locations.

214

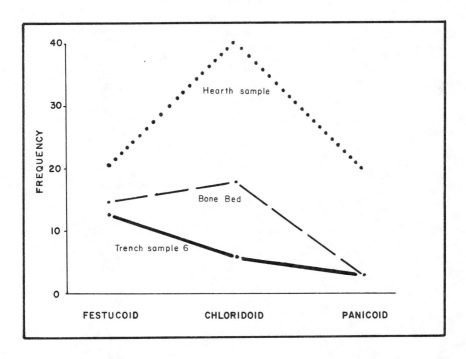

Figure 1. Comparisons of Phytolith Count from Trench Sample 6 and
Extrapolated Figures from the Bone Bed and Hearth Areas.

REFERENCES

Rovner, Irwin
    1971   Potential of opal phytoliths for use in paleoecological reconstruction.
            Quaternary Research. Vol. 1, pp. 343-359.

Twiss, P. C., E. Suess, and R. Smith
    1969   Morphological classification of grass phytoliths. *Soil Science Society
            of America Proceedings.* Vol. 33, pp. 109-114.

Wilding, L. P. and L. R. Drees
    1971   Biogenic opal in Ohio soils. *Soil Science Society of America Pro-
            ceedings.* Vol. 35, pp. 1004-1010.

Yeck, R. D. and Fenton Gray
    1972   Phytolith size characteristics between Udols and Ustols. *Soil Science
            Society of America Proceedings.* Vol. 36, pp. 639-641.

APPENDIX IV

VEGETATION AND FLORA OF THE HUDSON-MENG BISON KILL

LAWRENCE W. YOUNG II
UNIVERSITY OF WYOMING

RONALD R. WEEDON
CHADRON STATE COLLEGE

INTRODUCTION

One of the most interesting aspects of the Hudson-Meng Bison Killsite is that the present vegetation, largely intact, provides valuable opportunities for potential comparison with the vegetation and situation that existed at ca. 9820 B.P.

CLIMATE

The present climate of the Hudson-Meng Bison Killsite area is dry continental, characterized by warm summers, cold winters, light precipitation, low humidity, and frequent changes of weather. The weather patterns are modified by the physiography of the surrounding areas such as the Black Hills to the north and the Rocky Mountains to the west which act as climatic barriers. Moisture entering Nebraska from the south is often shunted to the east which results in less rainfall in the Panhandle. The result is a semiarid situation where the average annual precipitation is 15.3 inches, seventy percent of which falls during March through September, the greater portion of it in the spring. These spring and summer storms can be severe, often accompanied by hail and damaging winds. Precipitation during the winter falls as snow and is usually accompanied by days of cold temperatures. The snowfall is fairly evenly divided between the months with an average of four-tenths of an inch per month. The precipitation which occurs during the spring months from March to May provide most of the water available for plant growth. The average growing period is about 130 frost-free days starting about May 19 or earlier and lasting through to about September 24.

PHYSIOGRAPHY AND SOILS

The physiography of the study area is characteristic of the Pine Ridge Province. Its southern border is an east-west trending escarpment of the Pine Ridge. The upper slopes of the ridge are steep but do not form cliffs. The lower slopes consist of ridges and narrow canyons to nearly level plains. The parallel drainage pattern is towards the north.

The soils are of the Canyon-Bridget-Oglala Association. They are generally described as deep and shallow, moderately steep to very steep loamy silt soils formed in colluvium and weathered sandstone materials.

The parent material is of Tertiary sandstone from the Orella Member of the Brule Formation. The unit is characterized by brownish buff to orange silty clays and sandstones. The Orella weathers to a series of sinuous "knife" like ridges. The soils on the lower slopes may have layers of volcanic ash which have been weathered out of the overlying Whitney Member of the Brule Formation.

The Canyon Series are located on the rough broken ridges and upland drainage ways. The slopes are mostly 11 to 30 percent but may be as great as 60 percent along the tree-covered ridges. Rock outcrops may be visible intermingled with the canyon soils. In a representative profile, the surface layer is friable grayish-brown loam about 5 inches thick. Below this there is a transitional layer of friable light brownish calcareous loam of 6 inches thick. The underlying material is light gray loam over a white fine-grained sandstone at a depth of 15 inches.

The Bridget Series are deep well-drained soils on colluvial slopes and entrenched drainage ways that flow northward. These slopes are mostly 3 to 9 percent. The surface layer is 14 inches or less and can vary from a silt loam to a very fine sandy loam. The upper 6 inches are grayish-brown and the lower 8 inches gray to a brownish gray. These are above a 4 inch transitional layer that is a grayish-brown silt loam. Underlying this is a very pale brown material of very fine sandy loam to a depth of 60 inches.

Soils on the middle and lower slopes may grade into the Oglala Series. These soils are deep, well-drained soils formed from fine grained sandstone. Slopes range from 9 to 30 percent. The surface layer is grayish-brown loam about 14 inches thick, underlain by a transitional layer of pale brown silt loam 10 inches thick. The underlying material is very pale brown calcareous silt loam that contains fragments of fine-grained sandstone (Ragon, *et al.*, 1977; Witzel, 1974).

In summary, the parent material of the Hudson-Meng site has been and is being reworked as sequences of alluvial cuts and fills. The soils in the general area are easily subjected to impressively quick and severe erosion, once the cover of the vegetation is disturbed or removed. The grassland areas particularly have been susceptible to extreme erosion, leading to an expanding "Badlands" topography.

THE PRESENT VEGETATION

The vegetation is one of the most significant features of the landscape surrounding the Hudson-Meng Bison Killsite. The greater area of the vegetation is natural in that it has not been appreciably disturbed by man and/or has recovered in the most part from prior disturbance. Following use by Sioux peoples in the last century, the property in the area of the killsite was homesteaded by a Mr. Nance who may have had a significant influence upon the occurrence of certain exotic species found today at the site (Wiseman and Wiseman, 1972). Eventually the land came under the administration of the U. S. Forest Service and through lease from this agency as cattle range to a local rancher, Albert Meng. The influence of cattle no doubt has led to the introduction of other exotic species into the area. Given the various aspects of the influence of modern man on the present vegetation, discussed later where appropriate, the plant communities are still very comparable to the natural state, thus useful in discussions of what it was like in the past. The areas of greatest disturbance, for example, are localized near the site itself, since it is near the site where the greatest influx of people has been and where the greatest tendency of cattle to congregrate has occurred. Fencing techniques have controlled this potential problem to an extent.

The general area is covered by three major plant communities, the Eastern Ponderosa Pine Forest on the uplands, the Riparian Complex in the valley proper, and the Wheatgrass-Needle and Thread Community on the intermediate slopes.

THE EASTERN PONDEROSA FOREST

This plant community consists of a medium dense to open forest of medium tall needle-leaf evergreen trees with open ground covered by grasses (Küchler, 1964). Slopes are steep with both north and south exposures. In the area near the killsite, this plant community is found on the crests of hills.

Ponderosa Pine (*Pinus ponderosa*) is the most conspicuous and dominant species in the community. An occasional juniper tree (*Juniperus scopulorum*) and an occasional choke cherry (*Prunus virginiana*), can be seen among the pines, particularly on the northern slopes. The increased abundance of these species on the northern slopes as compared to the southern slopes is about three to one (Nixon, 1967). Conversely, there is a decrease in the grass cover and understory species on these same sites. Skunkbrush Sumac (*Rhus aromatica* var. *trilobata*) is a characteristic understory shrub in this plant community. The lower slopes and southern exposures have a greater cover of grasses. Their presence appears as crescent-shaped and oblong patterns among the pines. The dominant species present include Needle and Thread (*Stipa comata*), Western Wheatgrass (*Agropyron smithii*), and Sandberg Bluestem (*Poa sandbergii*). Yucca (*Yucca glauca*) is most abundant in this location and is spread in local colonies throughout the lower slopes just below the pines.

The Ponderosa Pine community is common to the Pine Ridge Escarpment, which covers approximately 2700 square miles, extending from northeastern Wyoming, across northwest Nebraska and into South Dakota (Weaver, 1965). Geographically the Pine Ridge Province separates the Pierre Hills and Gumbo

Plains of South Dakota from the High Plains and Sandhills of Nebraska.

THE WHEATGRASS-NEEDLE AND THREAD COMMUNITY

This community consists of short to medium-tall grasses of moderate to dense cover on upland mixed prairie sites. The dominant members of the community are Western Wheatgrass *(Agropyron smithii)* and Needle and Thread *(Stipa comata)*. These members are closely associated with Little Bluestem *(Andropogon scoparius)* which may be considered as dominant in this area. This plant community would be similar to Kuchler's (1964) Wheatgrass-Needlegrass *(Agropyron-Stipa)* type except for the conspicuous absence of Green Needlegrass *(Stipa viridula)* and Blue Grama *(Bouteloua gracilis)* as codominants in the community as locally represented.

Needle and Thread is a cool season bunchgrass of boreal origin. It is best adapted to sandy soils, heads of draws and drier sites. The basal area of the plant is quite small and with an increase in its apparent density the percent of bare ground also increases. This is particularly true when a decrease in the presence of Little Bluestem occurs.

Western Wheatgrass is a hardy sod-forming perennial grass. However it is present as individual culms on upland mixed prairie sites. With Thread-leaf sedge *(Carex filifolia)* and Needle and Thread intermixed, Western Wheatgrass has abundant long-branched rhizomes which spread rapidly and widely (Weaver, 1968). For this reason it is one of the major grasses which first establishes itself on disturbed sites.

In this community Little Bluestem appears as scattered buches to closely-spaced clumps where soil moisture is abundant. Little Bluestem comprises as much as 40 percent of the vegetative cover in the alluvial bottoms, then gives way to Needle and Thread along the slopes above.

The lower nearly level slopes are predominantly grass-covered, the dominants and their constituents forming dense stands. Prairie sandreed *(Calamovilfa longifolia)* appears as clumps and broad areas of pure stands. Kentucky Bluegrass *(Poa pratensis)* and Junegrass *(Koeleria pyramidata)* are abundantly placed throughout the community. The most common forb present is Silver-leaf Scurf Pea *(Psoralea argophylla)*, occurring as colonies on lower slopes and as scattered individuals on drier uplands.

The vegetation on the ridges and steeper slopes is more complex and varied. The dominant species and their constituents do not appear in dense stands but as clumps and scattered individuals. The percentage of bare exposed ground is much greater.

Some of these barren and sandy exposed areas are occupied by Fringed Sage *(Artemisia frigida)* and Broom Snakeweed, *(Gutierrezia sarothrae)*. Thread-leaf sedge *(Carex filifolia)* has a wide range of habitats but is primarily seen as bunches along the ridges and upland slopes. It is highly drought-resistant, surviving on dry ridges where other species do not.

THE RIPARIAN COMPLEX

This plant community has been so named as a result of several local phenomena which alter the description one would normally use for the open riparian woodlands of northwestern Nebraska. The particular shallow valley involving the killsite is consistently spring-fed and thus more species survive than in the intermittently fed, mostly dry stream beds in the immediate area. In addition, approximately fifteen years ago a dam was constructed very close to the killsite itself. The resulting stock pond has created a niche for a great many hydrophytes such as bulrushes and cattails that probably would not survive in the seepy soil near the springs at the head of the draw.

The open riparian woodland generally is dominated by American Elm, *(Ulmus americana),* Ash *(Fraxinus pennsylvanica),* Cottonwood *(Populus deltoides)* and Wild Plum *(Prunus americana),* Box Elder Maple *(Acer negundo)* Willows, and Red-Osier Dogwood are also present. Snowberry *(Symphoricarpos occidentalis)* forms dense local colonies and Choke cherry *(Prunus virginiana)* occurs in the draw above the pond. Riverbank Grape, Western Clematis, and Woodbine are characteristic vines found as part of the understory vegetation in this relatively open woodland of short to medium tall trees. False Indigo *(Amorpha fruticosa)* occurs in thickets along the valley floor, as does Buffaloberry *(Shepherdia argentea)* in the various draws in the general area.

DISTURBED AREAS

Locally disturbed areas are invaded by a host of what is commonly referred to as weedy species. These annual and perennial forbs and grasses are invading plants pioneering on disturbed soils. The species found in disturbed areas in the upland prairie are Downy Brome *(Bromus tectorum),* White Aster *(Aster ericoides),* and Wavyleaf Thistle *(Cirsium undulatum).* The largest and most conspicuous disturbed areas are in the vicinity of the pond and old farmstead. The sites around the pond include the cutbanks, dam and killsite spoil banks. The invading species include Lamb's Quarters *(Chenopodium album),* Russian Thistle *(Salsola iberica),* Clammy Ground Cherry *(Physalis heterophylla),* Western Ragweed *(Ambrosia psilostachya),* and Downy Brome *(Bromus tectorum).* Rocky Mountain Bee Plant *(Cleome serrulata)* is locally abundant along the bank east of the pond between the fence and dam. The only other major site which hosts the invading plants is the road which enters the study area from the north and extends south to the old farmstead then west across the dam to the dig site. Siberian Elm *(Ulmus pumila)* appears to have been planted at the farmsite and thus remains as an anthropogenic relict.

221

Most of these plants are common in disturbed areas throughout the Great Plains. Their abundance, particularly the annuals, will vary depending upon the climatic conditions of the particular year. Plants such as Broom Snakeweed and White Aster are native species that increase with disturbance while plants such as Downy Brome and Russian Thistle probably have increased on disturbed sites as invaders.

DISCUSSION

The dry slopes and ridges of the Pine Ridge Escarpment seem to serve as a refugium for *Pinus ponderosa* and associated species such as Rocky Mountain Juniper *(Juniperus scopulorum)* which are generally at or near the eastern limits of their distribution, coming from the Rocky Mountain Cordillera and the West. The narrow draws and stream canyons seem to serve often as refugia for species of eastern affinities particularly when moisture is consistent as with the springfed valley of the killsite which provides favorable habitats for Elm, Ash, Woodbine, Riverbank Grape, and other species. The Wheatgrass-Needle and Thread prairie has species of both southwestern and northern affinities represented. Characteristic species from the southwest include Skunkbrush Sumac, Red Threeawn *(Aristida longiseta)*, Fringed Sage *(Artemisia filifolia)*, Broom Snakeweed *(Gutierrezia sarothrae)*, Skeleton-weed *(Lygodesmia juncea)* and cacti. Characteristic species with northern affinities include Needle and Thread *(Stipa comata)*, Western Wild Rose *(Rosa woodsii)*, Snowberry *(Symphoricarpos occidentalis)* and others (Bare and McGregor, 1970). In the areas around the Hudson-Meng site, there may be species such as Skunkbrush Sumac found in more than one of the plant communities represented locally.

Both palynological evidence (Kelso, 1977, personal communication) and opal phytolith analysis (Lewis, Appendix III, this volume) generally tend to indicate that the area near the Hudson-Meng site was a grassland similar to that of the present with the possibility of conditions being somewhat more moist than currently. According to Lewis, "the high percentage of festucoid class phytoliths in all the trench samples indicates the constant presence of humid grass, possibly a micro-environment created by a stream or spring area." There is also the indication of sufficient moisture for the presence of tall grasses. The pollen data of Kelso would also indicate a condition similar to the present, except that the pine pollen is much more obvious in the modern samples.

It is thus possible to construct in outline a vegetational scene for ca. 9820 B.P. under a climatic regime generally more moist than present with grassland communities predominating. It is further possible to speculate that these communities consisted of more xeric grassland composed of mostly shortgrass species on the upper slopes and more mesic tall grass community occurring along the stream-fed or spring-fed valleys. It is known that the number and density of woodland trees, both pines and hardwoods, have increased tremendously in the general area during the last 80-100 years. This relatively very recent development

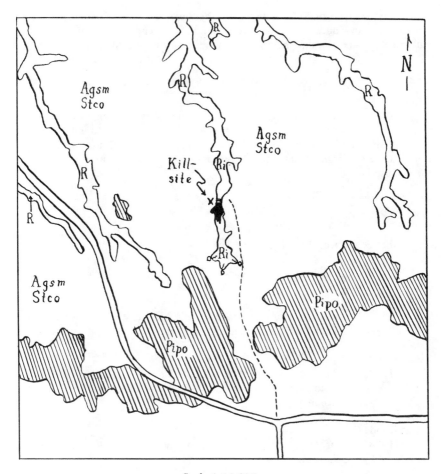

Scale 1:10,800

Legend

Pipo........................*Pinus ponderosa*
Agsm, Stco ......*Agropyron smithii, Stipa comata*
R.............................Riparian
Ri.......................Riparian complex
.............................Dam
♀.............................Springs
X .... Archaeological site, Killsite

Figure 1. Map of Plant Communities.

plus the pollen data of Kelso indicate that neither the Eastern Ponderosa Forest nor the riparian woodlands as they are known today occurred in the area near the Hudson-Meng site, certainly not nearly to the extent that they do now.

ACKNOWLEDGEMENTS

We thank the following people for their assistance regarding the field work: Gloria Aspinall, Betty Heiser, Gary Mason, C. S. Meyer, Joseph O'Brien, Joyce Phillips, David Spires, Joyce Stotts, and Jack Watson. We also thank Betty Heiser, Loretta Margrave and Robin Wasserburger for their assistance in preparing the manuscript.

REFERENCES

Bare, Janét E. and Ronald L. McGregor
  1970 An Introduction to the Phytogeography of Kansas. *The University of Kansas Science Bulletin,* Vol. 48, No. 26, pp. 869-949.

Kelso, Gerald
  1977 Personal communication. Tucson, Arizona, The University of Arizona Laboratory of Paleoenvironmental Research.

Küchler, A. W.
  1964 *Potential Natural Vegetation of the Conterminous United States.* American Geographical Society. Special Publication No. 36, 116 pp. with map.

Lewis, Rhoda O.
  1978 Use of Opal Phytoliths in Paleo-Environmental Reconstruction. Appendix III, this volume.

Nixon, E. S.
  1967 A Vegetational Study of the Pine Ridge of Northwestern Nebraska. *The Southwestern Naturalist.* Vol. 12, No. 2, pp. 134-145.

Ragon, Larry G., Larry D. Worth, Max A. Sherwood, and Michael L. Fausch.
  1977 Soil Survey of Dawes County, Nebraska. U. S. D. A., Soil Conservation Service with the University of Nebraska Conservation and Survey Division. 138 pp. with maps.

Weaver, John. E.
  1965 *Native Vegetation of Nebraska.* Lincoln, The University of Nebraska Press. 185 pp.

1968 *Prairie Plants and Their Environment.* Lincoln, The University of Nebraska Press. 276 pp.

Wiseman, F. A. and M. A. Wiseman
1972 Present Vegetation in the Vicinity of the Hudson-Meng Paleo Indian Bison Kill. Unpublished report, Tucson, Arizona, The University of Arizona Laboratory of Paleoenvironmental Research.

Witzel, Frank L.
1974 Guidebook and Road Logs for the Geology of Dawes and Northern Sioux Counties, Nebraska. Master's Thesis, Chadron State College, Chadron, Nebraska. 97 pp. with maps.

SUBJECT INDEX

A

Abraders, 25, 95-97
Agate Basin site, 125-126, 140
Alluvium, 15, 21, 103-111, 117
Altithermal, 17, 109, 111, 114, 138
Angostura (Long) site, 125, 126
Anzick site, 126
Arroyo, 5, 31-33, 103, 111, 114
Assiniboin, 48
Astragalus, 53-54, 56
Auger drill program, 13, 15, 21

B

Bison
    Age groups, 57, 61-64
    Bison antiquus, 61
    Bison bison, 45, 61
    Bison occidentalis, 45, 61
    Bone preservation, 19-20
    Drives (jumps), 30, 32, 125, 138-139
    Evolution, 56, 61, 137
    Meat products, 45-52
    Post-cranial analysis, 53-65
    Sex determination 53, 56-57
    Speciation, 27, 61,
    Time of year determination, 30, 48, 56, 61
Black Hills, 1, 73
Birch Creek, 56, 59-60
Boarding School site, 36
Bone tools, 36-37, 65-66
Bonfire shelter, 53, 56, 59-60, 126, 130
Brule formation, 15, 101, 103
Butcher marks, 19, 36
Butcher tools, 80-95

C

Calcium carbonate, 19, 36, 107-108,
110-111, 114
Campsite, 23
Casper site, 25, 36-37, 53, 56, 58-64, 116, 126, 130, 138-140
Ceremony, 27, 139
Chadron formation, 101
Chadron State College Research Institute, xiii, 132-133
Cherokee site, 126
Cheyenne River, 1, 17, 101
Chronology, 109, 111, 113-116, 123
Claypool site, 84, 87, 126
Clovis, 91-92, 95, 121, 125-126, 128
Cody Complex, 15, 75, 80, 91, 94-95, 115, 121-124, 137
Cody Knife, 80-81, 85-87, 94-95, 98, 122-124, 137
Colby site, 126, 128
Contour map, 112
Crow Butte, 101

D

Dawes County, 17, 101
Debitage (waste flakes), 66, 98
Dent site, 126
Distributional analysis
    Faunal remains, 25-44
    Hearths, 30
    Waste flakes (debitage), 66, 98
Dogs, 49, 51
Duffield site, 56, 59-60

E

Eden site, 126
Educational Expeditions International, xiii, 130, 132-134

227

228